TUPELO:
The Evolution of a
Community

TUPELO:
The Evolution of a Community

Vaughn L. Grisham, Jr.

with a Foreword by
William F. Winter

Kettering Foundation Press

DAYTON, OHIO

First edition 1999

Manufactured in the United States of America

Library of Congress Cataloging-in-Publication Data

Tupelo: The Evolution of a Community

p.c.m.

ISBN 0-923993-06-1

Library of Congress Catalog Card Number 98-89622

CIP

To
George A. McLean, Anna Keirsey McLean,
and
My parents, Vaughn and Margaret Grisham

CONTENTS

PREFACE

Economic development is a central issue in our times. Presidential and other national elections turn on the credibility of candidates to address issues of economic well-being. National economic policies help determine the degree of success of presidential administrations and are critical to the lives of all the nation's citizens. Such policies form a national umbrella and the national conditions are, in turn, shaped by international factors. In the final analysis, however, goods and services are produced in a specific locale. Consequently, the nation's towns and cities must be healthy if the economy is to be vibrant. Those cities and towns provide the setting in which the economy performs.

Tupelo: The Evolution of a Community engages in a dialogue about community revitalization. It argues that community development is often a vital component in economic development. Although community development is not synonymous with economic development, an expected consequence is improved quality of life. Moreover, successful community development almost always involves structural changes that enhance the creation and opportunities for jobs.

The book offers a model, Tupelo, Mississippi, as a concrete example of the power of community and community development to improve the quality of life. The story depicts the evolutionary transformation of Tupelo from its settlement to its status as a model for community development. By taking a historical perspective, it seeks to demonstrate the nature of growth experienced by many nonmetropolitan communities. The advantage of studying Tupelo is that it also can teach the *lessons* of community development. The book is not so much concerned with praising Tupelo as it is interested in learning from its example.

A study of community development should focus on the process, but no community development occurs without individuals — people, who contribute their time, talent, and resources. *Tupelo: The Evolution of a Community* is a tribute to all the thousands of people in Lee County, many whose faces and names I know, who have taken the time to be involved in some facet of community life. On a regular basis, between 5,000 and 6,000 Lee countians participated in Rural Community Development Council programs during the 1950s and 1960s. Many are still involved through this means. Others involve themselves through Community Development Foundation activities or myriad other community outlets. The educational associations and organizations, the recreational projects, the symphony, theatre, museums, all depend on volunteers. These individuals are deserving of praise and attention, but alas, neither space nor format permits such individual accolades. They, at least, have the reward of living in a good community, made so by all their individual contributions.

There are others, whose names and roles are described herein, so many names that I am including a list of participants for the sake of the readers.

A Preface also provides the added joy of thanking those who made a book possible. For the past 28 years, Lee County and Tupelo have taught me about community development. There have been so many mentors, not just the prominent citizens, but common people in town and country whose participation in the community set an example for the enriching possibilities of community involvement. Community leaders, busy people with crowded calendars, took the time to share their insights. I thank you all. Your graciousness is a perfect complement to your role as community leaders.

Lee County, the state of Mississippi, and all who learned community development from George McLean, sat at the feet of the master. There is none better.

Anna Keirsey McLean, whom I am pleased to call my friend, has been an inspiration with her strength, charm, and intellect. She has been a benefactor whose unselfish gifts gave life to the McLean Institute for Community Development and allowed the work of George McLean to spread throughout the region.

The successors to George McLean, Billy Crews and Tom Pittman, are my former students who have taught their teacher. These men, along with the capable staff of the *Northeast Mississippi Daily Journal,* provided me with a second home. Your insights and hospitality were invaluable.

Harry Martin and the staff of the Community Development Foundation, afforded essential access to material, which is at the heart of Lee County's community and economic success. For your time and energy, I am in your debt. You also have earned the respect of the community for all you do.

The staff of the Lee County Library demonstrated professionalism and kindness as they shared their riches with me. We began in the temporary quarters across from the courthouse and ultimately moved to your fine present facilities. We share a lot.

To all those I interviewed, I hope you feel that your time was justified.

The research and time for writing was made possible by grants from The Appalachian Regional Commission; CREATE; the *Northeast Mississippi Daily Journal* through the Community Development Foundation; and a faculty grant through the University of Mississippi. Your confidence and support made the project possible. You went beyond making a grant; you have been my partners in the endeavor. I am grateful to be associated with good citizens like you all.

Jerry Robinson, Jr., Billy Crews, Nick Chandler, Blaine Brownell, Ken Wilkinson, John Lovorn, and Steve Mayhorn provided insight with their reading of the manuscript. You strengthened the finished product.

Roger Lotchin read an early version of the manuscript and was a tough taskmaster whose mental toughness and knowledge of urban history added richly to the book before you.

Then there are the invaluable contributions of the family, who often suffer the most from my absence. To my children first, Cindy, Mike, Tonya, and Terri, the project too often took me away from you, but never away from your love and concern, and I give my heartfelt thanks to you all. Grandsons Will, Cam, and Jonathon; granddaughters Maggie and Rachel, provided joy away from the project.

My mother-in-law Ruth Hopper, went the extra mile. She not only did all the domestic chores with her gift for doing everything well, she is the best proof-reader I have known. This project could not have been done without you.

My parents Vaughn and Margaret, instilled the love of learning and the discipline, but more than that, they shared their love with me and my sister, Jane.

A special word of appreciation is due Governor William Winter for his gracious and eloquent Foreword to this book.

I offer my heartfelt thanks to the fine staff of the Kettering Foundation, especially David Mathews, Estus Smith, and my friend, now gone, Vicki Simpson. I offer a special thanks to Susan Willey for her time, insights, and professionalism in editing this book and Ed Arnone for his cooperation in helping me to bring closure in this labor of love. It is an honor to work with such excellent people.

Finally, how can I find the words to thank my wife, Sandy? She is my best friend, my toughest editor, my inspiration, my partner in every project, and light of my life.

While the acknowledgments are a moment of joy, there is also a note of sadness as I put the closing touches to the book. The research began in 1971 and there are many good friends who contributed to this effort who did not get to see the finished project. I want to especially note three: My mother, Margaret, was the most constant, positive, continual force in my life. She died in June 1998. Harold Kaufman, a giant in the field of community and rural sociology was my undergraduate and graduate mentor. It was he who first introduced me to Tupelo, but never completed his own community text. I have tried to continue in his tradition. Kenneth P. Wilkinson, a fellow student and colleague offered suggestions for this book. Ken died too young on November 18, 1993. His book, *The Community in Rural America,* is, I believe, the most brilliant theoretical treatment ever done of the rural American community. Ken, I stood on your strong shoulders for the theoretical understanding of community.

FOREWORD

I t has been my good fortune to have known and been associated with some authentic American heroes. A disproportionately large number of them have been citizens of Tupelo, Mississippi. They have been involved in the most important vocation that any American can be engaged in — that of community-building. The success of their efforts can be seen in the quality of life and in the human relationships that have been created in this relatively small city located in what once would have been regarded by some as the backwoods of northeast Mississippi.

Tupelo's geographical location in a landlocked rural area populated by struggling small farmers and removed from the main corridors of industry and commerce was not a promising site for economic and social progress. There seemed to be nothing to distinguish it from scores of other small communities scattered across America. There was, however, one element that made all the difference. It was the exceptional vision and persevering leadership of a group of local citizens who understood the importance and the techniques of community-building. To a considerable extent it was the drive and determination of one particularly far-sighted leader named George McLean that made it come together.

The incisive volume by Vaughn Grisham relates the incredible story of Tupelo's emergence as a national model for homegrown community development. No one is better equipped to write of the events in this remarkable saga than Dr. Grisham, since for a quarter of a century he has made a study of the Tupelo experience his consuming passion. Through his close personal acquaintance with so many of the individual players and his intimate understanding of the history of the community, he enables us in this book to occupy a special vantage point from which to view these impressive achievements.

Much has been written about community-building in the abstract. This book features real-life human beings and the series of events that shaped the body and soul of an actual community. No one can read this story without concurring in the ultimate thesis of George McLean; that the key to success in Tupelo, as it must be in every community, is "to treat every person as a resource and to develop that resource to a maximum."

There were obviously many factors that contributed to the success of the Tupelo Plan. One was to broaden the definition of "community." McLean and his comrades recognized that common interests transcended political and geographical boundaries and that community objectives needed to be looked at in regional terms. The result was that most of the turf protection concerns that frequently thwart efforts at cooperation were overwhelmed by a larger community spirit.

Always in the forefront of the community priorities was the advancement of educational opportunity. There was the commitment from the very beginning that the building of an educated citizenry had to be an indispensable element in the creation of a competitive community. The result has been the development in Tupelo of outstanding elementary and secondary schools and the addition of branches of two public institutions of higher learning.

It is generally conceded that much of Tupelo's success would not have been accomplished without the active involvement of the community's daily newspaper, the *Northeast Mississippi Daily Journal.* With George McLean as its owner and publisher, it was a consistent force for social justice and community development, a role it continues to play under McLean's successors.

None of this is to suggest that this account of Tupelo's ascendancy has been without conflict and controversy. As in every community, there were naysayers and nitpickers. There still are. But unlike many other less-inspired communities, Tupelo has achieved a basic unity of spirit and of purpose. This unity has been recently expressed in near unanimous support of bond issues for schools and physical improvements.

It is now into a second and even a third generation of community leadership, aided and expanded by many newcomers who have been attracted to the area by its burgeoning reputation as a good place to live. Most of them have become almost immediately caught up in the civic life of the city.

In addition to the practical lessons that this volume teaches about successful community-building, perhaps its most rewarding contribution is the refreshing picture it paints of a place where people have learned not to dismiss their own personal self-interest, but to equate it with the interest of their community.

Dr. Grisham makes it clear that pure altruism has not been the principal motivating factor in Tupelo's success. Most people there simply came to understand that the key to their personal success lay in their willingness to work together with their neighbors for the well-being of their community, as well as themselves.

This volume is a textbook for civic change. It articulates a vision that, if adopted by others, and especially our young citizens, can cause them to reject a quiescent status quo of disinterest and neglect. It speaks unforgettably to the importance of sustaining a society that recognizes the worth and dignity of every citizen. It imparts a message of faith and optimism that should give new resolve to all of us in the never-ending community-building obligations that we share.

WILLIAM F. WINTER

Former Governor of Mississippi

CHAPTER 1

An Introduction to
Tupelo, Mississippi, and the Community
Development Process

C ountless generations of human beings have delighted in tales of triumph over adversity. Americans in particular are fascinated when ordinary people do extraordinary things. It is uplifting when those who are among the lowly dream great dreams and then, with sheer willpower and determination, fulfill those visions. Abraham Lincoln, lacking physical grace or beauty, overcame poverty and repeated reversals of fortune to reach the pinnacle of public office. Andrew Carnegie and John D. Rockefeller rose to lead powerful corporations. A school-teacher from a modest community was selected to be the first nonmilitary passenger on a space vehicle. Though Christa McAuliff died in the *Challenger* disaster, her accomplishments were championed by an entire nation. Even such literary figures as Horatio Alger and *Lonesome Dove* heroes Woodrow Call and Angus McCrae become household words for overcoming adversity.

So it is with Tupelo, Mississippi. Here is a town set in one of the poorest counties in the poorest state in the nation, which against great odds has become a national and international model for community development. It is the tale of citizens bonding together into a community, and "community" is the key word, to escape the mean clutches of poverty. It chronicles what is possible when community is achieved and people learn to work toward common goals.

It is a timely account because almost two-thirds of the nonmetropolitan communities (towns and cities of less than 50,000 population) lost population between 1980 and 1990. The same trend continued in the decade of the nineties. This occurred despite the fact that a majority of the people in the nation consistently report that they would prefer to live in a small town. Moreover, residents of small towns do, in fact, express greater satisfaction with their community than people from larger cities. The challenge is to maintain the small towns for the present generation and those to follow.

In every state and almost every county, there are citizens working on ways to strengthen their place of residence. But where do they start and what are they to do to preserve their community? Many community leaders are looking for a concrete model of a successful community whose experience can help enlighten their own quest for an improved community. Shortly after *The Wall Street Journal* ran a front-page article on Tupelo, Mississippi, and mentioned a book on the town, this author received letters and telephone calls from every state in the union. This interest in the Tupelo story is consistent with my experiences for the past quarter of a century.

Leaders in both the academic and applied dimensions of community development are always seeking an effective model, and the quest that led to this book began with certain basic criteria in mind. The town or city selected had to be representative of the history of most small towns. It could not have special advantages such as coastlines or governmental installations. The town could not have special beauty or in other ways have unusual advantages for tourism. The town could not be a state capital or be home to a college or university. Nor could the site selected be a suburb of a metropolitan area. The primary concern was that this be a town or city whose development depended primarily on the human efforts of local citizens and that the process by which the development was achieved be transferable to other communities.

The town selected for the model is Tupelo/Lee County, Mississippi. To the distant viewer, Tupelo is known only as the birthplace of Elvis Presley, but like its famous native son, the town has its own Horatio Alger story. It is a small city of just under 34,000 people located in the hills section of northeast Mississippi. The county numbers approximately 72,000 and the bond between county and town make it almost impossible to talk about one without referring to the other. Its story and the lessons it has learned are a valuable tool for community development throughout the nation.

In 1940, Lee County had the dubious distinction of being one of the poorest counties in the poorest state in the union. Relying primarily on its own human resources, the county has now raised its per capita income to the second highest in the state. Only the county containing the state capital has a higher per capita income. Lee County's income level is near the national average, while the state remains mired as fiftieth in most categories. Its industrial development program was recently rated as one of the nation's ten best.[1] The county numbers 18 Fortune 500 manufacturers among its more than 100 industries. While other parts of the nation have experienced a decline in their employment base, Lee County has averaged more than 1,000 new manufacturing jobs a year for each of the last 13 years. Its jobs in the service sector are growing even faster.[2] As of June 1998, the county has more than 52,000 jobs.

The town has used its economic base to produce a series of local community achievements. Its reading aid program became the cornerstone of the first state Educational Reform Legislation in the nation. A subsequent citizens' effort on behalf of public education earned awards by Harvard's Kennedy School of

Government and the Ford Foundation as being one of the ten most innovative public-private projects in the nation. The local school is currently one of five programs in the United States selected by the Center for Educational Leadership as part of a research effort to radically reform education. In addition, the school system has the support of almost the whole community. In 1990, the town proposed the largest school bond issue in the history of Mississippi. The bond issue received approval by 88 percent of the voting public.

The school's academic decathlon team has won the state championship every year for the past 13 years and has ranked among the nation's top 20 for the past 7 years. Six of those eight years, its athletic program was also judged to be the best in Mississippi. It has won state championships in football and baseball in each of the past two years.[3]

The town has a symphony, an art museum, a theatre group, and an outstanding recreational program. Tupelo's Gum Tree Festival has more than 2,000 participants in its 6-kilometer run.

Its medical center is the state's largest. It employs more than 5,000 people and serves patients in 3 states in this relatively small city. It is the second largest employer in the whole state and was consciously designed to both provide health care and to serve as a nonpolluting high wage job source. The quality of the health service led the *U. S. News & World Report,* in a 1993 issue, to cite it as one of the four model programs for the nation.

The initial focus of the community development efforts were jobs and economic development, but as noted above, the results become cyclical in which the economic prosperity allows the funding of other community projects such as good schools and good health care. These achievements feed directly and indirectly into still better jobs and more prosperity. Moreover, the process of organizing a community gives it almost unlimited potential to achieve whatever it focuses on. The most recent accomplishment occurred over a period from 1997 to 1998 when a racially diverse neighborhood, tenants and homeowners, came together to revitalize their housing and neighborhood. This grassroots effort has gained the full participation and sponsorship of the newspaper, the *Northeast Mississippi Daily Journal,* and all of the community's banks. One is reminded of the words of George McLean, the father of the Tupelo Model, "There is no limit to what an organized community can do if it wants to."

For these and other achievements, Tupelo was selected many years ago as a model for community development. It was twice designated an All-America City by the National Civic League. This prestigious award is granted to only 10 communities a year. It is given for "creativity and innovation at the local level."[4] In 1967, Tupelo was the first southern city to win the award. Its second citation came 20 years later, making it the first city to repeat. Even before this celebration of the town's effort, the U.S. Department of Agriculture had selected Lee County as a national model for rural development. A 1992 Kettering Foundation publication on economic and community development used Tupelo as a model of a successful community effort.[5]

The national model label has helped to attract a steady stream of visitors eager to benefit from the area's experiences. Leaders from more than 300 communities have made the trek to Lee County to learn firsthand from this enterprising community. In addition, representatives from 63 nations have also made the pilgrimage. Approximately one half of these international delegates came to study the community. The other half came to do business and thereby benefit in a different way from its economic development.[6]

The town has no natural advantages that would give it a competitive edge. There is no waterfront or natural beauty. There are no resources deposited in the soil. Much of the agricultural land was depleted by the late nineteenth century.[7] The county was poor, so there was no reserve of capital. It has no interstate or four-lane highways. These are only now being built. Moreover, it is not near any metropolitan center. Both Memphis and Birmingham, its closest urban neighbors, are more than 100 miles away.

All of the basic components of its community development program were borrowed. None of the basic transforming ideas originated there. Tupelo sought and found these ideas elsewhere. Lee County's role was to supply the imagination and the will to first consciously locate other models. Subsequently, it adapted these ideas to fit its own culture. Following that, the community performed the tedious and daunting task of implementing the ideas.

Unfortunately, a short visit to the area is not sufficient to grasp more than the most simple principles. Persons studying the area see only the fruit of the achievements and not the process by which they were developed. As one leading economic developer is fond of saying, "economic and community development is not an event that can be witnessed. It is a process which requires ongoing effort."[8]

This community development process must be understood over a long period of time and within a historical context. The author spent six years of detailed study of the community, during which he read all one hundred-twenty years of newspapers, utilized public records, including city and county minutes, school and church record diaries, library materials, and personal memorabilia. The library of the Community Development Foundation opened their records, and he was invited to attend the executive session meetings of that organization. The county's industries were kind enough to permit multiple visits. Working alongside visiting industrial development analysts, the author learned to see the community through their eyes and experiences. More than 2,000 people, including key leaders from all segments of life cooperated through interviews. Living in the town for a period of time provided an opportunity to experience it from an insider's perspective. As part of the on-site experience, 16 months were spent living and visiting in the African-American neighborhoods.

The same basic question arose everywhere: "What gives Tupelo its advantage?" The answer was consistent. The citizens of Lee County have learned to work together.

While the respondents did not use the precise terminology, they were describing a fundamental characteristic of community. Community, following the interactionalist model as this book does, has three common elements. One of the most basic elements is the practice of recognizing common interests and problems and working together to address those problems, just as the local leaders recognized when they answered the question about the source of the achievements. A second component of community is locality or territory. Lee countians have learned, what rural sociologists have long known, that the town and country[9] are part of the same economic community. The community in Lee County today and for the past 50 years includes both rural and urban segments as a part of a "rururban" pattern. Lee County has gradually understood the relationship of the town to the surrounding area and that there is a correlation between the relative success of all parts. The third component of community is the local society including the interconnecting association and networks. The evolution of these ties is a central theme in this book.

The community one encounters in Tupelo today is a product of the community development of the past half-century. The Tupelo community development experience, like all community development, should be viewed in two different ways. There is development *of* community and development *in* community. The former usually refers to strengthening of the relationships and networks within the community. Emphasis is on the creation and maintenance of organizations and activities that link citizens to one another and to the community. Community leaders must continually tend to the elements that bind the community into a meaningful group. The community itself cannot exist without these structural elements that hold it together.

Development in the community views the community as "essentially a territorial setting for social processes." Community development within this context is a means of improving the social process to achieve some goal; i.e., making more money. Community economic development is an example of development in community.[10]

Leaders within Tupelo would not use such academic language, but they would understand its meaning and would recognize the truth of what is being said. In their words, "community development precedes economic development," implying, of course, that it is first necessary to build a sense of community before one can achieve meaningful economic development.[11] For them a strong community came before the economic fruits for which they have become known. Over a long period of time, the economic gains were pumped back into the community, enhancing the community's ability to remain viable and to further enrich itself with still more jobs.

The ultimate goal of Tupelo, as with any community concerned with development, is to become what Leonard Cottrell calls the "competent community." He describes such a community as "one in which the various component parts of the community: (1) are able to collaborate effectively in identifying the problems and needs of the community; (2) can achieve a working consensus on goals and priorities; (3) can agree on ways and means to implement the agreement; and (4) can collaborate effectively in the agreed actions."[12]

It is, of course, very difficult to become a competent community. Building community is not a natural process. The common tendency is to work toward one's own goals without recognizing the commonality of interest and problems, which might bring citizens together in a sense of community. Within all communities at almost any time, there are the forces for unity and turbulence; the strain between cooperation and self-seeking. It is the same in Tupelo.[13]

One of the keys to the success of Tupelo and similarly resourceful communities is that the community has been able to meet self-interest by working together. This does not mean that citizens do not sometimes behave in unselfish ways. They do, but altruism is not the basis of the success of the community.

Communities have strong internal disagreements. In this community self-interest is one of the most powerful motivations. The approach that Tupelo pursues is to achieve personal goals through working together, even when the participants do not always like one another personally. This is not only possible, it is a daily occurrence.[14]

During the course of one interview, the author commented to a respondent that he missed visiting with one of his now deceased former colleagues. "Hell," he said, "I don't miss the so-and-so." Surprised, he pressed on. "But, I thought you two had worked together for over 25 years." "Hell," he retorted, "I worked with the s.o.b. for more than 30 years and hated him the whole time." Not allowing the matter to rest, the interviewer tried one more time, "Well, why did you cooperate with him?" His answer came back faster than the question. "Because we needed one another and besides, I didn't want him to get all the credit." This, too, is part of the Tupelo Spirit.

Communities and Boundaries

For all of us, community is more than an abstract idea. It is a place. It is a setting with all the physical characteristics of towns or cities. It has streets, sites of work, trade, and recreation. It includes downtown and maybe shopping malls, tidy residential neighborhoods, and perhaps a few shabby areas. But where is the boundary of the community? Do the legal corporate limits accurately define the boundaries of the community? Does it stop at the railroad tracks where the fashionable neighborhoods give way to blighted areas? Are the commuters who live in the surrounding hinterland but who work and shop in the town part of the community? Are the suburbs and the inner city part of the same community? Is the community composed only of people of common race or ethnic origin?[15]

The answers to these questions are very important for day-to-day behavior. People are usually interested in their community, and they care about their community. They often support their community's athletic teams and turn quickly to the sports pages of the newspaper to see how their team did. They contribute to their United Way. They are concerned about the children in their community and worry that drugs, teen gangs, and AIDS might come to their community. Their community may provide a sense of safety and security.[16]

These informal bonds between the residents and their community are as real as the more tangible physical structures' dimensions. These ties link us to our community. Without these and similar ties there is no community and, consequently, no community development. Both begin with the ties that bind us to the community. Understanding that one's own self-interest is linked to the community is often the starting point for an individual's involvement in community development. Identifying the boundaries of the community and thereby the boundary of self-interest is equally critical. The community may be willing to invest its resources in its own development, but have little personal stake beyond the local boundaries.

It is essential, therefore, that people feel an involvement with their community, that they experience the benefits of being a part of the locale, that it truly be their community.

In all communities there are strong social barriers that retard or prevent interaction and therefore prevent community from developing among all the people. An essential part of community development is removing these barriers, whether they are rural/urban schisms, class or racial barriers. Too often the "community development" projects of towns focus on delivering primary benefits to those in the top echelons, who may be in fact the least in need of the benefits of "community development."

Sociologists have long sought to identify boundaries as a means of coming to grips with the nature of community. Charles Galpin, in his pioneer research to determine trade-area boundaries, studied the ruts made by wagons as they turned from their driveways. He could correctly identify the trade boundaries by noting the places within the county where the ruts pointed to different communities. Galpin's research demonstrated the two sides of the issue. While communities may be divided from one another, the town and its countryside are linked economically.[17]

Economic boundaries are real, as Galpin's research indicated. Determining where and how to draw those boundaries is fodder for the imagination. Defining the economic boundaries is often an initial step in community and economic development. The dynamics and often the economic health of the community are influenced by the placement of the boundaries. Obviously, these boundaries almost never approximate the political boundaries of corporate limits. In our own time, it has become almost a cliché to note that each community is part of a global economy and all communities must come to grips with their relationship to remote regions. Initially, however, it must consider its most immediate boundaries.

As this book will demonstrate, the beginning of Tupelo and Lee County's success was the recognition of the interrelationship between the town and county's economy. Community and community development, however, is more than an awareness of commonality. Community development requires action.

As noted above and throughout this book, the most fundamental action of community development is the removal of barriers to interaction and the building of social structures that enhance interaction. This is true in all communities and it can be clearly seen in the Tupelo experience.

Communities are dynamic and ever-changing. Boundaries, once defined for the purpose of conscious community development, will need to be redefined as the society changes. As can be seen in Tupelo's story, building community is much like building sand castles on the beach. Both the external and internal forces continually work to erode the structure. Community development is frequently community redevelopment. The sense of community must be reinforced regularly.

Tupelo, like all towns, constantly has had to draw and redraw boundaries. Sometimes the boundaries have been unnecessarily restrictive and have been the primary obstacle to progress. For example, the arbitrary boundaries between town and country or the boundaries between whites and blacks[18] have often deterred development. At other times the boundaries were drawn in such a way that they were more liberating than confining. A good example of such boundary identification occurred during World War I. At that time, some of the community's leaders recognized that the prosperity of the town was linked to that of the surrounding farmland. The town could only reach its potential by helping farmers to reach their goals. As long as farmers were poor, the merchants with whom they traded would also be economically limited. It was not enough to recognize the commonality of interest. It was also necessary to expend energy and resources to assist the farmers to earn more money. This was a way of serving both self-interest and community needs. Consequently, from that time to the present Tupelo has understood that its economic boundaries do not stop at the corporate limits. To remind itself of that part of its history, Tupelo later proudly hailed itself as "the city without city limits." While this phrase was neither original nor entirely true, it did formally acknowledge a vital lesson for both town and county. Lee County leaders, like many other visionaries, had learned the greater lesson that power is often increased by sharing it. That lesson has had to be relearned regularly in Lee County and its worthiness will be cited throughout this book.

A different but equally critical dimension of the boundary issue is the widely held concern that community boundaries may fade entirely and thus bring the death of community. Roland Warren's path-breaking work has instructed a generation of community scholars and leaders and has placed that issue on center stage. He notes that there are forces, that he describes as "horizontal ties" that bind a community together, such as community schools. There are even more dominant bonds or "vertical ties," which link the community to the external world, such as state standards for education. He, like other scholars, has seen a threat to the very nature of community, as the vertical ties become both more numerous and influential. No one who works in or with communities can doubt that threat.[19]

In summary, community development begins with a sense of community identity. It is the foundation of all that follows. This often starts with the awareness that locale or boundary maintenance is both relevant and necessary.

Moreover, the community needs internal structure that provides a sense of unity. There must be consensus that the community's problems are the rightful concern of all its citizens. There also must be institutional and cultural mechanisms to address those problems. Without the proper mechanism to engage the problems, there is both demoralization and defeatism. The very survival of the community depends on maximizing the involvement of the largest segment of population possible. Thus, community boundaries must be inclusive in order to maximize involvement of the population in their own development.

Social Structures and Community Leadership

Community development in Tupelo or any other place is always concerned with social structure. Community by its very nature is held together by local social institutions, networks, and organizations. The town may also have traditional symbols or local celebrations that unite the citizens. There are also personal ties such as home ownership and family linkages. All of these form a social framework or social structure that make the existence of community possible.

The internal bonds are also the basis for community development, which is best defined as "a group of people in a locality initiating a social action process (i.e., planned interaction) to change their economic, social, cultural, and/or environmental situation."[20] For any group to act, especially one as large as a community, there must be some internal order.

There are three approaches to community development: self-help, technical assistance, and conflict. For both the self-help and conflict approach, cohesiveness of purpose and action is essential. The basic assumption of self-help is that people working together can improve their conditions. Conflict works on a similar principle. The conflict approach sees a major division within the community that stimulates confrontation between the opposing sides. Both of these approaches will often require technical assistance to achieve their goals. Obviously, technical assistance can be gained without community unity, but community development must involve community participation. Without some order and structure, community action is not possible.[21]

One of the rubric lessons of the Tupelo experience is the power of organization. At any point in the community's history the group that is the best organized is the most likely to achieve its goal, whether that goal is road construction, industrial recruitment, election of candidates, or wage negotiations. When the community has been well organized it is more often successful than not. This is a lesson that can be seen throughout the nation. Studies consistently reveal that local organization is necessary for development. Development is impeded wherever organization and associations are weak or nonexistent.[22]

The organizational process that drives the community development process often begins as an informal interpersonal relationship among community power figures. This group of key leaders comprise what is herein called the coordinating association. In local parlance, they might be referred to as the movers and shakers. These individuals may or may not hold public office. In Tupelo, only a small percentage were public officeholders. They may or may not have democratic tendencies. They will hold key economic positions such as membership on the board of directors of banks, ownership of major businesses, and plant managers or CEOs of local companies. They may not originate all community development efforts, but they are at least the gatekeepers for such action and most community actions will have to gain their tacit sanction.[23]

Like leaders in any situation, one of their primary functions is to define reality.[24] Thus, similar situations occurring in different towns might be defined in quite different ways. Leaders in one town might see a situation as an opportunity. Their counterparts in another town might define almost the exact set of situations as a crisis. Leaders in a third locale might see the events as a situation requiring no formal response at all. Leaders are the actors who are expected to respond to change. They are the envisioning agents for the town. As such they are expected to give the town a vision and sense of direction. They must mobilize the community's resources, seek technical assistance when needed, raise capital for action, and provide linkage to the external society.

Their ability to respond depends on personal skills, but is also shaped by the readiness of the community to act. If proper community-building has transpired and organizations or service associations are in place, the coordinating association's responsibility is to coordinate the activities of these service associations. In the face of change, the coordinating agencies must use the existing service associations. This will usually include the use of the local government and its subparts or will call on some external agency for technical or other form of assistance.

The coordinating association plays the pivotal role in community development. This group must have knowledge or information and imagination. They must apply this information and imagination in a way that strengthens community organizations and thereby build community capacity. Because of the centrality of their role, community leadership development is now being viewed as the cornerstone of community revitalization. Almost all regional development programs begin with leadership development.[25]

Community coordinating associations are almost always working on two types of issues. There are the town building projects and the community-building efforts. Town building programs dominate the early history of a town, though town building continues for the life of the community. The town must have its basic infrastructure, which is created over a sustained period of time. Such efforts never entirely cease, since a growing town is constantly adding infrastructure of new roads, sewage, water, airports, industrial parks, or other infrastructure necessary for current residents or to create new jobs. Some of these activities are performed as a matter of course by city government, but items not deemed routine will almost require the leadership and mobilization skills of the coordinating association.

In Tupelo, it was a coordinating association of this type that decided the town needed a second railroad in the 1880s. A similarly functioning group worked to construct a power plant and build the town's factories in the 1890s and still other almost identical groups promoted a drainage program in the early 1900s, and paved roads during World War I. Although the specific membership changed, the structure and function rarely altered.

Community-building, as noted earlier, consists of strengthening the bonds among the residents. This occurs simultaneously with town building and it, too, is an ongoing activity. On some occasions in Tupelo, the town building efforts infused a sense of community in the participants. Unfortunately, many community leaders throughout the nation perceive the activities aimed at community-building as being fringe action and unconnected to the central business of the community, such as earning a living, family rearing, and other measures that consume most of our time. Research reveals, however, that community-building and organization construction are critical to the other town processes.[26]

The stages of action for any form of community development are remarkably similar. It begins with an awareness of the problem. While the problem may be observed by a number of individuals, there will be one individual who is sufficiently concerned to begin at least conversations about the issue. Successful projects often require a champion who is passionate about its implementation. He or she elevates the effort to its second stage, initiation of effort. At this point, the individuals concerned begin to consider goals and strategies. In the third stage, legitimation, the group seeks support from a wider audience including the formal structures, such as governmental agencies, which must be involved in the effort. Following this there must be a mobilization of community and external resources. Once this is achieved the association begins implementation. If the project succeeds, the community is now ready for future action. This readiness is itself a vital component of the stages of action. The experience and confidence tends to increase the probability that a community will act in the future.[27]

At each level beyond the awareness stage, organizations become critical for the continuation of the project. If organizations do not exist they need to be created. The relative strength of the groups often determines the degree of success.

Changing the Social Structure

Community development does not simply use the social structure as a resource. Community development changes the social structure.[28]

Tupelo and Lee County have gone through three broad stages of community action. The first stretches from the mid-1880s to World War I. The second from World War I to 1930. The third and longest stage began in the mid-1930s and extends to the present. In each phase the key elements are leadership, community-building, and organization.

The first stage was primarily a period of town building. Its signal accomplishment was the establishment of basic infrastructure. As noted above, a well-orga-nized group of community leaders were able to influence a second railroad to intersect the original line. Another group of equally well-organized leaders established electrical power and water for the town. This led directly to the town's early industrial base when these same leaders pooled their money to build a series of agriculturally related factories. A third set of leaders helped establish an effective drainage system for much of the county, then topped this achievement by helping to build the first concrete highways in the South. These were all essential for the subsequent growth of the town. They provided a physical basis for future growth and became the inspiration and model for subsequent community development. Some required extraordinary resourcefulness and foresight, but they were achieved by a relatively small group of well-organized key people. They did not depend on extensive involvement of the people. While the results might be praiseworthy, and brought benefits to almost all the citizens, these events did not significantly alter the structure of the community.[29]

Phase two, although the shortest period, brought important change to the structure of the community. The specific events were noted earlier, but are so critical to the Tupelo model that they bear deeper examination.

Lee County was cotton country when World War I began. Some of the region's soil was fertile, but much of it had been depleted by the turn of the century, contributing to some of the rural poverty. Most of the lint cotton made its way to the mills in England. The war, especially the German blockade, severely weakened the international cotton market. This problem was compounded by the arrival of the cotton boll weevil, which destroyed a large part of the crop. Farmers faced total disaster and so did their creditors, the banks. At that point, Jim High, vice president of The Peoples Bank, borrowed the ideas of fellow banks in the Pacific Northwest and started a countywide agricultural diversification program. The Bank of Tupelo followed the lead as did the Progressive Club, the businessmen's organization. The banks and other business leaders invested a significant part of their profits in this experiment. The program was a success and saved many of the county's farmers from ruin. The banks recouped their loans and made a profit; their fellow businessmen benefited from the farmers' prosperity through trade.[30]

The town building and community action cited above are important and even significant. In 1923, *The Wall Street Journal* called for Jim High's model to be used as a national model.[31] Unfortunately, however, these efforts were not sustained in the 1930s, not even in Lee County. Tragically, by 1940 Lee County was then one of the poorest counties in the United States.

The inability of Lee County to sustain its immediate postwar success demonstrates two principles of community development. First, the origins of many community troubles originate outside of the community and cannot be solved by local efforts alone. Most of these problems require national and state policies that can only be supplemented by local endeavors. Second, Tupelo did not institutionalize its community development efforts. There was no organization that assumed the responsibility for maintaining community development.

The changes of the High era had not gone far enough in reshaping the social structure. Nevertheless, the High era had laid the groundwork on which the next generation of leaders could build.

The key leader, or catalyst as he preferred to be called, was George McLean. McLean was a boundary spanner, a man who had traveled outside his own tribe, as political scientist Tom Cronin would call him. He was a native Mississippian, who in seven years away from his home had gained new knowledge and a new perspective. He was a pragmatic imaginist and innovative social architect who provided many of the blueprints for building a better community.

The building materials of that transition are sketched here, but their full richness in their historical setting are described in later chapters. The community development began with a plan. It was an excellent plan that years later would receive national praise.[32] But the plan lay dormant until the people became actively involved in its implementation. This was an early and valuable lesson. Leadership is not about doing things for the community, it is about empowering the citizens so that they can become central to their own community development. Moreover, this town learned that boosterism, that is "talking up the town," was not sufficient. Meaningful action involved changing the social structure.

Some of their work has been experimental and risky, but Tupelo leaders have gained knowledge by looking at other communities to learn from their experiences. They have consistently done their homework. They research, gain technical assistance, and constantly read for new ideas. Almost nothing is left to chance or luck.

Tupelo's effort at restructuring began on a small scale. In fact, it began with developing interpersonal ties among the leadership and between the leaders and their constituency. In hindsight, many of the early programs began as pilot projects, although that term was not used. While all successful projects started small, the goal was usually to gain maximum involvement by the population. Where this was possible the results were the most profound.

The projects began where the need was greatest, in this case the poor rural areas. Over the years, the programs with the greatest impact were those that led directly or indirectly to jobs. For example, every Tupelo generation has attempted a beautification program for the commercial district, but none has been successful. Why? One likely answer is that such projects were not perceived to create jobs.

One of the most crucial elements in Lee County's success is its willingness to recognize and address the reality of conflict. All communities have latent conflict that occasionally rises to the surface. Lee County has had its share of major conflicts; for example, the tension between town and country has existed from the beginning. It has sometimes emerged into active hostilities, as it did in the 1890s. There has also been tension between labor and management. In 1937, Tupelo was the scene of one of the most bitter labor strikes in the nation. Moreover, racial tension is an ongoing reality.

For much of the last half-century, the whole community, town, and county has engaged in the intelligent construction of win/win situations that both defuse much of the tension and are a source of the county's strength. Each rural community was organized at the grassroots level through a rural community development corporation (RCDC), which operates like a New England town meeting with full participation from all the community's citizens. Each of these RCDCs was linked to a Tupelo civic club that served as the sponsor of the RCDC. In this way, the town and rural communities became partners in community development. As a second method, the industries are scattered throughout the county. They are not Tupelo's industries. They are Lee County industries. This puts jobs close to the workers and perhaps, more importantly, it puts industry in the district of every county supervisor. This makes the board of supervisors active participants in the economic and community development programs.

Engaging the county supervisors, city officials, and businessmen in the economic development process helps to fuse the public and private sector, which otherwise would be another potential source of conflict. Industrial growth of the community enriches the city government with tax dollars just as it does for the county government. This helps make the city a partner in both community and economic development.

Businesses have come to realize that their own prosperity depends on the financial status of their customers, who are also the workers in the county. The community development efforts have established three primary means of raising the income levels of laborers. It is done by direct assistance. This was especially true of efforts in the 1940s to increase agricultural productivity. In addition, the county's factory jobs offer supplemental or alternative sources of income. As a third option, workers have numerous opportunities to upgrade their skills, which benefits them and the industry. Laborers can choose from vo-tech programs, a community college, literacy programs, and a branch of the state's university, all of which were created as part of the community development efforts.

Part of the centerpiece of the community restructuring is the formalization of the coordinating association. The town abandoned the Chamber of Commerce and in its place established the Community Development Foundation (CDF). The CDF takes a broad perspective of the community and is concerned with improving all phases of life through the whole county. It has a broad-based membership of more than 1,100 members.

The CDF, working in conjunction with the local newspaper, has invented or created more than 20 organizations, herein referred to as service associations, which work with some specialized segment of community development such as housing, health care, education, vocational training, or economic development. In this arrangement, the CDF serves as the coordinating association and the specialized organizations are the service associations.

During the past three decades, Lee County has continued to expand its economic boundaries. As part of that transition, the county has helped create new multicounty social structures. Consistent with its policy of building an economic foundation, its first multicounty organization was the North Mississippi Industrial Development Association, whose purpose has been to assist all of north Mississippi to establish a strong economic base. To extend communication ties to the area, the local newspaper deleted the name Tupelo from its masthead and has become the *Northeast Mississippi Daily Journal* in name and in philosophy. The newspaper now envisions its role to serve the whole area.

CDF serves as the hub of a multiorganizational leadership pattern. Detailed research reveals that Tupelo and Lee County have an unusually high number of leaders who are attached to numerous organizations.[33] Tupelo leaders are therefore more likely to take a broad or generalist perspective. In part, this is true because in creating such a wide number of organizations, the town has also multiplied the opportunities to work at community activities. These organizations are also training grounds for future leadership.

Many of the most effective leaders have learned to be social architects. They build new organizations and they create social bridges between existing groups.

One can observe the extensive number of community organizations from the litany of community activities cited earlier.

Community leaders are guided by the principle that local problems require local response. While the community's philosophy is deeply grounded in the importance of self-help, the community regularly seeks technical assistance. A cardinal premise is that the town must continually update its focus and skills. The town invariably draws on the expertise of national figures deemed to be near the cutting edge of change.

Such efforts are expensive as is the challenge to maintain gains and build for the future. Tupelo's norms expect widespread participation and financial investments in community development. Most businessmen have come to view their contributions as investments in the community and as part of the fixed overhead of doing business.

The community has established a second means of pooling local monies. George McLean, understanding the need to have local capital, founded a community foundation that he named CREATE (Christian, Research, Education, Action, Technical Enterprise). CREATE makes a good case to demonstrate the importance of developing service organizations as part of the social structure. This community foundation is an invention consciously constructed to fill a gap not being performed within the existing social system. It collects local money to be used in community development projects and is also an instrument for seeking external funds for the area. In addition, it heightens the sense of community as individuals make contributions to and in the name of the community.

The town has also become adept at gaining external resources. In rebuilding its internal social structure, the town did not neglect its vertical or external ties. Community leaders are well connected to state and federal agencies. They have become proficient at recapturing state and federal tax dollars. They constantly work to strengthen such linkages and to forge new ties to other innovative towns and regions. The community is ever attuned to ideas that can be borrowed, adapted, and put in place in Lee County.

Lee County's development approach may be accurately described as focus with flexibility. The central goal is to create a stronger community that enriches all its citizens. The leadership is receptive to a variety of means by which the goals are attained.

The local newspaper has been a beacon assisting the community with its vision and helping to maintain focus. There are few newspapers in the nation that can match it for community concern and involvement. It keeps the primary issues before the reading public. It has promoted some projects for half a century. Projects, such as four-lane highways and sound housing for all citizens have taken decades to accomplish. The newspaper has also been the model for community involvement. It has been the catalyst for a majority of the most innovative projects. It has invested a greater share of its wealth than any other business in town. It has been a reservoir and disseminator of ideas for development. It has been the champion for the common man.

This persistence and continuity of effort has also become a part of the local culture. Community development is a daily process. The community expects progress. The consistency of the daily operations combine to make the more spectacular achievements that capture the headlines. It is difficult to exaggerate the importance of this consistency. It means that community development is routine and that the county continually strengthens its ability to do community development. Newcomers, especially factory managers, report that they are drawn into this process as part of their earliest orientation to the town.

Tupelo performs. Outsiders who work with Tupelo constantly remark "Tupelo does what it says it will do." The town and county have worked diligently to establish its organizations and it makes good use of them. The daily implementation is often the least glamorous part of community action, but is obviously where the whole process culminates.

Community development in Lee County and Tupelo, even with its long history of community development, is as challenging today as it was when its fledgling efforts began. Community development may be achieved only because some of the social structure (i.e., organizations and use of them) is in place. Nevertheless, there are the dual challenges of holding the community together in the face of increasing diversity and the centrifugal force created by strong vertical ties.

In subsequent chapters we will examine the process by which the community has come this far and how it is preparing itself to address current and future problems. This story follows in the tradition of tales throughout history whose message is success in the face of adversity, beauty arising from ugliness, and heroes and heroines who can imagine. It is a story of ongoing community development.

Summary and Conclusions

There is no formula for community development. It is a complex process and there is no way to make it simple or easy. However, there are basic elements that are essential. The community development process usually begins with leadership. Leadership, using a combination of information or knowledge, and imagination establishes a social structure that can solve community problems. One useful way of understanding the community development process is to examine a successful model. The model chosen for this study is Tupelo/Lee County, Mississippi.

This community has a number of qualities that make it an excellent model. During the past 40 years, it has been cited as a model by 4 different agencies representing 4 different criteria and perspectives. The community has established a strong economic base that has greatly increased the per capita income of its citizens. That base has served as a productive seedbed. Out of it has grown a quality medical center, a multibranched educational system, affordable housing, cultural and performing arts programs, and recreational opportunities. The medical center and educational programs are the choice plums that feed still more development.

These achievements are the attractive fruit of a consciously planned and implemented program of community development. But this is not ornamental fruit for display only. The economic and social gains provide the nourishment or resources for subsequent community development. This is part of the cycle of development in which the development *in* community feeds back into the development *of* community.

Lee County makes a useful model also because it is almost devoid of natural resources. The community has relied on its human resources and supplemented its own capacity by borrowing ideas from sister communities. It has borrowed all of its basic ideas. Now the cycle can be complete as other communities borrow from the borrower.

Lee County's community development has withstood the test of social change. The program has evolved over a half-century. During that time its economic and social gains continue to increase. The economic base remains resilient after making the transition from agriculture to industry and service.

Community development involves both development of the community and in the community. In the case of the former, the concern is with strengthening the community itself. A simple starting point is to identify the boundaries of the community and by this means help to establish the nature and scope of the community to be affected. All communities require a critical mass of population and services to be viable and, therefore, the community boundaries must be wide enough to incorporate those minimal necessities. By contrast it must also be restrictive enough that the community has clear identity to its inhabitants.

Community is difficult to achieve because of the barriers posed by inequality and distance. Moreover, personal agendas often force community issues aside. Effective communities are also able to meet individual needs through community development. Interests are the driving force in communities. The key is in recognizing and acting on common problems. By so doing, the community attends to both personal and community needs.

The Lee County community-building process has gone through three stages. During the period from the 1880s to World War I, the town established much of its basic infrastructure, but made little change in the internal social structure.

During the second period, from World War I to 1930, key county leaders helped to redraw the community's economic boundaries. As a result, Lee County became the basic economic community. For the first time in the county's history, Tupelo leaders actively invested in a community development effort to improve the economic condition of the whole county.

These efforts were curtailed by the Great Depression. The decade of the thirties was a period of little or no community progress and the county actually lost ground when it was unable to sustain earlier gains.

From 1940 to the present, the community transformed its social structure leading to a period of continual community development. The catalyst for the transformation was the owner and publisher of the *Tupelo Journal,* George McLean. The effort began with a carefully developed plan that was firmly grounded in sound community development principles. The plan itself was not activated until McLean established a bond of trust with community leaders.

The leaders, who composed the county's coordinating association, strengthened their own unity and resolve. Thus, the restructuring began at the top. Their efforts produced a vision for the county. The next step was to build ties to the large rural population. This was achieved through sustained interpersonal contacts aimed at improving the rural economy. The second phase was to enhance each rural community's capacity to improve itself.

The plan concentrated on organizing rural community development corporations in all rural communities. Each rural community was linked to a Tupelo civic club that served as a sponsor and could provide ongoing assistance.

Through a series of win/win approaches, the community leadership drew the rural area into the overall economic gains of the county. For those who remained on the farm, Tupelo provided direct assistance. The remaining rural population that constituted the majority of the work force was drawn into industrial employment after their displacement from agricultural jobs. To assist in this transformation, the community took two primary actions. Industries were built in the rural areas to bring the jobs closer to the workers. The community established a broad range of educational opportunities including programs in literacy, vocational education, and university classes to allow workers to upgrade their skills.

The county and city governments were made partners in the benefits and economic process, thus laying the groundwork for strong public-private cooperative efforts. This has evolved to include cooperative efforts in education, health care, and between industry and the local governments.

The coordinating association was formalized into a broad-based community development association. Henceforth, the coordinating association focused on community development on an ongoing basis. No longer did the coordinating association come forward only in moments of crisis.

Among the most salient actions, the CDF and *Tupelo Journal* helped to invent or create a variety of service associations that addressed specific community needs. This and similar programs provided services and helped to integrate the social structure. As a result, the community's social structure has been radically altered from the grass roots to the top and linked together by a series of social associations. The structure has been put in place for ongoing community development.

CHAPTER 2

Town Building

Town building, unlike community-building, may require little local community effort. Town building is more competitive than cooperative and is infused and driven by entrepreneurial energy. It often requires the efforts of strong-willed, well-focused individuals. In the final analysis it is men, in the generic sense, who build cities. Men, who can attract or build transportation lines and who can utilize the natural advantages, are among the most essential components of town building. However, towns and cities by their very nature are part of a much greater economic system and, therefore, local efforts must be supplemented by external elements. This requires imaginative coordination of local, state, and federal activities.

Town building in Lee County had its origin in the exciting speculative mania of the 1830s. The nation as a whole was aflame with the expectation of great riches acquired quickly through land transactions. Nowhere did the passion for fortunes burn hotter than in Mississippi. John Moore, one of the state's leading historians, sums up the motivational factors: "Although people migrated to other regions of North America seeking economic opportunities, religious liberty, or the right to govern themselves after their own fashions, the early settlers of Mississippi moved there for no other reason but to make their fortune."[1]

Fortune seekers in Mississippi were the embodiment of privatism as described by the urban historian, Sam Bass Warner. The essence of privatism, as he used the term, is the concentration on the individual and the individual's search for wealth.

"Psychologically, privatism meant that the individual should seek happiness in personal independence and in the search for wealth; socially, privatism meant that the individual should see his first loyalty as his immediate family, and that a community should be a union of such money-making, accumulating families; politically, privatism meant that the community should keep peace among individual money-makers, and if possible, help to create an open and thriving setting where each citizen would have some substantial opportunity to prosper."[2]

This accurately describes the dominant sentiment of the settlers and the "community" that they sought to create.

The initial step was the removal of the indigenous population. After several decades of pressure, Choctaw Territory was ceded in 1830 with the Treaty of Dancing Rabbit Creek. Two years later, the land from which Lee County and Tupelo were carved was transferred from the Chickasaw Nation to the United States.

There had been a series of treaties extending over a decade by which the Chickasaw land was taken. The final treaty was made on October 20, 1832, at Pontotoc Creek in the southeastern part of what became Pontotoc County. The agreement was between the Chickasaw Nation in general council assembled and General John Coffee of Tennessee, the United States Commissioner.[3]

According to the terms of the treaty, the Chickasaw Nation ceded all their lands east of the Mississippi River, which brought an end to all Native American ownership of land in Mississippi. The proceeds of the land sales were to go to the Indians. The Chickasaw were to decide on a location west of the Mississippi. Based on an amendment in 1834, they were to be protected against hostile tribes after their move. Until that time, they were to live on specified reservations. Four years later, in 1836, the Chickasaw departed their ancient homeland.[4]

The acquisition brought Mississippi an additional 6,283,804 acres covering over 10,000 square miles. From that territory were carved twelve new counties. Several kept alive the memory of their previous occupants with county names like Tishomingo, Itawamba, Pontotoc, Tippah, Tunica, and Chickasaw.

Original Counties of the Chickasaw Cession

These counties, along with Marshall, Lafayette, DeSoto, Panola, Monroe, and Bolivar composed the original units. From these still other counties would emerge, including Lee, which was at that time part of Pontotoc and Itawamba counties.

The official opening of the land in 1836 launched one of the wildest and most spectacular periods in the history of the South. The presence of abundant land brought the promise of quick riches, and the intoxicating scent of profit lured speculators like jackals to a fresh kill. Mississippi grew by more than 175 percent in the decade of the 1830s, the largest growth in its history. The 1830 population of 132,621 swelled to 375,651 by 1840.[5]

The mood of these flush times was captured by its most famous chronicler, Joseph G. Baldwin.

"The country was just setting up. Marvellous accounts had gone forth of the fertility of its virgin lands; and the production of the soil were commanding a price remunerating to slave labor as it had never been remunerated before. . . . Emigrants came flocking in from all quarters of the Union, especially the slave-holding states. The new country seemed to be a reservoir, and every road leading to it a vagrant stream of enterprise and adventure."[6]

Looking back on those days of glittering greed, Baldwin recalled the fierce competition.

"What country could boast more largely of its crime? What more splendid felonies! What more terrific murders! What gorgeous bank robberies! What more magnificent operations in land offices . . . the romance of a wild and weird larceny!" [7]

Another contemporary, Reuben Davis, wrote that the people of the 1880s would be "horrified" by the "excitement and pleasures of such a carnival." He depicted the times as a period of "strong passions." "It was a new country teeming with wealth and full of adventurous spirits. There is no tameness, no satiety."[8]

The mood of the time reflected the national mind-set. Between 1835 and 1837, an estimated 29,000,000 acres of the 38,000,000 acres of United States public land sold were acquired for speculation.[9] The Mississippi speculation was a part of that national activity. All of the big land speculators were eastern land companies. There was the New York and Mississippi Land Company, Boston and Mississippi Land Company, Boston and New York Chickasaw Land Company, the New York, Mississippi, and Arkansas Land Company, and the American Land Company, which was formed in New York.

Their representatives were men from the East who had come to the then southwest frontier to make their own personal fortune. Five of these men are worth noting. There was Robert Gordon, originally a native of Aberdeen, Scotland, whose quickly amassed fortune demonstrated the potential of the times. Gordon, a merchant and lawyer, was one of the first speculators in the area. His land holdings in time would rival that of land barons anywhere. From his palatial mansion, Lochinvar, still occupied in Pontotoc, he seemed the lord of the great manor so recently taken from the natives.[10] Gordon became the friend and business partner of John Bell. Bell was the only speculator with long ties to the area. His father, Robert Bell, had been a Presbyterian missionary in what became Monroe County. Bell's intimate knowledge of the area and his skill as a surveyor led to his being appointed as the surveyor general for the territory. He and Gordon eventually sold much of their land to other land speculators, Richard Edward Orne and Henry Anderson.

Orne, a short stout man, was a native of Massachusetts. Originally he had sought adventure and fortune as a seaman. He became a sea captain but abandoned that life to seek wealth in Mississippi. His partner, Henry Anderson, had gradually moved to the Southwest in a series of stages. He lived for a time in Florence, Alabama, but saw the opportunity for even quicker riches in Mississippi. Richard Bolton completed the quintet of key speculators. Bolton was a native of New York. He was trained as an engineer and had been hired by the Eastern land companies to survey and claim much of the land. At times all five men worked as a unit or individually. Orne, Anderson, and Bolton bought 35 percent of the Chickasaw allotments, more than 2 million acres. It was big business on a grand scale.[11]

They were the generals in this army of speculators. Their invasion moved with the speed of a blitzkrieg. In a short time, an estimated 80 percent of the Chickasaw land was owned for speculative profit.[12]

The appetite of the speculators was being fed by the demand for cotton land. The timing was fortuitous. On the one hand much of the tobacco land of the upper South, of Virginia and the Carolinas, was fast becoming exhausted from intensive farming. By the 1830s, cotton was promising even greater profits than tobacco. Cotton had now become the dominant crop in Mississippi. Prices for the fleecy staple was stirring excitement throughout the region. One visitor to Mobile during this period reported that he had heard the word "cotton" at least 3,000 times in a short visit.[13]

This region was almost perfect for this white gold. It had a long growing season. The annual rainfall of more than 50 inches assured all the water needed for the crop. The land to the east of the Pontotoc Ridge was too hilly for some row crops, but the land to the west of the ridge was excellent. Within a decade, Marshall County was the leading cotton producing county in the state.[14] The advertisements for the land were calling it the richest cotton land in the nation. Of course one must consider the profit-seeking mentality of those offering the land. Often there was only a thin line between truth and outright lies. More often there was little or no truth to the claims. One of the favorite ploys was to note that this was formerly Indian land and that the natives had unlimited choice and they had chosen to settle here. These ads did not note that the Chickasaw were primarily hunters and not concerned with farming and certainly not with cotton.

Much of the land sold quickly, and by 1838 there were only 24 sections of land in Pontotoc that had not been sold at least once. Fortunes on paper were almost commonplace.[15]

The greatest profits, however, were not to be made in selling farmland. The great fortunes were to be made in creating towns and selling town lots. Land could be purchased for a little more than one dollar an acre. A single acre could be subdivided into three one-third acre lots and sold for $500 per lot or $1,500 for a one-dollar investment.

With that kind of profit at stake, speculators wasted no time in building towns. Pontotoc was established two years before the legal sale of the Chickasaw allotments. Town lots in Holly Springs in Marshall County were being advertised in 1835, a year before the official opening of the land.[16] Robert Gordon, John Bell, and Richard Bolton found an excellent town site on the blue bluffs of the Tombigbee River where they created Aberdeen, so named in honor of Gordon's hometown in Scotland. Henry Anderson worked to develop Holly Springs. Richard Edward Orne platted Hernando, originally named Jefferson. After their initial success, Anderson, Orne and Samuel McCorkle, representing three different land companies, pooled their efforts to establish the town of Commerce on the Mississippi River. Within six months they had sold $160,000 in town lots in their aptly named village.[17]

The town builders continued at a hectic pace. By 1839, these five primary "movers and shakers" were responsible for originating eight of the twenty-one towns created in the former Chickasaw territory.[18]

The specific site of Tupelo was not developed in this initial round. The property was owned jointly by Anderson, Orne, and Christopher Orr. Orr had just platted a town that he named in honor of his native state of South Carolina, calling his town Palmetto. This town was only a short distance from the eventual site of Tupelo.[19]

The commerce of almost all the towns centered around two businesses: taverns for the youthful extant population and the newspaper, whose primary role was to lure still more settlers. The newspapers delighted in portraying their towns and the surrounding hinterland as a veritable promised land for distressed farmers. They were also careful to characterize their immigrants as persons of the highest quality. An ideal combination was hit on by the *Hernando Phenix (sic)*. The newspaper described their migrants in language later used by Avery Craven's narrative of farmers driven from the upper South as the result of soil exhaustion.[20]

"Our citizens consist not of the refuse of cities, who are generally indolent and extravagant; but of those who seek a livelihood in the culture of the soil, and the pursuit of the most useful and necessary trades and professions. Our population, too, is chiefly of the elder states whose enterprise and perseverance led them to abandon the worn out lands of their inheritance, and with their source and industry cultivate the rich soil of Mississippi. . . ."[21]

Boosterism of this sort was rampant and much of the empty claims were silly in their simplicity, but there were also ambitious individuals who both planned and delivered on their promise. Holly Springs had created a university by 1837. Unfortunately it was one of the casualties of the depression later that year.[22] Nearby Oxford had a different fate. Its university, established in 1844, became the

State University.

The same type of individuals who founded universities knew that empty boost-erism would not build towns. Towns by their very nature required trade and commerce. Trade, in turn, required adequate transportation. Even those towns such as Aberdeen and Commerce, which had the natural advantage of river transportation, were not linked to the hinterland on which they depended for raw materials and commerce.

There were a series of existing trails. Gaines Trace was used to transport goods on pack trains from Colbert's Ferry on the Tennessee River in northwest Alabama to Cotton Gin Port on the Tombigbee River. The Baldwin Trail, also called the Choctaw Trail, ran from Chickasaw Bluffs (Memphis) southeast to Chickasaw Fields, in the vicinity of what became Tupelo. The Natchez Trace by contrast, one of the oldest trails in the area, had never been suitable for transporting goods from farm to market. Lastly there was the Jackson Military Road, that traverses the area between Columbia, Tennessee, and New Orleans and had been forged by troops under Old Hickory's command, but it too was not adequate for routine commerce. A continual problem was the 50 inches of rain a year that helped to grow cotton, but made the roads virtual quagmires during the winter and spring.

The strategy, therefore, became to link the interior towns to the river towns by railroad. Many of the towns closer to the west would run rail lines to the Mississippi. Those to the east of the Pontotoc Ridge would build roads to points on the Tombigbee. Other towns sought to link to any nearby navigable stream. The plans themselves seemed reasonable and possible under good economic conditions. The problem, however, was always a shortage of capital.

Town builders all understood that without adequate transportation their towns would soon languish. They wasted little time in devising an institution that would provide the impetus for the capital and the rail lines. Like other town and railroad builders, they created banking-railroad companies. Speculators/town builders took the initiative. Anderson, Orne, and McCorkle, for example, created the Hernando Railroad and Banking Company with the objective of linking their interior towns with their river towns.[23]

In 1836, the first year that the territory was legally open to settlement, three railroad companies were chartered in northeast Mississippi: the Aberdeen and Pontotoc Railroad and Banking Company; the Tallahatchie-Tillatoba Railroad Company, and the Tombigbee Railroad Company. The following year, two more companies were granted charters: the Pontotoc, Oxford, and Delta Railroad Company and the Grenada Railroad Company. In 1838, the Paulding and Pontotoc Railroad Company was chartered.[24] This gradual slowdown of railroad charters was one of the signs of the impending economic disaster. The panic of 1837 was devastating to the South's economy. It was triggered in large measure by the reckless speculation in which most of the purchases had been made with worthless currency. Presidents Andrew Jackson and Martin Van Buren had advocated the specie circular, a system of payment by which land purchases from the government could only be made by the use of hard currency, silver or gold. This severely curtailed the land speculation and revealed the absence of any foundation for the paper fortunes. These newly formed banking companies exacerbated the problem by adding more unsecured credit.

Compounding the problem, the price of cotton was soon cut in half. In 1834, Mississippi's main staple sold on the New Orleans' market for 15.5 cents a pound. Prices dropped two cents a pound two years later and were down an additional four cents a pound by 1837. This downward trend continued until 1844 when cotton prices reached the lowest mark of the century, selling for 5.5 cents a pound.[25]

The population became even more fluid. During the 1840s Pontotoc County's population increased from 4,291 to 17,112, a net increase of 12,821. The rate of increase was the greatest in the state.[26] The slowdown was reflected in the following census when the county experienced a new growth of 5,001, less than 40 percent of what it had been during the 1840s. Itawamba's rate of population change was less dramatic, but was consistent with the trend in Pontotoc. It added 8,153 people to its 1840 population of 5,375 to establish a total population of 13,528 in 1850. Ten years later, the increase of 4,167 was only 51 percent of the gain experienced in the prior decennial count.[27] As early as 1842 it was clear that the big profits from land transactions were coming to an end. In one Tunica County newspaper there were almost one thousand pieces of land for sale. In the 20-page *Hernando Phenix,* almost 18 pages listed land for sale.[28] Selling land for taxes became commonplace. A contemporary political figure, Reuben Davis, stated the problem directly. "We had no currency. Insolvency was the rule, and judgments accumulated against nearly all citizens. . . . By means of executions, sheriffs were seizing real and personal estate all over the country, and advertising for immediate sale. On the days appointed for such sales, the people assembled in angry mobs, and the feeling was evidently so desperate that sheriffs were compelled to postpone proceedings."[29] Merchants were asking for cotton, corn, or even peas as payment rather than money.[30] As the financial situation grew progressively worse, the Mississippi legislature attempted to reverse its own imprudent actions in chartering the banking railroad companies. Banks, which had completed in whole or in part any railroad work or other internal improvements, were to forfeit only their banking privileges. Otherwise the entire charter would be revoked.[31]

This brought all railroad work to a halt in northeast Mississippi and in most of the state. When the effects of the depression lasted to almost the 1850s, railroad construction remained at a standstill for the decade of the 1840s.

The town builders sought alternative means of building the necessary roads but when these efforts failed, key figures began to depart the area as the stagnant period persisted. Orne moved to Memphis where he remained for the rest of his life. Thomas McMacline, one of Pontotoc's principal designers, soon joined him in Memphis.[32] Potential leaders such as Lyman Draper and Charles Hathaway Larrabee moved to Wisconsin where they became vital leaders in that state.[33]

Lesser known people also left. Land in Arkansas and Texas was just being opened and the magnet of this land drew rootless settlers. The new territory offered an alternative to persons who might have otherwise migrated to northern Mississippi. It also provided an avenue of escape for those living in the region. Deeply in debt as a result of the easy credit, falling prices in cotton, and soaring prices, some of the farmers faced obligations they could not meet. J. A. Orr told of people from this area stealing silently away in the night, leaving meat in the smokehouse, chickens and pigs in their pens, and even carriages in their usual place so as not to raise suspicion. "The first object was to get to the county line, the next across the Mississippi River, and the next to cross the line of the Republic of Texas." Others more boldly painted the letters "GTT," (Gone To Texas) on their houses or fence posts.[34]

The slumping economy removed much of the incentive for town building. After incorporating 21 towns in the first 4 years, only 5 new towns were incorporated during the 1840s. For all its fanfare, Mississippi remained without a single major city in 1850. Even Natchez, the cultural capital of the state, had a population of less than 5,000 at the midpoint of the nineteenth century.[35]

The prolonged depression retarded railroad development throughout most of the South. Only Georgia and Virginia developed the model of railroad success; the state became a central partner in railroad construction.[36] These rail lines laid the foundations for Atlanta's emergence as the economic capital of the Southeast. One of the railroads planned in 1837 was the Mobile and Ohio Railroad that was chartered to run from Mobile to a point near the mouth of the Ohio River. A decade after the collapse of the first plan its original promoter, M. F. D. Baldwyn of Mobile, initiated a new program. As he envisioned it, the road would cross the Mississippi line just north of Mobile and would traverse all of eastern Mississippi passing through the heart of the Chickasaw cession and reach its journey's end near Columbus, Kentucky. His idea gained quick support from Mobile merchants who were losing business to New Orleans. A preliminary survey in 1847 demonstrated the feasibility of such a road and gained popular support.[37]

Baldwyn faced the persistent problem of acquiring capital. His plan varied from the aggressive competitive approach of a decade earlier and relied more on cooperation. The city of Mobile levied a special 2 percent tax on real estate within its boundaries to provide initial start-up funds.[38] He called on assistance from the Mississippi legislature for additional support. Mississippi, like most southern and western states had long supported the notion that government should be involved with bearing the cost for internal improvement and as early as 1842 had called on the federal legislature for assistance in building roads in the Chickasaw territory.[39] The state legislature provided initial assistance and ongoing support until the road was completed. It began by issuing the Mobile and Ohio a charter to build a road in Mississippi. Subsequently, the legislators called on the United States Congress to provide public land to assist in the construction of the railroad.[40] Beginning in 1850, the state legislature permitted counties to call a special election to permit qualified voters to determine their wishes in subscribing to stock in the Mobile and Ohio Railroad.[41] A critical part of the financing came when Senator William King of Alabama worked with Senator Stephen Douglas, the senator from Illinois and stockholder in the Illinois Central Railroad. They proposed federal land grants to the Mobile and Ohio and the Illinois Central as a means of funding the railroad construction. Eastern investors, who either owned Illinois Central securities or who planned to make subsequent investments, added their endorsement of the land grants. Together they carried the day. Illinois, Mississippi, and Alabama were granted alternate even sections of land to the extent of 6 miles on each side of the proposed 200-foot right-of-way. In cases where the land was no longer in government hands within the six miles, the states could extend the distance an additional nine miles for a total of 15 miles. Land retained by the government in the odd-numbered sections within the six-mile limit was to be sold at double the required minimum price to compensate for any revenue lost through the grants.[42] As the construction proceeded, the Mississippi legislature made good on its promise to provide continuing support. In 1856, it provided a loan of $181,850 from the Chickasaw School Fund.[43] Later the legislature made it easier to acquire land for the right of way by applying to the circuit court of each county for a writ of *ad quod damnum*. A jury would be impaneled to make a judgment as to damages.

The proposed railway and the subsequent flurry of activity kindled interest in the Tupelo site. Despite the fact that much of the immediate area was still wilderness in 1850, it offered some important advantages as a town site. The earliest settlers, the Chickasaw, had built their capital, Chichafalaya, on the highland ridges overlooking the broad rich valleys near the eventual site of Tupelo. Subsequently, the old Indian trails that connected their villages were improved by military and overland travelers to form a primitive road system. That nearby transportation system, though of poor quality, was actually better than that of most towns in the area. The Pontotoc-Fulton Road formed an East-West axis of the system and the Natchez Trace a Northeast-Southwest crossing.[44] Old Town Creek, which flowed past the original eastern boundary of the original Tupelo was a navigable stream from a point just south of the town.[45] The potential farmland surrounding the town was part of the prairie belt and some of the richest land in Northeast Mississippi.[46]

It did not take long for two experienced town builders, William Harris and George Thomason, to recognize the potential for quick profits. They had platted Harrisburg, a tiny village to the west of the Tupelo site in order to be closer to the Natchez Trace, but by 1851 the modest village had shown little growth. There were three stores, a blacksmith, a saddler, a post office, and a justice of the peace.[47]

Clearly, if any meaningful growth were to take place, it would be necessary to be in the path of the planned railway. Stock in the Mobile and Ohio Railroad sold well in the area and rivalry for access to the rail lines began to mount in the early fifties.[48] The record is not clear at this point, but it appears that Harrisburg and Christopher Orr's Palmetto were the two villages most in contention for the line. The road was certain to miss one site and could bypass them both. Rather than risk the loss of the road altogether, Harris and Orr began to work together. In

1853 Judge Harris purchased a quarter section of land adjoining the Orr property, which the latter had held since 1839.[49] Harris apparently had some knowledge of the final route of the railroad when he was willing to pay twice as much per acre for an additional half section of land in 1857.[50]

The anticipation and expectation of the two men were achieved when the track was laid in 1859. The road brought the town into existence and the construction process also suggested the name Gum Pond for the community. Once the railroad was completed the most conspicuous landmarks were the tracks themselves and a swampy pond formed by the levee of the railroad a few hundred yards north of what became Main Street. Only cypress and tupelo gum trees would grow in the marshland surrounding the pond. The name Gum Pond was attached to the swamp and the settlement on the railroad map. Tupelo, the proper name for the gum trees and a Chickasaw word meaning "a lodging place" was substituted when the town was platted the following year.[51]

The first stage of Tupelo's development ended in a flurry of activity. George Thomason, Harris' old partner, was drawn into the founding group to help with the land sales.[52] Tupelo's plat was recorded in Fulton, the county seat of Itawamba County, in July 1860.[53] Within a week the trio of town builders offered 62 lots for sale, many of which sold quickly.[54] As their last contribution to the Mobile and Ohio Railroad, the founders provided the company with a large lot as a site for a depot.[55] With the completion of the railway most of the Harrisburg citizens were drawn to Tupelo to be closer to the railroad and to share in the expected boom.[56]

Tupelo's first quarter-century, 1860-1885, was a time of private development that produced a town, but not a true community. During that time the town was transformed from a motley collection of saloons and hotels to an established rural trade center, but the horizontal patterns that bind the citizens together took much longer to evolve.

Even before the town was platted in 1860, saloons were hastily constructed to take advantage of the presence and thirst of the railroad construction crews. Initially, the saloons constituted the heart of the commercial activity. The completion of the railway and the coming of the Civil War threatened to destroy this prosperous saloon trade. Business, however, temporarily increased after the hotels were converted to a jail for the incarceration of pro-Union sympathizers and a garrison of soldiers was stationed in other hotels to guard the prisoners.[57]

Both the prison and hotel-saloon business was destroyed during the military clashes in 1864. The rail lines that had promised to bring land-hungry immigrants brought instead battle-weary soldiers as the war slogged toward its ultimate conclusion. Two major battles were fought in the Tupelo vicinity, one north of town at Brice's Crossroads and the other on the immediate outskirts of town near the original site of Harrisburg.[58] In time local citizens would recount the glories of the two encounters, but by the war's end these events were responsible for the almost total devastation of all man-made structures in the area.

The war left Tupelo with few material resources on which it could draw. Tumbledown ruins marked the location of recently erected edifices. Capital was in short supply and equipment of any sort almost nonexistent.[59] The railroad, which served as the lifeline in the cotton economy, was in desperate straits. All of the rail-road's bridges, trestleworks, warehouses, and station buildings were destroyed within a 180-mile radius. The rolling stock of the Mobile and Ohio Railroad was reduced by three-fourths. The Confederate government and the state of Alabama owed more than $5 million to the company.[60] The only immediate resource was the rich soil surrounding the town. The Black Prairie belt, in which Tupelo is located, stretches westward from mid-Alabama and then curves north like a broad scimitar coming to a final point north of Tupelo. Within its plains were located all of the county's main villages. Farmers who tilled the fertile soil were directly involved with most of the commerce of these hamlets.

Competition among the villages for the trade of the husbandmen was the hall-mark of town activity in the postwar period. In 1865, the settlements competed with one another on equal ground. Each village was almost exactly the same size. Looking at a railroad map of the time they appear to be identical beads strung together by the tracks of the Mobile and Ohio Railroad. Only by some manipu-lation of existing affairs, could the standoff be altered.

The most expeditious strategy in gaining an advantage for one of the settle-ments lay in creating a separate county and then throwing open the competition for the seat of justice. A new county could be justified as being consistent with the practice of having no part of a county more than a one day's round-trip journey from the county seat. This strategy appealed to all the aspiring hamlets and each voted overwhelmingly for a separate county.[61] The first step was completed when a new county, named in honor of Robert E. Lee, was established on October 30, 1866.[62] The desperate rivalry that followed was common to towns in almost every part of the nation.[63] Becoming the county seat was one of the most coveted plums in every county. As one national historian noted, for towns which could not become the capital of the state or the site of the state's university, the next best thing was to become the county seat. For many villages, failure to attain this goal curtailed any economic hope for the future.[64]

The initial advantage went to Saltillo when it was named temporary seat of jus-tice. But the proviso that selected Saltillo attached the stipulation that there would be a countywide election to be held within a year to determine the permanent site.[65] The ultimate outcome of the election was loaded in favor of Tupelo from the beginning. Either by design or accident, the county's boundaries were drawn so as to locate Tupelo in the center of the new county. In the election, Tupelo out-polled Saltillo by a vote of 1,135 to 667. Tupelo's geographic centrality, rather than any developed attributes, determined the election.[66] They were probably correct.

The stakes were significant and in such a bitter contest it was too soon for rival towns to capitulate. Town rivalry is too great for a single setback to end the feud. County seats can be changed. Neighboring Monroe County had four different seats by 1865. Therefore it was no surprise that the issue resurfaced after the Lee County Courthouse burned in 1873.[67] There were accusations that the fire had been deliberately set by henchmen hired by neighboring town Verona. These suspicions were elevated when less than a week after the fire, some citizens of Verona came forward with an offer of $15,000 to build the next courthouse in their town.[68] After prolonged wrangling, charges and countercharges, a handsome new courthouse was built on the original site in 1874.

Becoming the county seat provides any town an enormous advantage. There are important and vital jobs that come with the courthouse. Moreover the courthouse is a drawing card for rural citizens who need to conduct business at the county seat. Attorneys are lured to the county seat and soon these attorneys provided leadership for the town and county. Perhaps most important, the county's roads become focused on the county seat and are maintained at the expense of the whole county. Farmers going to market tend to follow the best roads. As a result, business grows in the town. In Tupelo's case it became the center of the lucrative cotton trade. The county's most ambitious businessmen gravitated to Tupelo. They provided leadership and their financial success provided the town with jobs and the county's largest reservoir of capital. The multiplier effect of jobs, capital, and other elements continued to add to Tupelo's economic advantages.

With the county seat issue resolved, Tupelo now found itself with an internal rivalry. The commercial center, small as it was, had two loci that were divided by the railroad tracks. On the east side of the tracks were the saloons and hotels that served also as bordellos. On the west side were those businesses that catered to rural trade.

The choice commercial lots were considered to be those facing the tracks on Front Street or Front Row as it was commonly called. In 1870 there were four saloons, two hotels, and two boardinghouses. This section catered primarily to a transient population of railroad men, drummers, drifters between jobs, and rough-hewn locals. The business and brawls of this section established Tupelo's well-deserved reputation as being one of the wildest towns in the region. Drunks occasionally shot up the whole town and rode their horses into the stores.[69] A local historian told of an incident in which "one man killed three men before breakfast and nothing was done about it."[70] So difficult and deadly was law enforcement, that there were eight sheriffs in the first thirteen years of the county.[71]

Compounding the lawlessness of the town, Tupelo shared the unruly appearance of most frontier towns. The buildings were unpainted, poorly constructed shacks in the words of even a local town booster. Packed earth served as the sidewalks and the dirt streets were dust trails in the summer and muddy quagmires in the winter and spring. Garbage lined the streets, adding to the inconvenience of travel and the ugliness and smell of the town. Pigs and dogs rummaged through the streets searching for meals among the trash. Rumors of rabid animals was a common occurrence and brought forth a round of dog executions by civic-minded locals using rifles and shotguns. In a gesture of progressive action the local board of councilmen established an ordinance preventing the dumping of dead livestock inside the corporate limits.[72]

This image was well known throughout the county and was frequently used to argue against the selection of Tupelo as county seat. Merchants and the newspaper fought against that view. The editor conceded that the town had lacked polish when it was first selected as the county seat, but argued that it had righted itself in the interim. "Tupelo was at that time a very small unincorporated town with a very bad name. . . . Since that time Tupelo has grown to be quite a respectable county-town in size. It has improved in morals more than the most hopeful could have expected, and is now one of the best regulated towns in our state."[73]

This initial division between the saloon trade and the rural trade helped to shape some of the growth and the ecological pattern of the town in ways that could be seen a century later. In the nineteenth century, most of the more "respectable" business located on the west side of the railroad and spread in a westerly pattern along Main Street away from the railroad. The homes of these merchants and other white residents outlined the business district on the north and west. Most African-Americans were segregated on the poorest site selections to the east and northeast. The largest and most completely segregated section was "Shakerag," a single story slum area situated on the mud flats east of the railroad. Residents of that slum rarely escaped the harsh poverty except by migrating from Tupelo. A second black neighborhood in which most of the black property owners lived centered around Gum Pond.[74] Still further to the east, far beyond "Shakerag," poor whites came to live in their simple "shotgun"-style houses. It was there that Elvis Presley would be born more than a half-century later.

When the remnants of the saloons and hotels burned in the 1890s, it provided a large building space in the center of town, but so strong was the old image that some of the area was converted into wagon yards and later parking lots, which were present in 1993. The area in the southeast was used for fairgrounds when no businesses were willing to occupy that land. Those fairgrounds remained in the same location until 1992.

By the middle of the 1870s, the town was beginning to shed its old saloon business and becoming a rural trade center as reflected in the occupations of its residents and almost total focus on the production of cotton. Over three-fourths of the male population was directly involved with agricultural commerce. There was, however, a basic occupational division along racial lines. In 1870, all but 5 of the 58 employed African-American males worked as unskilled labor, much of which was seasonal activity created by the marketing of cotton. The remaining five black men were skilled workers. Thirty-eight of the white males (40 percent) were merchants or clerks in stores, all of which catered primarily to rural trade. Eleven white males (10 percent) offered skilled services to farmers, i.e., millers, blacksmiths, wagon makers, and saddlers. The town's nine attorneys served farmer-clients in most of their work. Ten percent of the white employed males were farmers who preferred town life to that in open country neighborhoods. An additional 11 white men (10 percent) transported goods, primarily agricultural products. By 1880, almost all people in town were involved with rural trade in one way or another.[75]

Agriculture for Lee County, as with much of Mississippi, meant cotton. One agricultural historian noted that the South was even more dependent on a one-crop economy than it had been before the Civil War. By 1859, Mississippi had become the geographic center of cotton production, a position it would hold for the next half-century. The county was in the top one-third of the counties in Mississippi in cotton production. Cotton and corn accounted for 75 percent of the tilled acreage in Lee County in 1870 and 1880. The corn was used primarily as feed for the mules, horses, and other livestock and was not a major cash crop.[76]

To accommodate its rural customers, the town built a large wagon yard complete with privies and firewood for persons who had to stay overnight. The wagon yard was not only a convenience, but in time the center of social activities and a permanent fixture in the town's landscape.

Perhaps the most common gathering place and landmark was the covered well in the center of the intersection of Main and Spring Street. It, too, was a town convenience, but when it became an inconvenience in the age of the automobile, it was covered over, leaving no trace of the tales and laughter that were a part of the environs.

This was a time of town building and there was little attention to social matters. The all-day church services and dinner on the grounds in good weather and the church camp meeting served to feed both the soul and social needs. There was a town baseball team formed in 1873, but the efforts to create a town brass band and a city park never came to fruition.[77]

There were very few horizontal ties to hold the community together. The town had a Baptist Church as early as 1850, ten years before the town was platted. The Methodists and Presbyterians formed congregations in 1867 and used the Baptist Church for services. By 1885 there was still no permanent minister in town.[78] Mississippi's public school system began in 1870, but in 1885 the town had still not built a schoolhouse, choosing instead to use the private academies that offered four months of public school and private lessons after the end of that four-month period. In 1873, only 12 students were enrolled in the private academy.[79]

The absence of strong horizontal ties is obvious from the amount of personal mobility that took place between 1870 and 1880. In that single decade, 67 percent of the people who lived in Tupelo in 1870 had moved by 1880. Whites were more likely to move than blacks. Sixty-nine percent of the white population migrated and 54 percent of the black population left the town. This was not an unusual rate of migration for towns and cities in the United States at that time. Cities as different from Tupelo as Poughkeepsie, New York; Newburyport, Massachusetts; Rochester, New York; and Boston all had migration rates of 60 to 68 percent.[80]

The people who remained in town were those with structural ties such as home ownership, business, or marital ties. Eighty-two percent of the migrants owned no property such as a home or land. By contrast only 42 percent of property owners left town. Eighty-four percent of the migrants were not married. Almost half of the married people persisted, that is, did not move. Moreover, most of the migrants were under 35 years of age.

For Tupelo and Lee County, these were not the times and this was not the population for community-building. These were strong-willed individuals, who valued their individualism. They were seeking their own fortune by means of privatism. Reuben Davis, who was among those fortune seekers, captured the sentiment of the time. "A man ought to fear God and mind his own business. He should be respectful and courteous to all women; he should love his friends and hate his enemies. He should eat when he is hungry, drink when he is thirsty, dance when he is merry, vote for the candidate he likes best, and knock down any man who questions his right to those privileges."[81]

This individualism and privatism frequently has a dimension that benefits the public, but not all the public. In this highly competitive environment there are winners and losers. By the mid-1880s, Tupelo was the winner vis-a-vis the other villages in the county. Its success or good fortune in being selected as the county seat had brought some of the direct and indirect benefits cited earlier. The courthouse became the magnet for businesses. The county-maintained roads literally were the paths that brought economic gains to the county seat. It is difficult to exaggerate the importance of having the good roads of the county focused on the town. Without that transportation base the town's future would have been bleak.

That transportation system and the courthouse, however, paid additional dividends. Shortly after the town became the seat of justice it began to attract some of the brightest and most talented individuals in the county.

One of the first to move from one of the surrounding Lee County villages was John Mills Allen. Allen would become a keystone in the Lee County leadership network for the next 40 years. He became the United States congressman from the First District. He had a role in almost every major development in the town throughout the remainder of the century. Because of his presence and the courthouse, his nephew, John Quitman Robins, a Phi Beta Kappa graduate of the University of Virginia also moved to Tupelo.[82] John Clark, the county's leading businessman, along with his brother Berryman Turner Clark, made the short move from Verona to Tupelo. Clark, in turn, persuaded C. B. Hood to become his partner in what became the largest mercantile company in northeast Mississippi. Clark also brought in Neil Troy as a bookkeeper. Troy, in turn, became a key businessman and town alderman.[83]

Tupelo's early success also attracted the county's newspaper. The newspaper began as the *North Mississippian* in 1867. It became the *Lee County Journal* in 1870, then in 1872, Lee County native George Herndon bought the newspaper and it became the *Tupelo Journal*. The *Journal* became critical to both the town building and community-building process.

These human resources became the most fundamental forces in the development of the town and county. They were also the resources for the community-building process.

Summary and Conclusions

Community, meaning a sense of unity and common identity, was almost completely absent for much of the early history of northeast Mississippi. Long before community developed, there was a protracted period of town building. The area first attracted white immigrants in the 1830s. They were drawn to the area in search of quick riches. This earliest period was a time of strong privatism, of fierce competition among a relatively young male-dominated population who were not yet ready to put down roots and develop a sense of community.

The greatest riches were earned through land speculation. While much of the land sold as cotton land, the greatest riches were earned by creating towns and selling the land for commercial purposes. The land speculators, therefore, became town builders as a way of maximizing their profits.

Because towns depended on transportation to provide access to raw materials and markets for any would-be towns, these speculators/town builders also became experimenters in railroad building. Railroad construction, however, was foiled by a lack of capital and never existed more than as plans to link inland towns with waterways. The failure to develop transportation was the first step toward the end of land speculation. Almost all land speculation came to a complete halt with the depression of the late 1830s and 1840s, a depression caused in part by the speculative mania. With the end of land speculation also came a marked reduction in town building.

North Mississippi developed little during the early 1840s. New growth began again with the proposed construction of new rail lines at the end of the decade. M. F. D. Baldwyn, who sought expanded trade areas for his native Mobile, spearheaded the new development project. His plans called for a railroad from Mobile up the east side of Mississippi, crossing through the old Chickasaw territory before it traversed Tennessee and terminated its route on the Ohio River in Kentucky.

To build such a railroad called for a coalition of private and public segments. The coalition began when Mobile businessmen established a local tax to gain the initial funds to develop the plans. They forged a partnership between local government, private businessmen, state governments, and the federal government. Working in concert with the cities of New Orleans and Chicago, Senator William King of Alabama and Senator Stephen Douglas of Illinois were successful in persuading the federal government to contribute land as a way of subsidizing the railroad construction and thus making the construction possible.

Within the old Chickasaw territory, town builders William Harris, Christopher Orr, and George Thomason formed a partnership to help lure the Mobile and Ohio Railroad through their property. When they were successful, the village of Gum Pond, quickly renamed Tupelo, became one of the towns along the newly laid tracks.

Town development was delayed by the Civil War and its destruction in the area. After the war, Tupelo became distinguished from its sister communities when the new county of Lee was carved from Pontotoc and Itawamba Counties and

35

Tupelo was selected as the county seat. Young Tupelo was an unruly, unattractive collection of unpainted shacks, earth-packed streets, and a bawdy service trade. The merchants who came to form the core of the economy opted to earn their living through trade with farmers. Subsequently the town became a rural trade center, trading finished products and services for the products of the farms.

During the first quarter of its life, the town was unable to establish strong horizontal ties that pull inhabitants together as a community. By 1885, the town had neither public schools nor a resident minister. Its population was highly fluid and the town had not exhibited the ability to work together to form a sense of community.

CHAPTER 3

Expanding the Economic Base

At each phase of Tupelo's history, the primary issues, challenges, and agenda tend to be set by regional and national forces. As in other towns, development depends on the historical, cultural, and economic environment of the time.[1] Consequently, it is not surprising that the burst of urban energy in the latter half of the nineteenth century set the tone in this relatively remote rural trade center.

The modern American city emerged between 1860 and 1910. Following a series of sporadic population influxes the number of persons living in urban incorporated communities had increased from 6,216,518 to 44,639,989.[2] Moreover, the dominance of cities, the expansion of transportation lines, and the complexity of the interrelated economies served to draw America's communities into an urban network.[3] Not even remote rural trade centers such as Tupelo were immune to the changes that resulted.

After 1885, Tupelo's participation in this urban network became increasingly active. By that time the mid-South was astir with urban development. In the 20 years after 1880, Memphis' population grew from 31,000 to 102,000. The Bluff City's annual value of trade expanded from $72 million in 1881 to $200 million by the early nineties.[4] Birmingham, incorporated three years after Tupelo, grew from 3,000 in 1880 to more than 26,000 by the end of the decade and had a population in excess of 132,000 by 1910.[5]

At the vanguard of the urban growth was the resurgence of railroad construction. Memphis gained seven new rail lines between 1880 and 1892.[6] In 1885, there was still no railroad connecting Memphis and Birmingham. As early as 1869, Kansas City had attempted to expand its railway network to include direct ties with Memphis.[7] After years of failure, the effort was renewed in the 1880s with the hope of gaining a direct route that would extend to Birmingham. Talk of this road stirred more excitement in the Tupelo area than had existed since the struggle for the county seat. Almost every town between Memphis and Birmingham was caught up in the rivalry to have the route pass through its location.

Tupelo shared the dream of all the rival towns that sought that railroad crossing. A second railway would open up new markets both for selling and buying.

The alternate outlet would be an added incentive for farmers to bring their cotton to the locale of the railroad crossing for processing and shipping. These same farmers could also be expected to become regular customers in the town where they sold their products. More customers meant more jobs and workers to swell the resident population, bringing increased land values. Competing railroads might be expected to reduce freight rates and provide access to a variety of wholesalers and distributors. The loss of the rail line to a rival community possibly meant a reversal of these effects.

The situation was filled with multiple possibilities. Two companies received charters to construct a railway between Memphis and Birmingham. Since their charters prescribed different routes, the alternative rail lines were spread over a 75-mile wide course in north Mississippi.[8] Each company was searching for a route that could bring subsidies in the form of stock purchases and land grants. The field was wide open for aspiring towns. From the standpoint of the competing communities, no one of them had an advantage that would not be offset by a superior organization of one of its rivals. Consequently, each town sought to mobilize its citizens.

Commercial towns, such as Tupelo, are attuned to fierce competition and privatism. Cooperation and organization — the cornerstones of community — are not easily achieved. In addition to a culture better structured for commercial competition, there are also deep schisms which inhibit cooperation and organization.

Class clearly separated the population, from the earliest stages of the town. The economic dominants took pride in their distinctiveness. After the Civil War, many had assumed military titles that reflected class differences and served as a badge of distinction. Few were entitled to the military ranks that they now carried before their surname. These military titles seemed to order the local power structure. Hence the town's first mayor, Harvey Clay Medford, become Major Medford, although he had never risen above the rank of private.[9] The examples could be extended almost endlessly. Captain W. L. Clayton received the unofficial promotion to "colonel," which showed proper respect for his social position and age as distinguished from the younger Lieutenant Frank Goar, who became Major Goar, or the still younger Private John Allen, who became Captain Allen.[10] With only one exception, the young John Clark, whose father preempted the title "colonel," all other prominent leaders in 1885 bore the honorary rank of an officer. This included the ludicrous affixing of the rank "captain" to the newspaper editor, John Miller, despite the fact that he was only 14-years old when the war ended.[11]

There were other schisms that retarded broad-based cooperation and organization. Race proved an often uncrossable chasm. Relations between town and country, unlike the persistent schism between races, tended to fluctuate between lukewarm and cold, but came to a boil in the 1890s. Other differences sometimes became volatile and made cooperation almost impossible. Chief among these was the consumption or prohibition of alcohol. The struggle to prohibit alcohol kept the citizens in continual turmoil in the latter decades of the nineteenth century.

Lacking a broad-based organization, the town managed to organize only business people. Even among this group there were strong personal disagreements and antagonisms. In such a divisive setting the person often best able to pull the community together is the newspaper editor.[12] Tupelo's John Miller was an unlikely bearer of an olive branch. During his career he was more often a contributor to controversy. He was, however, one of the state's finest newspapermen. His keen wit and quixotic temperament never served him better than they did in the railroad campaign. Under his guidance, the contest to gain the railroad took on the trappings of a religious crusade and Miller was the chief evangelist. The content of his regular column "Railroad Notes" was a mixture of factual information and pleas for a full commitment to the "cause."[13]

Miller and John Allen, the U.S. congressman, were often the voices of a loosely organized coalition of merchants and professionals. They were the embodiment of the private-public cooperation. Most of the actual work was conducted by a formal committee of local businessmen who kept in touch with the railroad officials. On the local scene they sought to lure the railroad by purchasing stock in the company and gaining land for the right-of-way.[14] In his official capacity Allen worked to secure at least one of the two routes for his district. Unofficially he encouraged the Tupelo course. Little was left to chance. John A. Blair, the state representative, worked in the state legislature to promote interest in the railroad and to help shape its charter.[15] Every survey crew was greeted, wined, and dined. The town named one of its main streets in honor of the engineer in charge of the survey, Captain Gloster. Surveys in the local area were paid for by contributions from Tupelo's citizens.[16]

This did not assure Tupelo of being on the rail line. Both routes as outlined in their separate charters of incorporation passed through the more densely populated communities to the south of town.[17] Only a last-second agreement with the Memphis, Birmingham, and Atlantic Railroads permitted representative John Blair to amend its charter deflecting the route away from Verona and toward Tupelo. The stories that circulated in later years implied that Verona had feared that this railroad would disturb the peacefulness of the village and was not unhappy to see Tupelo get it. There is no evidence to support such a tale.

The story of how Tupelo was able to divert the railroad from Verona to its own site is not entirely clear. Existing sources suggest that a number of Verona merchants sought to gain the crossing, but their efforts lacked the organization that Tupelo was able to achieve.[18] Verona was without the communication advantages provided by a newspaper. Moreover, none of its people could match the visual and strategic leadership provided by John Allen. Allen, as noted above, had pledged to be neutral toward sites in his district, but he was often blatant in his support of Tupelo.[19] John Blair, the state legislator from Tupelo, was even more open in working in behalf of his hometown.[20] Tupelo sought the double advantage of securing Memphis and Birmingham investors who would bring capital to the area, plus the added self-interest of influencing the railroad to cross at the site of their investments. The town succeeded in attracting a Birmingham cotton investor who planned and later built a cotton compress in Tupelo after the final railroad route was announced.[21] His influence on the course of the rail line can only be surmised as being positive. Tupelo's leaders, because they had mobilized only the top echelon of the town, had ignored one of the most basic premises of leadership, the involvement of all the stakeholders. Unfortunately, the town lacked the foresight to involve the rural population in the project as was done in very successful railroad programs such as that in Kansas City.[22] Once construction began in 1886 there were a number of farmers who were extremely exercised over the town's indifference to the interests and the construction damage done to their property. One small group threatened to bring all road building to a halt unless they received compensation for this destruction. The immediate problem was treated, but the controversy that swirled around the incident was a factor in the farmers' revolt, which will be discussed in Chapter 4.[23]

Farmer displeasure continued to grow, but at least one dimension of the tension ended when the Memphis, Birmingham, and Atlantic Railroad was sold to its rival, the Kansas City, Springfield, and Memphis Company. The newspaper's sigh of relief was indicative of the town's feelings. "The threats of the Kansas City Company to parallel the Memphis, Birmingham, and Atlantic Railroad has been a serious menace to the interests of this place, producing a feeling of suspense, retarding improvements, and deterring many persons from moving in.[24]

The final stages of the construction seemed almost anticlimactic after all the other hurdles had been negotiated. In October 1886, the rail line was complete. At the concluding ceremony John Allen and J. M. Keating, the editor of the *Memphis Appeal,* who had long championed a road between his Bluff City and Birmingham, drove the final spikes near Guion, Alabama.[25] There was a delay before the engines began rolling, but in March 1887, the first train on what was now called the Kansas City, Memphis, and Birmingham Railroad and later named the Frisco Railroad passed through Tupelo where it was greeted by the cheers of a large crowd. Later that month regular passenger service began.[26]

The coming of the second railroad brought immediate changes in Tupelo's relationship to nearby villages. Even before the railway was completed Tupelo was luring important businesses away from neighboring hamlets. The county's only bank, the Bank of Lee County, made the short but significant journey from Verona to Tupelo in 1886.[27] The J. J. Rogers Company, which dealt in cotton and wholesale groceries, moved from Verona in 1888 to be at the center of the cotton trade in Tupelo.[28] Merchants from Saltillo and Baldwyn, reacting to the changing winds of fortune, drifted to the county seat as early as 1887.[29]

Tupelo experienced a short-lived boom period after the arrival of the railroad. In a single year, more than 50 new buildings were constructed. As a sign of the improved conditions and the fear of fire, one of the new blocks consisted of all brick structures.[30]

This "development in the community" provided Tupelo the economic strength to engage in the "development of community." By this means, it could also escape its "Front Street Image" and claim the respectability it so desperately sought. By the end of the decade the three largest religious denominations, the Baptists, Presbyterians, and Methodists, had all improved their church buildings. Moreover, they all had resident ministers. It was noted by one local historian that for the first time in its 30-year history, the number of churches exceeded the number of saloons.[31] Community leaders capitalized on the improved economy and the concern for respectability to promote the construction of a school building.[32] It was the town's first public school, and a vital step toward the development of a sense of community. Tupelo saw its school as both a means of educating the children and as a symbol that this ragged rural village was becoming a city. The crowning structure in the new building program was the new 900-seat opera house, the epitome of respectability.[33] For the next quarter of a century this structure and the performances within it were described and displayed in almost all the boosteristic literature.

These symbols of community were vital to the town's future, but most of the focus was on the economy. Because Tupelo shared access to some of the same basic types of raw materials as the dominant city of the region, Memphis, it too built its economy on cotton and hardwood. Involvement with the lumber industry began with a furniture factory shortly after the completion of the railroad in 1887.[34] The new railroad supported these efforts by alerting wood processors in the Midwest to the potentials of the area.[35] The idea of tapping the hardwood forests spread rapidly. By 1890, there were a number of factories turning out finished products: chairs, tool handles, spokes and wheel hubs, and brooms.[36] A planing mill, a long overdue asset to the community, began operation in 1890.[37]

Unfortunately, the hardwood relationship was short-lived. Within a year, a nonunionized group of workers brought consternation to the town leadership when they marched en masse to the office of one of the factory owners in protest of their low wages.[38] Tremors of the incident lingered long afterward and it was more than a year later before another wood factory was established.[39] Attempts to rekindle the industry were shackled from the outset. The depression of the nineties reduced the demand for the products and brought a major decline in production. Subsequent attempts to revive the hardwood industry by outside interests in the early twentieth century were unsuccessful. By then, a lumber company in a nearby hamlet had badly depleted the hardwood timber reserves. There was a gradual decline in the lumbering industry and by 1907 it had ceased to be a major factor in the town's economy.[40]

Tupelo's relation to the wood-processing industry was little more than flirtation rather than full-blown romance. The town was wed to the cotton industry and in many ways the second railroad strengthened those bonds. The new cotton compress built in 1886 was the only one in the county. In its first year's operation before the trains were running, the company pressed 9,000 bales. The following year the number of bales almost tripled to 25,000.[41] Clark and Hood built a new brick warehouse that had a storage capacity of 7,000 bales. The company's newest rival, J. J. Rogers, brought much of its trade from Verona and constructed a similar-sized warehouse.[42] When the wood-product industry began to slow down there were attempts to locate outside capital to build a textile mill. Unfortunately, investors were not forthcoming, and those plans were temporarily shelved.[43]

Shortly after the arrival of the second railroad, the newspaper began to speak boastfully of the town as the cotton center of north Mississippi. It was especially fond of comparing Tupelo's cotton market with that of Memphis. Cotton merchants, however, were not prospering. In an effort to promote Tupelo as a cotton market, the *Journal* urged merchants to sponsor a county fair. Unfortunately, the depressed cotton conditions of 1889 rendered businessmen unable to generate the needed capital for the project.[44] Efforts to enlist the Town Council as a sponsor similarly failed. The town government had initiated a number of civic improvement programs of its own and the town budget was strained to the limit.[45]

Tupelo's expanded involvement with the cotton trade was similar to B'rer Rabbit's experience with the tar baby. When the collapse of the cotton industry came in the nineties, the town was virtually immobilized. Signs of an impending agricultural disaster were posted throughout the eighties but the warnings went unheeded. The constant cotton farming without adequate fertilizer had exhausted much of the soil outside the bottomlands. By 1890, Lee County's cotton yield per acre was among the lowest in the state.[46]

The miseries of low production yields were compounded by the continuing decline in the cotton market. The price of the staple dropped below ten cents a pound in 1890 and did not rise above that level for the reminder of the decade.[47] By the mid-nineties it was bringing only six-and-a-half cents per pound, a half cent below the estimated cost of production.[48] One disillusioned farmer complained, "the basest fraud on earth is agriculture." He further charged that Thomas Jefferson's reference to farmers as the "chosen people of God" constituted a blasphemy. "No wonder Cain killed his brother. He was a tiller of the ground."[49]

Even before the final collapse of the market in the nineties, the small farmer with no cash reserves was being driven from the rural areas. As a dramatic response to the sagging agricultural economy, 85 African-American families left Lee County at the height of the railroad excitement in 1887.[50] A steady drain of the rural population took place during the entire decade of the eighties. By 1890, the county had suffered an estimated gross population loss in excess of 3,000 persons and a net reduction of more than 800 persons outside Tupelo's corporate limits. Tupelo absorbed only a small percentage of the displaced farmers. Its population expanded slightly from 1,006 in 1880 to 1,447 ten years later.[51]

Tupelo's narrow economic base and deep involvement in the sick cotton trade limited its usefulness as a safety valve for the migrating farmers and left the town vulnerable to the brunt of the depression. The community was totally unprepared for the economic downturn. So oblivious was it to the changing conditions that it was caught with posts in the ground and gas lights enroute when the town government realized it was out of funds and there were no new sources of revenue in sight.[52] The new school's budget was completely crippled. In four successive years, beginning in 1889, four different superintendents wrestled with the dilemma of shrinking funds and a growing enrollment.[53] Numerous merchants were forced out of business by the hard times.[54]

During the early depression years, Tupelo businessmen maintained a sense of unity. However, they found themselves in an economic desert in which economic profits dried in the relentless heat of controversy and depressed prices. A Board of Trade was organized in December 1892, to generate economic activity. Initially its promotional ideas suffered the same fundless death that befell the county fair project.[55]

Stereotypes notwithstanding, this small Mississippi town had no illusions of self-sufficiency. Following its initial failures, the Board of Trade initiated a series of projects that extended the town into an increasingly broader network of towns. For the first time, the county attempted to cooperate with surrounding counties. In January 1893, the Tupelo organization sponsored the North Mississippi Immigration Union involving four other counties. This group in turn originated a joint program with the Mobile and Ohio Railroad to sponsor excursion trips for persons interested in buying land in the area. A third linkup was directed by Tupelo insurance and real estate agent P. M. Savery. Working through the North Mississippi Immigration Union, Savery set up a cooperative association with other real estate agents in three midwestern states. The midwestern companies were asked to suggest north Mississippi as an alternative to people who were leaving the Midwest. The midwestern companies were to decline a commission for their efforts.[56]

In a characteristically optimistic manner, the *Tupelo Journal* boasted that more than 500 families from Illinois and Iowa would be moving to north Mississippi within the year.[57] For its part, the *Journal* urged farmers in Lee County to sell land at sacrifice levels in order to encourage immigrants and fresh capital to the area. Advertisements for such land would be placed in the newspaper at no expense to the seller. The newspaper also printed handbills at no charge to the advertisers, proclaiming the cheap land and advantages of living in Lee County.[58] In an attempt to hold its present population, the editor used a tactic common to newspapers in areas of declining population. He routinely printed letters that reported the "terrible conditions" in other places, especially Texas.[59]

Tupelo had not yet faced the fact that it had very little to offer immigrants from the Midwest or from its own surrounding rural areas. Consequently, the trains came and a few land speculators looked at the available offerings and then passed on to other areas. Hope for the program melted slowly and it passed from the scene leaving the town relatively unchanged.[60]

The crucial juncture came in 1898. In that year the price of cotton dropped below five cents a pound on the Memphis and New Orleans markets. The quotation figures for the staple had been dropping steadily for a decade. Its average market value for the nineties was 20 percent lower than the average price for the preceding decade.[61] The sustained depression was sapping the town's strength as surely as a deadly cancer.

The editor of the newspaper, writing in 1899, recalled the nightmarish nineties.

"The depression of all classes of business was great, confidence was destroyed, money was high…lands were reduced in value. The entire farming fraternity was disposed to emigrate…. It looked at one time like the entire population had been seized with the 'moving craze'…. Every train going westward was packed with humanity of all sorts, sizes, ages, and sexes."[62]

He did not exaggerate the amount of migration. The trend of the eighties continued into the nineties. Out-migration from Lee County exceeded immigration by an estimated 2,000 persons.[63] The loss of these potential customers was further aggravated by the bitter feelings of the rural population toward some Tupelo merchants, leading in some cases to boycotts.[64] As the largest cotton market in the county, many farmers blamed Tupelo cotton merchants for the low prices received for their products. Tupelo's emergence as a cotton center during the depressed nineties was not unlike Jonah's decision to flee from Joppa by boat. The town was being swallowed by the economic turmoils.

In this blackest hour, according to a favorite story of Tupelo boosters, the people of Tupelo rallied around their leaders, collected the capital and built the industries that saved the town. Much of this is true as far as it goes. Certainly if one reads only the newspapers and fails to read between the lines, this is the conclusion that would be reached. Stanley Elkins and Eric McKitrick describe similar events in other new towns on the frontier in which the people banded together in a democratic fashion to conquer their problems. In such a setting, according to Elkins and McKitrick, widespread cooperation "presents itself much less as bright possibility than a brutal necessity."[65] To a certain extent this too is applicable to Tupelo.

The transformation began when James Kincannon purchased the *Tupelo Journal* in 1898. Over the years the *Journal* had gained respect as one of the most active newspapers in the state. Unfortunately, John Miller had carried his attempts at social involvement to destructive lengths. Following his temporary role as peacemaker during the railroad construction, Miller returned to his more familiar routine as agitator and found himself going against the current of the rural revolt. Before he finally sold the paper in 1892, he had become the center of the town-country schism that threatened to destroy the community.

After Miller's bitter experience, the *Journal* became rather timid, afraid of offending another segment of the population. Perhaps the depression would have overwhelmed even the ablest of journalists, but the *Journal* and town seemed rudderless as they were battered around by the stormy times. What began as a cooling-off period for the *Journal* lapsed into aimless drifting.

After Kincannon became the owner in 1898, he reasserted the *Journal's* leadership role. He began by healing personal wounds between him and other town dominants, especially John Allen to whom Kincannon had become a political rival. Following this, he printed a series of letters prior to the 1898 elections calling for a strong town administration.[66]

Shortly thereafter, the town's most influential figures placed their names on the ballot. All of these men were subsequently elected. The voters selected perhaps the most able and vibrant collection of businessmen and professionals ever to sit in the executive positions of its town government. Tupelo's concern for change was partially motivated by the same discontent with local governments that existed throughout the nation.[67] It was not a reform that sought to bring about greater democratic participation, but reflected instead the pragmatic desire to bring a practical and efficient touch of solid business practices to local government.[68]

The single most influential member of the new Board of Councilmen was John Clark, who for three decades had been Tupelo's leading businessman. Despite his wealth and business skills, he had been overshadowed by his father, Richard Cottrell Clark of Verona, before his father's death in 1894. Subsequently, John Clark seemed to be catapulted into almost every phase of Tupelo life. With seemingly inexhaustible energy, he brought vibrance to every enterprise he touched after 1898. Between 1899 and his death in 1906, Clark was president of the county's largest retail outlet, the area's largest cotton firm, the Tupelo Cotton Oil Company, the Tupelo Compress Company, and the Bank of Tupelo. He was vice president and chairman of the board of the Tupelo Cotton Mills.[69]

With one possible exception, the other members of the Board of Councilmen between 1899 and 1907 were not quite the equal of Clark in economic or political power. D. W. (Will) Robins was his closest rival. Robins, the nephew of Congressman John M. Allen, was a strong-willed individual, already well on his way to becoming the county's largest and most successful farmer and cotton gin operator. Like Clark, he was a man of boundless energy. Between 1909 and 1929, Robins served as one of the strongest mayors in the history of the town. He also was to serve as a highway commissioner on the state's first highway commission.[70] The remaining members of the board were Dr. T. T. Bonner, the county's leading physician; C. W. (Neil) Troy, an old resident of the town and longtime employee of John Clark; and Van C. Kincannon, wealthy landowner, who came from one of the oldest and most prominent families in the county.[71]

The mayor was William Dozier Anderson. One of the town's most brilliant men, Anderson was the most prominent attorney in Lee County, who in time sat in the state senate and for over 20 years on the state's supreme court.[72] He had served for two terms as a member of the board of aldermen and knew local government well. As one of the most respected men in the county his presence commanded a wide following.

Added to these public officials was John Allen. Allen's name was easily the most recognizable in town. To many persons outside Lee County, Tupelo was thought of as "John Allen's town." A man of enormous intelligence and ability, he was regarded by the editor of the *Memphis Commercial Appeal* as "perhaps the ablest man in public life in Mississippi" at the close of the nineteenth century.[73] After eight terms as the congressman from District One, Allen fell victim to populist revolt when he sought the position as United States Senator in the 1899 campaign.[74] He returned to his native Tupelo as a hale and active man of 55 where he became one of the foremost figures in the transitions of the new century.

Despite internal schisms that divided John Clark and Will Robins and the fierce competition between the Clark-Anderson-Troy Bank of Tupelo and the Robins-Allen-Rogers First National, the men were able to work together on almost all issues. Their unity seemed to be imposed by the stringent opposition of the various farmer-based organizations that sought to wrest power away from the town dominants.[75]

As in so many small towns, these businessmen tended to equate their self-interest with those of the community. Both their rhetoric and action make clear their commitment to the premise that their own interests represented the interests of the community. When this perspective was challenged, especially by agrarian leaders, the agrarians were chided for their lack of citizenship as exhibited by their opposition to the unity proposed and controlled by the businessmen.

Once the businessmen assumed public office, their highest priority was to address the economic crises caused by the falling cotton market. Their focus was not to assist the struggling farmers, but to diversify their own economy and thus make it less dependent on the trade of the depression-draped yeomen. It was clearly a much more narrow definition of "community" and "community development" than would emerge in later decades.

Their action proceeded in two stages. The first task was to complete some of the basic infrastructure; namely, the development of electricity and a public water system for the town. The second stage was to use that infrastructure to add industries to the town. It was these goals that had drawn these businessmen into public office. Soon after assuming office, the councilmen called for a referendum on a publicly owned electrical plant.

The vote was in two parts: the initial concern was a vote for or against the electrical plant, and the second called for a decision as to whether it would be publicly or privately owned.[76] The town was nearly unanimous in its support to bring electricity to Tupelo, with only eight negative votes on the issue, but these taxaphobic residents of northeast Mississippi voted overwhelmingly for private ownership.[77]

After a six-month cooling-off period, the mayor embarrassingly announced that the vote was only a straw poll and should not be considered binding. When the board sought to proceed against the will of the electorate, a furor erupted.[78]

The disgruntlement subsided slowly as the town became excited about the prospect of electrification and with it new industries and jobs. Between the period of the initial vote and the controversy over a tax-built electric plant, John Clark assembled a group of businessmen who pooled their resources to establish an oil mill for pressing cotton seed.[79] The ease and speed with which the money was gained prompted a more ambitious project. Businessmen organized themselves into committees to seek financial support from local townsmen for a cotton mill. John Clark's brother, Turner, called a meeting at the courthouse with the announced intention of laying the groundwork for the factory. As in other southern towns, the goal of industrializing took on the trappings of a crusade.[80] John Allen used his enormous rhetorical skills to persuade the group that this was more than a business venture; it was "a move to save Tupelo."[81] Subsequently, Tupelo businessmen were caught up in the same crusading mania for cotton mills that spread across the South.[82] Improved economic conditions made investments possible and the emotional appeals added a sense of theater to the efforts. Within a week, 38 investors had pledged a total in excess of $100,000. Of that number, only one of the men was not from Lee County and only three were not from Tupelo.[83] Enthusiasm for the project was running so high that for some of the men the investment represented their life savings.[84] An additional $100,000 was secured from Tupelo citizens to complete the financing within six months.[85]

An excellent location at the crossing of the two railroads was selected and construction commenced. The mill began operation in the late spring of 1901. Originally, the plant manufactured only brown domestics. A year later it was making blue denims and blue suitings.[86] It was by far the largest factory in the county and by the end of 1903 it was operating with 170 looms and 500 spindles. Two hundred persons were employed with a monthly payroll of $3,000. Moreover, the mill served as an excellent market for the farmers since the operation consumed 2,500 bales annually of locally grown cotton.[87] The plant continued to manufacture a heavy cotton material called cheviots and was turning out 25 miles of cheviots or 1,000 work shirts per day by 1920. Employment at this time rose to 450 people with an annual payroll of over $400,000.[88]

The cotton mill remained the largest factory in the area, but a series of smaller plants soon supplemented it. A group of businessmen led by William Anderson's law partner, Charles P. Long, combined their capital to begin a fertilizer factory. This company not only provided employment and useful products for the surrounding area, it added a boosteristic note with its brand names, "Cotton Belt" and "Tupelo."[89] The cotton oil company added an ice plant to its operations. In 1901, John Allen and W. F. Riley opened separate planing mills. That same year Allen and his partner, J. R. Frazer, also established a company that manufactured scales for weighing cotton. The brick and tile company doubled its capacity.[90]

Once a locally owned industrial base had been established, an effort was made to secure outside capital for additional industries. In 1902, the Board of Councilmen offered a five-year exemption from local taxes to any new investors.[91] The town used the channels of communication, which had been designed in the mid-nineties to attract immigrants from the Midwest. A hosiery factory based in St. Louis established a branch factory in Tupelo that provided employment for more than 100 women. This was followed by a Muncie, Indiana-based handle factory which sought to revive the hardwood industry.[92] To accelerate the influx of new industry, a Businessmen's League was formed in 1904 with the objective of promoting Tupelo as a site for industry. The new organization was influential in getting the Swift Company to build a small processing plant in Tupelo in its first year, but this was the last factory of the era.[93]

Tupelo's industrial development stopped as abruptly as it began. Once again the town-country cleavage emerged but in a slightly different form. Throughout the state the political winds were blowing directly into the face of any attempts to expand industrialization. The state's newest champion of agrarianism, and future governor and senator, James K. Vardaman, spoke for a large segment of the state in one of his editorials. "I believe the 'ark of the covenant of American ideals' rests in the agricultural sections of the South."[94] Vardaman's biographer defends his subject against the charge that as governor his policies and behavior prevented industries from locating in the state.[95] He offers, however, no evidence that Vardaman took any action to encourage industry into Mississippi and Vardaman's posture has been seen by students of Mississippi economics as critical in deterring industrial development.[96] Vardaman was not acting alone and one scholar of Mississippi estimated that the antibusiness sentiment of Mississippi politicians during this period set back industrial development in the state by 30 years or more.[97]

The rise of the new agrarian sentiment voiced by Vardaman paralleled improving conditions in the agricultural market. This turn of events placed the Tupelo leaders squarely in a dilemma. Many of the county's largest farmers who lived outside Tupelo viewed the rise of industry with alarm. For some time, they had been losing their labor in the out-migration movements of the preceding two decades. Now they faced the possibility of new competition for their workers in nearby Tupelo. Charles P. Long, one of the industrial leaders, wrote of that concern. "Many of the prominent farmers in the area did not share our enthusiasm for industry. Some of them came to me and said flatly that they didn't want to hold their own people back, but they couldn't afford to continue losing their best tenants."[98]

The coolness of the large landowners toward industry is reflected in their failure to provide capital for the new factories. It was noted above that only three persons outside Tupelo purchased stock in the cotton mill. There is no evidence to suggest that they owned stock in any of the other factories. Gerald Capers' suggestion that large planters retarded urbanization by withholding capital from industry may be accurately applied to Tupelo.[99]

Most of the Tupelo leaders could empathize with the plight of the larger farmer. At least 21 of the 25 persons most deeply involved with industrial development in Tupelo also owned some farmland.[100] Their divided commitment to both rural and town needs is reflected in part by their support of factories that employed women. Almost two-thirds of the jobs created between 1899 and 1903 were filled by female employees and consequently did not compete with the farmer for labor. Only one of the male-employing industries had more than 20 employees and town leaders showed no inclination to alter that arrangement.[101]

Industrial development of all types gradually slowed to a halt between 1904 and 1907. Wilbur Thompson suggests that "victories" during crisis times may frequently be followed by a period of complacency in a town's economic growth pattern.[102] The older, more prominent leaders withdrew almost entirely from industrial development projects. The Businessmen's League formed in 1904 was led by the manager of the cotton mill and was composed primarily of smaller merchants.[103] They were unable to regenerate the enthusiasm that accompanied the industry building at the turn of the century. After a year's service in his position, the president of the league left town with little progress to show for his efforts.[104]

In his absence, the league seemed to fade from existence.

The abruptness with which the industrialization ended suggests two conclusions about the industrial phase and a sense of community. The first is that the drive for industrialization was clearly linked to key economic dominants and not the broader community. When these individuals ceased to press for industrialization, the process ended. The second is that the dominants insisted that their efforts were done on behalf of the whole community; however, when their own self-interests were threatened by reducing the labor pool and therefore driving up wages, the industrialists ceased to promote industry. This suggests that town interests are often best served where the activities meet both the self-interest of the dominants and the community as a whole.

Tupelo dominants never abandoned the interests of farmers where their own interests were at stake. Will Robins, one of the area's largest farmers, directed a major drainage plan that helped reclaim some of the county's best farmland. Robins took advantage of state legislation that permitted farmers to tax themselves for purposes of flood control. In a masterful piece of leadership, Robins coordinated the Lee County Board of Supervisors, the Tupelo Board of Councilmen, and local farmers in an ambitious program that provided fresh farmland to farmers, enhanced yields per acre, and new tax revenues for the county.[105]

Even at the height of the efforts to industrialize, the town never reduced rural trade to a secondary consideration. Merchants and the Board of Councilmen paralleled their industrial development with efforts to renew the confidence and trade of the rural sector. Beginning in 1900, Tupelo secured the responsibility to maintain all roads within three miles of Tupelo.[106] It was hoped that better roads would lead to stronger bonds linking Tupelo to its surrounding hinterland. Tupelo's streets were to be kept in better repair and the wagon yards were to receive more attention.[107] Shortly thereafter, a series of shopper promotions were initiated.[108] There is no available raw data to determine the effect of the program; but R. W. Reed, the town's most prominent twentieth-century merchant, observed that Tupelo was already the leading trade center in the area when he moved there in 1907.[109]

By 1907, this action-filled era was drawing to a close. The central figure, John Clark, died in 1906.[110] A year later, W. D. Anderson left his mayoral post in favor of a seat in the state senate.[111] John Allen drifted into semiretirement, and D. W. Robins took a furlough from his public career to attend to personal business. In 1908 there was only one carryover, C. W. Troy, from the earlier Board of Councilmen.

The participants in the activities between 1898 and 1907 had achieved some of the important goals they had set for themselves. The reclamation programs had greatly improved agricultural conditions. Utilities were established, an industrial base was developed, and a usable past forged. One measure of their success was the reversal of the out-migration patterns of two successive decades. The fear of a continued decline of the labor supply was not justified. Lee County's numbers grew from 21,956 in 1900 to 28,894 in 1910, an increase of 32 percent. Tupelo's count was enlarged from 2,118 to 3,881 for an 83 percent increase.[112]

Summary and Conclusions

Much of Tupelo's basic infrastructure was developed between 1885 to 1907. The town was able to avail itself of the opportunity to be on a route of a crossing railroad. It built its electrical infrastructure. It finally developed some core community institutions by creating public schools, strengthening its churches, and building community symbols such as the opera house. Moreover, the town broadened its economic base to include manufacturing.

The town had become potentially stronger and better able to compete in the broader economy. The railroad linked the town to a broader commercial network and gave Tupelo a competitive advantage over surrounding towns. By that advantage, it attracted both trade and businesses from the nearby towns. The transportation helped make the town a cotton trade center for a subregion, which then fed its cotton to the larger regional center in Memphis.

In establishing itself as a subregional hub, the town was tied more closely to the economic status of the hinterland. The town was dependent on the rural area for both raw materials and trade.

These strengthened linkages to the rural hinterland came in the midst of a devastating agricultural depression. The town sought to diversify its economy as a way of buffering itself against the impact of the depression. This diversification effort proceeded in two stages. In step one, key businessmen were elected to local offices from which they established an electrical generating plant. They then pooled local capital and using their new energy source proceeded to build local industries that used local raw materials. The newly established industries had some of the intended effect. The town gained population as it absorbed some of the displaced farm families and the economy stabilized. Wages in the factories, however, were not sufficient to raise the quality of life for the town.

The town had now positioned itself in a central role of the economy for the whole county. It was being thrust into the role of county leadership. As part of the town's response it helped sponsor drainage programs to reduce flooding and reclaim valuable farmland. The town also took the initiative to maintain the roads within three miles of its corporate limits. With its newly acquired advantages came new responsibilities.

CHAPTER 4

The Agrarian Revolt:
A Study in Community Conflict

A key community leader in a southern city recently suggested that Tupelo outperformed his city because Tupelo has been a unified city whereas his own has been divided. It is true that Tupelo has often found a way to work together, but as seen in earlier chapters, Tupelo and Lee County have had severe schisms from the outset. In this regard, Tupelo is no different from any other town.

Conflict is a common component of all towns and cities, in part because it is ingrained in the culture. Conflict is a by-product of the fierce competition of these successful commercial towns. Moreover, the diversity of values and perspectives that are central to the culture are also breeding grounds for conflict. Democracy, in order to be true democracy, protects and encourages the right to disapprove and voice that discontent.

Conflict is one of the basic methods by which the powerless are able to engage in community development. It is frequently used as a community development technique in American towns and elsewhere. It is a common tactic by which citizens in totalitarian regimes have expressed their discontent and desire for an open society. This and other positive functions of conflict have been clearly documented by the scholar Lewis Coser.[1]

At no time did conflict become such a dominant part of Tupelo's life than during the last decade and a half of the nineteenth century. Tupelo, of course, was only one of many rural trade centers that was embroiled in the fierce struggles of what became known as the Populist Revolt. Its experience, however, is instructive in an understanding of the processes that promote, shape, and blunt community conflict.

As noted in previous chapters, Tupelo's vertical ties to national and regional forces have consistently shaped the local agenda. As a small town, the community is trapped between the broader economic issues and the conditions of immediate localized hinterland. Because the economic and social trends are filtered through the town, local farmers have frequently mistaken the town as the locus of their economic and social problems. Consequently, farmers often blamed Tupelo merchants for the hard economic times between the 1870s and 1890.

Rising agricultural costs and declining market prices during the period shaved profit margins and left the area's economy on a precipitously thin foundation. The value of cotton slumped from twenty cents a pound in the early seventies to less than half that level a decade later. The downward spiral continued through the eighties and became even more acute in the nineties.[2] The fate of southern businessmen paralleled the agricultural decline. Business in the South failed at a rate well above the national average during the economic descent.[3] Small merchants, like most of these in Tupelo, were especially hard hit. As noted in the previous chapter, almost half of the businesses established in Tupelo in 1887 and 1888 were no longer operating after 1890.[4]

In a situation like this, the less powerful, in this case the farmers, are likely to turn to the more powerful for leadership.[5] Farmers in Lee County were shackled by the same problems of ineffectual leadership that handicapped other contemporary farm movements. In these settings, the rural population looked to the larger villages for guidance and leadership. The husbandmen had numerical strength, but even in rural locales the established political and economic power resided in the larger villages.[6]

Originally, the town and farmers worked together. Both sides understood that organization and leadership were critical. Tupelo's merchants and newspaper were the vanguard of the earliest farm organizations beginning with the Grange activities in the 1870s. Townspeople urged farm operators to join and participate in the Grange programs as their best hope to improve life in rural areas. Planter-merchants from Tupelo assumed leadership roles and the *Journal* served as the organ for the countywide organization. When farmers sought a more active voice, including the development of cooperatives that would compete with Tupelo stores, Tupelo's leadership sought to derail the entire movement.[7] The data are vague on subsequent events, except to note the demise of the once vital program two years later.[8]

The byword in major events was "unity" behind Tupelo leadership. When the early Greenback movement indicated their attempt to gain more political strength for farmers vis-a-vis the eastern establishment, it had the hearty endorsement of town spokesmen.[9] Once it became apparent that the organization would challenge the local Democratic Party, the Greenback leaders were denounced as "traitors to the Democracy and the Anglo-Saxon race."[10]

Relationships between town and country continued to ebb and crest in such a manner for the remainder of the eighties. For a brief time in the early eighties, the two populations were united by their opposition to eastern corporations. Tupelo citizens were often the most vocal in denouncing the "monsters who grow rich from the sweat of farmers." Local merchants urged agrarians to "stand shoulder to shoulder with all citizens of Lee County for protection against that grinding monopoly, the Standard Oil Company."[11] An exception to their attacks on eastern corporations came in 1883 when they jointly muted their discussions of corporations for fear that a regulatory agency would discourage railroad construction. The editor of the *Aberdeen Examiner* joyfully proclaimed that Democrats, Republicans, Greenbacks, and Independents were working in harmony to promote railroad building in northeast Mississippi.[12]

Even during periods of relative calm the latent tension was present and an effective leader could trigger a fresh outbreak of hostility between town and country. Community conflict tends to begin with specified issues and then move to more general disagreements. As a leading scholar noted, community conflict is a "process of events occurring in real time and space — not as a set of cultural patterns."[13] Not surprisingly, then, the warm relations that characterized the railroad promotion were chilled by charges of corruption in construction of the Memphis to Birmingham road. Frank Burkitt, a leader in the Grange and Farmers' Alliance, and editor of the *Okolona Chickasaw Messenger* 20 miles south of Tupelo, led the assault against the railroad company. Burkitt had worked to secure the original route for the railroad in the 1870s. The initial charter was granted to a company headed by Confederate war hero Nathan Bedford Forrest, for a course that would pass through Pontotoc and Chickasaw counties. Forrest toured the proposed route soliciting subscriptions for capital stock from counties, towns, and individuals. After the coalfields opened in north Alabama, the promoters of the line sought an amendment to their charter that would permit it to deviate from its proposed course. Burkitt attempted to block the amendment. When this failed, he offered his own amendment requiring the railroad to repay subscriptions with interest. This too was rejected. Following this second reversal, Burkitt took his case before farm supporters charging that "corrupt political rings" involving politicians and corporate leaders were working against farmer interests.[14] Burkitt cautioned rural citizens of Lee County that the railroad would not only take their land but would also do damage to their farm property for which they would be unable to collect.[15]

Burkitt's warnings were taken to heart by a number of Lee County farmers who insisted on being paid immediately for damages being done to their farms by railroad construction. John Miller, the editor of the *Tupelo Journal,* only made matters worse with his contemptuous comments concerning these complaints. "We hear," he began one of his more vitriolic columns, "of one or two persons along the line who insist that their five hundred dollar farms will be injured seven or eight hundred dollars by the railroad passing through it, but if these persons prove implacable and persist in refusing to donate the right of way, resort will be had to the provisions of the railroad charter, and the tax book will cut an important figure in determining the value of lands."[16]

Not all of the farmers were intimidated by the threat. R. D. Freeman interrupted construction of the railroad when he appeared among the construction crew with a shotgun and asserted he "would be damned" if any more work was done before he received damages. Following this bold action a number of neighboring farmers joined with Freeman in his stand. They received some satisfaction after a jury convened and ruled in favor of the plaintiffs. Tupelo taxed itself the $278 in damages and paid the men. Miller concluded the episode in a flurry of alliteration. "It is hoped that the parties receiving it [the money] will be happy; that the shotgun will be turned into a plowshare, and that the piping tunes of peace will reign once again on the placid banks of Old Town Creek."[17]

Community conflict begins with a threat and now the threat of economic loss to many farmers was more clearly evident. In stage two, tensions begin to develop as they were doing in Lee County.[18] As the tension mounts, positions tend to become polarized and new leaders and organizations reflecting that polarization emerge.[19]

The economic and railroad tensions served as an incubator that hatched a new round of agrarian unrest and gave birth to that new set of leaders. In 1888, R. D. Freeman and his brother, Thomas, helped establish the Farmers' Alliance. This organization and these new leaders were no longer content to allow Tupelo merchants to serve at the vanguard of the unrest.

The most conspicuous examples of the leadership in 1888 were Thomas Freeman, James Gillespie, and John Hansell. Freeman had served as an officer during the Civil War and afterward was given the title "colonel."[20] He and his brother R. D. Freeman were merchant-farmers in Tupelo in 1880, but Thomas regarded himself primarily as a farmer by 1888.[21] Colonel Freeman had been on the fringe of the Greenback movement, offering more moral encouragement than actual leadership.[22] His activist role in agrarian matters stemmed from his consistent squabbles with John Miller. In time, he became a member of the state's executive committee in the Populist party and served as a delegate to the national conventions in 1892.[23] His marginal political status left him on the outside of the county Democratic machinery that was dominated by Congressman Allen and John Miller, the president of the county's Democratic executive committee.

James Gillespie was co-owner, along with Joseph Ballard, of the *Tupelo Ledger*. In 1888, at the age of 23 he was the youngest member of the Mississippi House of Representatives.[24] Fiercely ambitious by his own admission, he had his eye on John Allen's seat in Congress and from 1888 to 1891 was Allen's most vicious antagonist. His rivalry with John Miller stemmed both from the competition between the two newspapers and also Miller's support for one of Gillespie's opponents in the race for the state legislature.[25] Despite his differences with Allen and Miller, his loyalty as a Democrat was unquestioned.

John Hansell was better acquainted with third-party politics than any other alliance leader. He had been one of the most prominent figures in Lee County's Greenback party.[26] His work in the Greenback movement, however, made him a pariah in the Democratic camp. Frozen out of his original party, he subsequently became the county's most conspicuous spokesman for the Republican party. The Republican presidential victory in 1888 brought Hansell the reward of postmaster in Shannon, which identified him as the titular head of the G.O.P. in Lee County.[27]

The initial task of this new leadership was to form a strong organization. The rural population, like its town counterparts was quick to take advantage of national trends and movements. Therefore, beginning in 1888 they built their organization around the National Alliance, a newly formed farmer organization that had just had its first annual meeting October 12, 1887, in Shreveport, Louisiana.

The primary goals of this organization were to gain more grassroots involvement in politics and to regain lost political power. It hoped to reverse the shift of power from the countryside to the city. In short, it hoped to educate farmers and their families in "the science of economic government" and to "give farmers a clear and united voice in political and economic debate."[28] In time, the National Alliance would give birth to the People's party as a vehicle to directly engage in the national and state political process.

The local Alliance, with its national ties, set out to establish grassroots support, and by July 1889 they were well under way. The *Tupelo Ledger* gave the movement a powerful voice and Gillespie championed their cause weekly. Farmers were counseled to organize as the only means of contending with the corporate forces that were reshaping their lives.[29] Suballiances were formed in almost all rural neighborhoods, although membership figures were not reported. The year brought no new demands, only the reiteration that county politics become more responsive to agrarian needs.[30]

By 1890, the county was alive with talk of the alliance. James Gillespie kicked off the year by sponsoring a strong antitrust bill when the state legislature returned to session in January.[31]

Often at this point a kind of Gresham's law sets in by which many of the moderate leaders are driven out.[32] John Allen, long a stabilizing political force, sensed the shifting political winds, and announced that he would not seek re-election, at least not until he could further test the water.[33] Frank Burkitt was sure the tide had turned and urged Lee County farmers to flex their muscles in selecting delegates to the upcoming state's constitutional convention as well as the congressional elections.[34] If the agrarians could rewrite the state constitution in their own favor it was hoped they could shape state policy for much of the next century.

By this point in community conflict it is very difficult to bring the conflict to a halt. The determining factors are internal structures and ties of the community and the quality of the leadership.[35]

The individual and collective response to the crisis was shaped by cross-pressures similar in consequence to the cross-pressures experienced by the agrarian Midwest. On the one hand, it was tempting to farmers to stand united and solve their problems on their own without involving themselves with townsmen. Numerically, Lee County's husbandmen in 1890 outnumbered all other occupations combined by almost three to one.[36] Moreover, they might have felt justified in independent action. Judged by the rhetoric of the time, most Lee countians accepted the Jeffersonian ideal that rural life was superior to life-styles in town.[37] Concurrently, many local farmers saw Tupelo businessmen as key links in a monopolistic chain. In the absence of banks, merchants controlled all credit in the area. This gave them the power to insist on the type of crop they would accept as security. The primary market for farm produce was again the merchants. The same proprietors were also the source of goods needed for home consumption.[38] Under these circumstances, the protests by merchants that they too were victims of the price squeeze and corporation-dictated policies often fell on unsympathetic rural ears.

The countervailing pressure was the multiple ties that bound the farmers and townspeople together. It was difficult to draw hard and fast lines between farmers and merchants. Many storekeepers also owned farms. Most of them had been born and reared on farms. In other cases, agricultural leaders had sons, brothers, or other relatives who were businessmen in Tupelo.[39] Moreover, the single crop economy compelled a common interest in promoting cotton. Businessmen were keenly aware of agrarian suffering. The plight of agriculture was recorded in the cash register of every store in Tupelo.[40]

Held together during the week by the cotton economy, the people were bonded together intellectually and spiritually on the Sabbath by a firmly rooted Protestant faith that was as ubiquitous in the South as cotton, cornbread, and catfish. Protestantism permeated the life-style as surely as sunshine bathed the landscape. "The South is by a long way the most simply and sincerely religious country that I was ever in," observed a contemporary English traveler.[41] The religious unity was enhanced by the limited number of clergymen. Because of the shortage of ministers, the same men preached in village and country churches on a rotating basis, generally using the same sermon and services in all of the churches.[42] Moreover, the practicing theological differences between the two largest denominations, Baptists and Presbyterians, were sufficiently minimal to permit joint services on a weekly or biweekly basis.[43]

Moreover, Lee County farmers were bound together politically as Democrats. While there had been multiple party allegiances prior to the Civil War, afterward, the county was very solidly Democratic. Although the Alliance spectrum permitted a variety of views, the overwhelming majority of its members were Democrats. The initial political efforts, therefore, were to work within the existing Democratic structure. In their first move the Alliance called for a reorganization of the county machine in a way that would give farmers a greater voice.[44] Somewhat startled by this action, the county's Democratic executive committee cautioned the fledgling group against any rash action, but failed to comply with the Alliance's command.[45] When the Alliance attempted to bring pressure on the Democratic leaders, the motions of the farmer organization were like those of an uncoordinated giant that grew tired of trying to move its own body. No one faction was in control and each suballiance sought to chart its own course.[46] Temporarily at least, John Miller merely laughed at the comical antics of his quixotic challengers and the first round ended with essentially no change in the party's form.[47]

An additional component of the cross-pressures was race. Would poor white farmers be willing to set aside cultural traditions and vote with similarly beleaguered poor black farmers? For those who opposed this grassroots movement the racial issue was often seen as the trump card used to bring unity among the white population and almost all knew that it would be played when the time seemed appropriate.

These cross-pressures were not so restrictive to the agrarian leadership. Almost all of these men had experienced earlier breaks from the dominant group and had established a much stronger independence. Only James Gillespie, the newspaper editor, whose ties to both the agrarian leadership and the Democratic Party was strongly affected by the cross-pressures.

On the other side, the leader who seemed to oppose radical change was John Allen. After Allen's initial reluctance to seek re-election, he reassessed his political strength and concluded that with proper fence-mending he could regain his congressional seat. Moreover, he foresaw a time when he might be able to secure a senatorial seat if he could hold his ground in the era of political change.

Allen was in fact a political moderate though some locals thought that Allen himself had a streak of Populist in him. He had been the first to break with the established Tupelo leaders by denouncing his assumed military title of "captain." Although he was from a prominent Lee County family, which in this postbellum time was sufficient grounds for taking a pseudo-military title, he abandoned its use when he realized that his lowly rank in the Confederate Army provided him with a positive link to a majority of the votes. The occasion for the switch in ranks came in his first congressional election when he campaigned against General William F. Tucker. Tucker closed one of his speeches by reminding the audience of his role in the Civil War.

"Seventeen years ago last night, my fellow citizens, after a hard-fought battle on yonder hill, I bivouacked under yonder clump of trees. Those of you who remember, as I do, the times that tried men's souls will not, I hope, forget their humble servant when the primaries shall be held."

John Allen assumed the stump and responded to his opponent.

"My fellow citizens, what General Tucker says to you about having bivouacked in yonder clump of trees on that night is true. It is also true, my fellow citizens, that I was vidette picket and stood guard over him while he slept. Now then fellow citizens, all of you who were generals and had privates stand guard over you while you slept, vote for General Tucker; and all you who were privates and stood guard over the generals while they slept, vote for Private John Allen."[48]

He was Private John Allen from that time forward.

By the last decade in the nineteenth century, the question was whether Allen was enough of a Populist to hold the agrarians and a sound enough Democrat to win the town vote. The test of the consequences of these pressures and counter-pressures was close at hand.

Beginning in 1890, the Alliance faced three consecutive years of critical elections that determined its fate. The impending constitutional convention marked 1890 as a pivotal year. The new constitution was certain to address itself to the issues of Negroes' voting rights and the state's position vis-a-vis corporations. With Frank Burkitt spearheading the movement, the state's Alliances were a driving force in creating the momentum for the constitutional convention.[49]

Senator James Z. George shifted the course of events and provided agrarian forces a sign of things to come when he stole Burkitt's thunder by placing himself at the vanguard of the constitutional bandwagon.[50] Fearful that they might be excluded altogether, Lee County's Alliance urged its members to select both of the county's representatives to the historic meeting in Jackson.[51] Tupelo's Democratic leaders countered by rigging the ballot to allow the Alliance only one place on the ticket.[52]

It was the most severe challenge to date, and Alliancemen had no intention of giving ground. A county meeting was called to determine the course of action. The majority of the members renewed their intention to select both constitutional delegates. Moreover, they ignored the regular party's nominees for office and put forth a slate of their own including a candidate for John Allen's congressional seat.[53]

The bold action was not without its dissenters. John Allen had not given up the race as easily as his political enemies had hoped. Following his original announcement not to seek re-election, the "noncandidate" addressed almost every suballiance within the county. His wit and charm recaptured the lost ground and perhaps won him new friends.[54] The decision by the main body to support his opponent brought the first major schism within the ranks of the Alliance. Less than a month after the county rally, four suballiances announced their endorsement of Allen.[55]

This stage of the conflict, best described as "the tension development stage" of community conflict was now mature and moving toward the stage of "role dilemma" in which sides must be chosen. The cross-pressures contributed heavily to the dilemma of the farmers. As this "role dilemma" stage rose to its height, the anti-agrarian forces played their trump card on the issue of race.

The race question was the Southern Alliance's "greatest ideological hurdle."[56] The official position of the Southern Alliance was to deny membership to African-Americans, but the organization was seen to be a threat to white unity. As Tom Watson, one of the National Alliance's leaders suggested, "The great fear is Negro Rule."[57]

The local Democrats attempted to exploit that fear and bolster their own ranks by stirring racial prejudices. The key issue was a new Colored Alliance at Palmetto. The president of the Palmetto organization, D. D. Edwards, attempted to alleviate white fears and ward off the attack by circulating a carefully prepared letter. "I wish to say that I don't aim to teach anything but Alliance principles and not create strife between the two races, but to teach unity and respect and it must be supported by law abiding people. If any should doubt me, you can get my recommendations from the white Alliance at Palmetto."[58] The Democrats gave the message their own interpretation by emphasizing the last sentence, implying that the white Alliance had sponsored its Negro counterpart.[59]

The resulting confusion and cross-pressures had predictable results. Allen's opponent, Newman Cayse, not wishing to appear in sympathy with the Colored

Alliance, withdrew from the campaign, leaving "Private John" unopposed and removing an emotional element from the canvas.[60]

The results were those which would be predicted by community conflict theory. Most white Lee County husbandmen avoided the role dilemma and pressure to choose sides by avoiding the decision.[61] They either could or would not vote either as a farmer or loyal white Democrat. Thus they did not go to the polls.[62] The delegates to the very important state's constitutional convention were chosen by the smallest vote in Lee County's history. A total of only 527 votes were cast in the entire county. In the end, the Alliance and the town each sent one delegate.[63]

There was little time for despondency, however. The election of 1891 presented another crucial test for the Alliance. It provided the opportunity to select officeholders for every major state and county post. Moreover, the senatorial race between incumbent Senator James Z. George, and former Congressman Ethelbert Barksdale was a measure of popular support for the subtreasury scheme that had gained the endorsement at the 1890 National Alliance Convention in Ocala, Florida.

Even at the National Convention, the subtreasury plan was the most controversial position approved.[64] Under the terms of this plan all national banks would be replaced with "subtreasuries" in each congressional district throughout the nation. These subtreasuries would loan money "to the people" at rates of interest not to exceed 2 percent per annum. These subtreasuries were designed to especially assist cotton farmers. Loans could be secured by nonperishable farm products. Under the terms of this proposal, farmers could withhold such products as cotton off the market to await favorable conditions by storing staple items in a federal warehouse and securing a loan of up to 80 percent of their current market value.[65]

The popular Senator George, who had won respect among farmers for his attack on trusts at the constitutional convention, risked losing favor with the Alliance by opposing the subtreasury. Barksdale, on the other hand, supported the plan and gained the endorsement of the Mississippi Alliance.[66]

The Lee County Alliance seemed prepared for the campaign. It was more confident than it had been previously. The resolutions, which came out of the national convention at Ocala, Florida, gave the local organization a sense of direction missing in earlier years. The demands called again for the abolition of national banks; 2 percent loans by the federal government; expansion of currency until it reached $50 per capita; lower tariffs; a graduated income tax; economies in government; curbs on future dealings; alien land ownership and the unearned land holdings of railroads and corporations; government ownership of railroads and communications; and the direct election of senators.[67]

The Ocala convention left the question of a third political party unresolved. Following a district Alliance meeting in Tupelo, the delegates addressed themselves to this issue and at the same time sought to extirpate themselves from the defensive image of 1890. "Whereas we are surrounded by a large Negro element; and whereas white supremacy with us is paramount to everything else, therefore resolved that we seek redress only through the white man's party, which in Mississippi is the Democratic Party."[68] Their statement of principles also insisted that the local Alliance would not support any man for office who did not endorse and support the platform as set forward at the Ocala convention. They pointed specifically at John Allen and called upon him to work toward the implementation of the goals stated at the Florida meeting.[69]

As part of their more aggressive tactics, the Alliance regenerated its attempt to gain control of the Democratic machinery. As in most community conflicts, the attacks became increasingly personal. Those attacks focused heaviest on John Miller, the county chairman of the Democratic Party, and the owner of the *Tupelo Journal*. In order to underscore their determination, many Lee County alliancemen boycotted the *Tupelo Journal* and the businesses that advertised in John Miller's paper.[70] Meanwhile, the honeymoon between the *Tupelo Ledger* and the Alliance was waning. James Gillespie's efforts to encourage the Alliance to work within the Democratic Party was his last major role in the farmer organization.

As any community conflict increases in intensity it tends to drive moderates from its ranks, "the process of stripping for action" in the words of community conflict theorist, James Coleman.[71] Consequently when Gillespie was seen to have a stronger attachment to the Democratic Party than to the Alliance, he was increasingly pushed from the Alliance.[72]

The Lee County Alliance further asserted its independence within the Democratic Party adhering to the pattern of other southern Alliances of nominating their own slate of candidates within the Democracy.[73] This action brought a critical break between town and country. James Gillespie referred to the move as a "reckless step" and urged the members to reconsider.[74] The implacable John Miller attacked the movers as "anti-Democrats." He charged his readers, "Let every man show his colors — either hoist the proud banner of Democracy or run up the black flag of anarchy."[75]

Tupelo businessmen reacted more moderately and sought to heal the schism before it became wider. Desperate for any constructive ties between the town and county, businessmen proposed again that a county fair be established as one means of bringing farmer and merchant together.[76] A Democratic-Alliance was formed with James Gillespie as a leading spokesman, in hopes that common ground could be found for a large number of the participants.[77] John Miller was encouraged to soften his language in response to the Alliance challenge.[78]

Many farmers also discouraged a division within the Democratic Party. Two suballiances urged the county organization to reconsider its efforts to offer a rival slate of candidates.[79] Their protests led to a second county meeting within a month. The group was badly split, but the majority reaffirmed their determination to support their own candidates.[80]

When the Alliance nominees were omitted from the Democratic ballot, the stage was set for a head-on collision between the Alliancemen and the Democrats. Over 800 farmers attended a mass rally in Tupelo to consider the best plan of action. Now that the break with the Democratic Party seemed inevitable, the old

Greenbacker and Republican, John Hansell, was asked to be the keynote speaker. The crowd cheered enthusiastically when Hansell called for a third party. Before the meeting adjourned, the majority of those assembled agreed to support the Alliance nominees named earlier.[81]

Democrats all over the state were fearful that other county Alliances might follow this pioneering effort to establish a third party. The *Aberdeen Examiner* referred to the movement as the greatest threat to white solidarity since the end of Reconstruction.[82] Newspapers throughout Mississippi echoed this sentiment.[83] The *Tupelo Ledger,* which for almost three years had been the voice of the Lee County Alliance, was the most emotional in its response. "Down With Radicalism!" Gillespie wrote, "Down With Third Partyism! Down With Every Other Ism! Organize, Democrats, Organize! White Supremacy Must Be Maintained At All Hazards In The State!"[84]

As might be expected in community conflicts, the personal attacks continued and by reciprocity each side responded in kind.[85] The *Journal* and the *Ledger* worked in unison by dredging up Reconstruction hatreds and racial fears. John Hansell was subjected to scurrilous attacks. His role in the Republican Party was made a central issue and farmers were continually warned that they were being used as part of a "Republican conspiracy" to reintroduce G.O.P. influence in the state.[86] In community conflict, formal channels of communication are often replaced by word of mouth and in some of the worst situations, the rumors are then reported as facts by the formal channel of communication. In this case, the newspapers repeated or initiated rumors that the Alliance had formed Negro political clubs throughout the county. Gunplay seemed inevitable and Alliance leader Thomas Freeman threatened John Miller and demanded a retraction of the statement that he had addressed a Negro meeting and asked for black support in his campaign for a seat in the state legislature.[87]

After the accusations and counteraccusations came the voice from the ballot box. Lee County's election results reflected the cross-pressures involved in the political decision, but it also revealed an intervening variable. Racial distribution, for example, was not the critical factor in the vote. Areas with concentrations of whites and blacks were in each of the political camps. Tenancy rates also fail to explain the vote since areas of high tenancy divided their vote between the opposing parties. The vote seems to have gone to the party with what might be described as organization with a personal touch.

Wherever the third party had an established leader it tended to poll well. The agrarian campaign was built around eleven men: T. H. Freeman, John Hansell, R. C. Cunningham, J. S. Stevens, W. C. Kyle, L. J. Rhodes, C. S. Brice, B. E. Harris, L. H. Dabbs, L. O. McCarty, and J. S. Howerton, who represented nine communities or open-country neighborhoods. The third party carried seven of the nine communities, losing only Tupelo and Corona. Moreover only their 4 percent margin at Saltillo was not a one-sided victory. The maverick party garnered 66 percent of the ballots cast in their winning boxes. The farmer-based group received 32 of the 33 votes at Unity for a 94 percent total and 44 of the 52 votes at Macedonia (85 percent).[88] The agrarians fell short, however, because of the non-voting. Too many people opted to avoid the cross-pressures by not voting.

Democrats, on the other hand, with a strong Tupelo-based organization were able to carry the county. The Alliance's all-out attack on Tupelo solidified the community and prompted the development of a political group of 90 men, most of whom were Tupeloans who canvassed the town and county. Tupelo, too, had organization with a personal touch. Rather than retaliating directly against the agrarians, they stressed Democratic unity as the best insurance of white supremacy.[89]

Among the personal losers, James Gillespie finally succumbed to Alliance pressure and left town. Subsequently, Democrats portrayed the young editor as a martyr who had been crucified by his former friends.[90]

The tactics brought Democrats one-sided victories in all boxes outside the home territory of the agrarian leaders. The key victory came in Tupelo where the Democrats received 268 votes of the 323 cast (83 percent). In the other boxes won by Democrats, they captured 380 of the 564 votes (67 percent).[91]

The election results were an ominous sign for farmers in future elections. Their failure to win any of the major offices deprived them of this strategic advantage. Moreover, some members expressed a sense of futility toward upcoming elections. Farmers, like the underdogs in other community conflict, felt an impotence in improving their situation. One of the most frustrating aspects of the election was the party's inability to counter successfully the racial fears generated by Democratic rhetoric.

The 1892 election offered the final major challenge, but the demoralized farmers were never able to establish a strong organization. There were some signs of life in the early spring when the Lee County Populist Party was formally established, but only 100 persons attended the opening rally.[92] Agrarians took heart after the Democrats nominated Grover Cleveland and longtime rural leaders such as Frank Burkitt made a clean break with the Democratic Party to align themselves with the Populists.[93] This hope, however, was counterbalanced by a coolness toward the Populist nominee, James Weaver. Some farmers let it be known that they sympathized with Populist ideals but could not support General Weaver.[94]

Although the outcome seemed inevitable, the congressional campaign between John Allen and James Burkitt, the younger brother of Frank, was filled with emotional fireworks. For a time, the candidates ran a close race. The complexion of the campaign turned quickly after the release of a letter attributed to Burkitt while serving as the superintendent of education in Chickasaw County. In the letter, addressed to a Negro schoolteacher, Burkitt allegedly advised the instructor that he was entitled to an assistant because of the size of his class enrollment. The communication suggested that the teacher would be sent the pay for an assistant with the stipulation that half of the money be returned to the superintendent of education. The bold words at the top of the letter were said to instruct the receiver to "Read and Burn," thus providing Democrats the convenient handle of attacking the "Read and Burn Letter."[95]

The contents of the brief note were continually kept before the electorate. John Allen hammered away at his opponent, using the note to imply a conspiracy between Populists and Negroes to misuse public funds.[96] Joe Ballard, who succeeded James Gillespie as the editor of the *Ledger,* got into a fistfight with James Burkitt over the letter.[97] John Miller and Frank Burkitt exchanged blows during a quarrel about the authenticity of the letter.[98]

Populists saw the hand of John Miller in the drafting of the letter and indicated their intention to boycott the entire town if necessary in response to Democratic tactics.[99] The *Journal's* editor was vulnerable to economic attack. Both his advertising and circulation had dropped below those of the *Ledger.*[100] Under this intense pressure, he announced the sale of the *Journal* to the owner of the *Ledger.* In his final editorial, Miller closed with the expressed hope that his departure "would benefit town and country."[101]

The alleged Burkitt letter supported Populist suspicions that Democrats planned to steal the election. Since many believed that the previous election had been stolen at the ballot box, the Populist leaders requested federal officials to monitor the polls and vote count.[102] Democrats argued that this confirmed their charge of a Populist-Republican-Negro conspiracy to return federal control to the South.[103]

The presence of the federal poll watchers may have hurt the Populists' chances. Grover Cleveland and John Allen received approximately 90 percent of the Tupelo vote, winning by totals of 217 to 28 and 209 to 22, respectively. Even in the rural areas of Lee County, Weaver received only 351 votes or 37 percent of the total, and Burkitt garnered 360 ballots for 40 percent. Populists received majorities in only four of the fifteen boxes.[104]

Subsequent elections in 1894, 1895, and 1896 confirmed the deterioration of an agrarian party. In 1894, both town and country gave John Allen more than 80 percent of the vote over his Populist rival.[105] Not even Frank Burkitt's bid in the 1895 gubernatorial race could stem the decline of the Populist Party in the county. Burkitt's opponent, A. J. McLaurin, received 90 percent of the vote in Tupelo and 60 percent in the rural areas.[106] The following year, both Tupelo and the rural areas gave the Democratic Party 90 percent of its vote.[107]

Tension between the town and country surfaced sporadically through the remainder of the decade, primarily in the form of caustic complaints by disgruntled farmers. One embittered yeoman vowed that he would haul his cotton 50 miles rather than take it to Tupelo.[108] Such protests frequently sparked fresh threats of boycotts, but the organized effort was never forthcoming. Nevertheless, the editor of the *Journal* acknowledged that Tupelo business was hurt by the tension and that many farmers in the southern part of the county made good their threats to trade in Aberdeen rather than in Tupelo.[109]

The community conflict had not ended. A final ironic twist remained. In such a mood of community conflict the final break normally occurs where the ties are the weakest. And so it did. The final split was not along town/country lines, but along racial lines.

There were specific overt clashes, but it was more a degeneration of existing ties and the failure to build new linkages. Prior to the 1890s, blacks had been making gains and there was evidence that these separated societies of white and black might grow closer, at least as coequals. Blacks had served on the Board of Police and there was a black policeman.[110] Black teachers were unified in support of better schools and making their collective voices heard.[111] The Colored Alliance was becoming a vibrant organization and was attempting to forge unified ties with their white counterpart. Blacks were regularly featured in the newspapers including the usage of surnames.

All of these efforts failed and the state's new constitution virtually disenfranchised blacks. Blacks along with all poor people lost political power under the new constitution. In 1892, there were 120,000 voters in Mississippi. Two years later the numbers were virtually cut in half to 68,000 as a result of the poll tax and literacy requirements for voting.[112] Black farmers were rejected as political allies by fellow white farmers. Even worse, African-Americans were becoming the political whipping boy for white Democrats and Populists.

Tensions mounted as blacks saw their gains being torn out by the very roots.

As the heat of the agrarian conflict mounted, the local newspaper printed articles that were seemingly designed to portray blacks in a bad light. Stories of Negro crime or rumors of black coalitions were increasingly frequent.[113] Financing for additional rooms in the black school was cancelled.[114] In 1896 a black prisoner, accused of killing a white man, was forcibly removed from the local jail and hanged on the courthouse lawn.[115] It was the first and only act of its kind in the town's history and it fueled the already volatile emotions of both sides. The fires of anger, frustration, mistrust, and prejudice smoldered for another two years and then burst forth in a near race riot in 1898.

The specific event that triggered the conflict was the alleged mistreatment of blacks being quarantined during a smallpox epidemic. According to the word-of-mouth rumors in the black community, the blacks in the "pest house" were being mistreated. Moreover, there was discussion of burning the houses of the smallpox victims as a means of curbing the epidemic.[116]

Only quick and decisive action by Mayor W. D. Anderson and the board averted a riot. The mayor and board members went through the separate communities calming fears and refuting rumors. The mayor went to Jackson, Mississippi, to discuss the situation with the state's health officer and returned to Tupelo with enough vaccination for 1,200 people.[117]

Tensions subsided, but the political and cultural segregation erected strong barriers between the separate white and black communities. Channels of communication were cut off. Blacks found themselves with virtually no resources. Their schools were poorly subsidized. Lacking political clout, they were unable to make their frustration known either about schools, poor streets and services, or the myriad other features that reduced their quality of life. And so for the coming decades the communities continued their drift apart punctuated occasionally by manifestations of the underlying community conflict.

Summary and Conclusions

Conflict is a normal and routine component in the experience of all towns. It grows out of the economic competition, the culture itself, individualism, and principles of democracy. Moreover, conflict is a legitimate technique in the community development process.

As a technique of community development, conflict, like the self-help approach, is rooted in the ability of the developing group to organize and act in concert. As noted in Chapter 3, when businessmen organized effectively they were much more likely to achieve their goals. The same principle was true for the farmers of the late nineteenth century.

Farmers were losing ground economically and politically. The most enlightened agrarians understood that the economic fortunes of farmers were linked to their ability to act in the political arena. They sensed that without the power that comes from organization and unity, the economic and political fate of farmers was set on a downhill course.

In a very real sense, farmers of the late nineteenth century faced fundamental problems very much like the problems that face small towns at the end of the twentieth century. They find themselves losing ground economically and unable to control their fate politically.

Townspeople in places such as Tupelo understood and sympathized with the dilemma of farmers. Indeed, most contended that the towns were the allies, not the oppressors of farmers. Small towns saw themselves as victims of distant and powerful forces that were making gains at the expense of the more helpless. They placed themselves as among the less powerful.

Because they were suffering a common fate, townspeople and farmers worked together in a loose partnership during much of the economically stressful times. But what most townspeople did not understand, then or now, is that community development does not benefit all segments of the population.

Community development often has winners and losers. In the case of the railroad development, the town was the winner. Farmers could see no improvement in their lives. In fact, they may have lost land and had their farms dissected by intrusive railroad tracks and noisy disruptive trains that scared livestock, to say nothing of posing a threat to the safety of the livestock. After all, trains were equipped with cowcatchers for good reason. The very act of community development, attracting a new railroad, had now come full circle and was one of a number of specific points of community conflict.

The community conflict in Lee County tended to proceed through the basic stages common to community conflict. Almost all persons involved with the study of community conflict agree on the basic steps. Jerry W. Robinson depicts six basic steps or stages of community conflict as shown below.

James Coleman describes three rubric changes that occur in the dynamics of community controversy: issues change from (1) specific disagreements to more

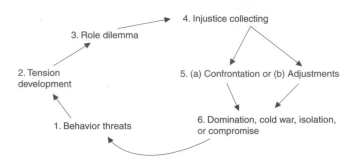

general ones; (2) elaboration into new and different disagreements, i.e., old wounds or grievances are recalled and brought into play; and (3) a final shift from disagreement to direct antagonism. During the course of these transitions polarization occurs that drives the two sides farther apart, new leaders appear, and a Gresham's law occurs in which the "harmful and dangerous elements drive out those who would keep the conflict within borders." Attacks on the other side become more personal and the reciprocity causes an equally aggressive response.

Elements of all these stages were part of the Lee County experience. Agrarians tended to rally around the Farmers' Alliance that gave the movement some cohesiveness and a guiding set of principles. As the issues became politicized, the townspeople tended to center around the Democratic Party.

Farmers, especially white farmers, experienced strong cross-pressures in the conflict. There were common elements that held them together as farmers, especially farmers with real grievances. At the same time, these husbandmen were linked to townspeople through culture, common economy, religion, race, and kinship, to cite only a few of the bonding forces.

Agrarian leaders were much less susceptible to these cross-pressures. They had broken with the dominant political culture and thus felt more freedom to stay away from conventional ties and positions.

One of the key leaders was Frank Burkitt, who was the single most powerful voice for agrarians in the state and the region. His efforts in northeast Mississippi made it a focal point in the agrarian revolt.

There were other local leaders who were very significant at the community level. Each of these individuals was able to gain unity among farmers at the very base grassroots level. The ties seemed to have been between leader and constituent in a very personal way rather than constituents being wed to agrarian principles.

Despite the efforts of Burkitt and local leaders, the agrarians were unable to form an organization sufficiently strong to win elections and thereby place themselves in a position to help make policy. The cross-pressures placed on the rural voters appear to be the key. Rather than having to take sides, most of the voters opted not to cast a ballot. Because many eligible rural voters remained on the sidelines, the rural vote was too small to counter the well-organized, unified town voters. Thus, in three consecutive elections, the agrarians fell short of a majority of the votes.

Perhaps the key election was to elect representatives to the constitutional convention. There they were to write a new constitution for the state. Some of the measures taken there, especially the limitations on the franchise, greatly reduced the number of persons eligible to vote in subsequent elections.

In each election, agrarians were frequently divided by the issue of race. Opponents of the agrarians argued that unless whites maintained unity, blacks would gain political control. Thus, blacks were used as whipping boys in each of the elections.

This tactic helped arouse racial fears and racial tension and contributed to a weakening of any ties or potential links between the races. During the 1890s, there was a gradual deterioration of the horizontal ties between blacks and whites in the country.[118] There were overt acts of violence between the biracial communities, but many of the ties seem to have dissolved slowly until there were few avenues of cooperation.

CHAPTER 5

The Development of Good Roads: Tying the Community Together

The changes of the early twentieth century, which saw the establishment of an industrial base and the development of public utilities, included also the emergence of a system of good roads for the town and country. The inter-regional development of a railway system that had led originally to the birth of Tupelo and countless parallel towns, had established a galaxy of communities strung along rail lines that crisscrossed the nation. Nevertheless while Tupelo and similar towns had frequent and easy access to their sister communities along the tracks, much of the farming regions were as inaccessible as they had been from the time of the first settlers. A traveler could make a round-trip train ride from Tupelo to Birmingham faster and much easier than many farmers in the county could make the one-way journey from the farm to the market. Riding the train from Tupelo to Memphis often meant a pleasure trip; crossing Main Street on a rainy February day generally proved an adventure. It was not uncommon for heavy rains to halt commerce, delay the court, and prevent the opening of church doors on the Sabbath. The sad truth of the matter was that Mississippi's roads became bottomless quagmires in the winter and were as bad in the early part of the twentieth century as they had been a century before.[1]

Until better roads could be built, Tupelo pragmatically accommodated itself to the reality of the poor ones. The wagon yards provided by the merchants were a necessity to farmers who could not conduct all of their business and return home in the period of sunlight.[2] Because it often required as long as ten hours to make the 34-mile round-trip from Pontotoc or to traverse the 34 miles from Fulton, the yards were filled to capacity on marketing days.[3] The parking lots themselves became the focus of much of the day's activities. Friends socialized, exchanging news and gossip. As in other communities where such facilities existed, the grounds became a center of trade. Farmers brought surplus goods or old items for which they no longer had use and exchanged them for other goods.[4] Tupelo's merchants were most willing to accommodate their customers, the trick was to get the farmers to the market. The slow transportation tended to limit the range of the community and confine much of its trade to a small radius.[5] Even the railroad's effectiveness to link the town with the hinterland was limited by its policy of favoring the long haul and discriminating against the short haul.[6] Consequently, towns like Tupelo entered the twentieth century clustered around their railroad, restrained even in their own physical dimensions by slow transportation.[7] Only good roads and the automobile would expand the range of these towns.

The community had never been satisfied to have good rail transportation only. Both the town and county had dreamed of improved roads from the time that the first load of cotton had struggled through sometimes axle-deep muck to reach the cotton gin and railroad. By the twentieth century, the community wanted more than ever to enhance the convenience of town living with streets and sidewalks that would be serviceable in all weather. The town sought also to encourage a greater flow of traffic from the country as the farmers brought their products to market and stayed long enough to purchase new goods and services. An important step was noted in Chapter 3, when Tupelo assumed responsibility for the maintenance of all roads within three miles of the town limits.

The town and the state as a whole had verbally supported the building of improved roads on a regular basis during the last two decades of the nineteenth century and into the new century. Every major rain revived discussions of improved roads. Everyone seemed to favor good roads. Speaking affirmatively for better streets and highways came as easily as applauding the virtues of the Democratic Party or extolling the blessing of clean living. Editorials and letters endorsing good roads were almost as much a part of the newspapers as advertising.[8]

The state underscored its interest in better roads when in 1901 it played host to the president and secretary of the National Good Roads Association who spoke to enthusiastic audiences.[9] Governor Andrew H. Longino, in turn, expressed the state's view at the International Good Roads Congress later in the year at Buffalo, New York. "My friends, the importance of good roads seems to me to be so apparent, so self-evident, that the discussion thereof is but a discussion of truisms."[10] The state cooperated with the Office of Public Roads in constructing objective-lesson roads to demonstrate the advantages of good roads as well as the techniques of their construction.[11] One such road was built in Clarksdale, Mississippi, but neither the Tupelo newspaper nor the minutes of the Board of Supervisors reflects any awareness of the program or this model road.[12]

The collective breath expressed in support of improved transportation facilities might have served a more useful purpose if it had been used to dry the soggy roads. By 1910, the South was far behind the nation in the construction of hard surfaced roads.[13] Mississippi, in turn, was lagging behind the remainder of the region in good roads mileage. Ten years into the twentieth century the entire state had only 185 miles of improved roads as compared to 4,375 miles in neighboring Tennessee.[14] Unfortunately, the existing legislation almost assured no systematic approach to road maintenance or construction. The state had modeled much of its government on the plans of older southern states, principally Georgia and South Carolina, with their prevailing philosophy that counties were largely self-contained and that all their fiscal and administrative interests should be centered in county-seat towns and about courthouses rather than the state capital.[15] Consequently, Section 170 of the state constitution provided each county would have a board of supervisors who would "have full jurisdiction over the roads, ferries, and bridges in their respective counties."[16] There were five board members representing the five beats or wards that served also as the road districts. The board, in turn, appointed overseers who were supplied with a list of all able-bodied males between sixteen and sixty who were required to work at least ten eight-hour days a year on the roads.[17] This system and its weaknesses were widespread throughout the South. One strong advocate of good roads stated the problem succinctly. "If you got for overseer one of those ill-natured men who does not like his neighbors, he would get some work out of the hands; but as a general thing no man likes to fuss with his neighbors, and consequently they would come late and after a few hours stop working, so that by the end of the day very little had been done."[18] The key figure in Mississippi's drive for good roads in the late nineteenth century gave the same dismal appraisal of the system at a Good Roads Congress in Atlanta. "We have laws that are not carried out. Our law regulating the work on the roads makes every man from 18 to 60 liable to duty unless he is a professional man. . . . They work on an average of two days, when they are required by the law to work ten days in the year on the roads."[19]

The board members and the overseers often worked at cross-purposes with the interests of the towns. Almost all of these men were farmers whose primary concern was in holding down taxes.[20] Because the existing maintenance program operated at almost no expense to the county, the supervisors were reluctant to change. Seldom did the men responsible for the maintenance and construction of the roads have any training for their positions. Moreover, they rarely sought professional advice. Most counties, including Lee County, were devoid of road equipment, depending instead on the workers to provide their own tools.[21] There was no basis for taxation that could have provided the state with a decent road system. The constitution specified that the necessary funds to defray the cost of road construction must be provided by the board of supervisors. Bond issues would only be permitted in the construction of bridges.[22] Such a set of circumstances proved a deadly combination in the prevention of improved roads.

In development projects such as an improved transportation system, the town and state often needed an outside impetus. Such a potential catalyst came with the development of the rural delivery system at the turn of the century. Under the provisions of this action, the rural areas would receive home delivery provided that the service was desired and the roads were kept in good condition. The state responded with the legislative Road Contract Law, which made only minor revisions and the adoption of this law was optional with the counties.[23] Unfortunately, the law did not go far enough in making the necessary provisions to improve substantially the state's roads.

When D. W. Robins assumed the mayoral responsibilities in 1909, Tupelo also had not been motivated to the point of making major street improvements. The Anderson administration had given some indication that it might upgrade the quality of the streets and sidewalks, but the intentions were too seldom translated into action. At the time that Robins became mayor, the town had no paved streets and just the one concrete sidewalk on the south side of Main Street. Only the main intersections were covered with gravel.[24] The town had passed an ordinance requiring property owners in specified sections of town to provide granitoid walks in front of their property, but when many townsmen chose to ignore the ordinance no action was taken to force compliance.[25]

Tupelo's response to the announcement by the postal authority was delayed by six months. Shortly after Will Robins took the reins of government, he converted the requisite to an asset. The new mayor and his board seized upon the requirement of the postal authorities and fused it with a burst of ongoing civic activities to create enthusiastic support for paved streets and sidewalks.[26] A group of leading merchants surged into the foreground with the familiar tactic of creating a formal organization to respond to the challenge. The newly formed Commercial Club distributed circulars calling on citizens to be willing to tax themselves for good roads.[27]

The first progress came downtown.[28] Soon thereafter persons living on the busiest blocks in town were required to construct functional sidewalks, preferably granitoid. Everyone living within the city limits was required to place numbers on his house.[29] Gravel was poured on all roads within three miles of town to improve the ease of travel.[30]

The town's interest in good roads stretched far beyond the town limits but the existing legislation stood in the way of any realistic road improvement program. At this point Will Robins and former mayor W. D. Anderson, now a state senator, combined talents to draft legislation to permit the implementation of their good roads program. Robins and Anderson were convinced that the time had come for their road program. Increased automobiles made good roads an imperative; improved agricultural conditions made it economically feasible to finance the roads. The drainage program was complete and more than 20,000 acres of farmland had been added since 1900.[31] Moreover, this good land had allowed Lee County to increase greatly the acreage yields so that it became the state's pacesetter in corn yield per acre and tied with three Delta counties for the lead in cotton yield.[32] If the county could act at this time it could not only capitalize on its ascending fortunes but assure even better times for the future.

Even with the upswing in agricultural conditions, farmers in the county and throughout the South gave only vocal support to good roads, shrinking from the prospect of higher taxes.[33] The impending legislation would have to provide a means by which the town could get around the certainty that the rural areas would defeat a bond issue to improve the roads. Such tactics reflected the continuing tension between town and country and were in marked contrast to the cooperative efforts of the Community Development Foundation that would emerge in the late 1940s. Anderson's bill, Senate Bill 66, would allow a single supervisor's district within a county to issue bonds and levy taxes for the construction of roads. Senator Anderson sought help from any possible quarter. He notified Governor E. H. Noel of the bill and gained the governor's endorsement in his annual message.[34] As the representative from Lee County, he introduced his legislation on January 19, 1910, the birthday of Robert E. Lee.[35] Final passage came March 3, 1910.[36] A week after passage, Anderson went before the county board of supervisors and asked this body to act immediately on the measure.[37]

Under the terms of the bill, District Three, in which Tupelo had the greatest vote, was permitted to act alone in developing the state's first hard-surfaced road. When the bond issue came before the voters of the Third District, every rural community in the district voted against it. Only the overwhelming vote it received in Tupelo permitted the passage of the bond issue.[38] The voting by polling places is given below.

Community	For	Against
Belden	8	47
Auburn	6	51
Eggville	2	7
Gilvo	8	14
Mooreville	18	19
Tupelo	268	111
Totals	**310**	**249**

D. W. Robins, H. B. Heard, and Emmett Whitesides were appointed by the board as the road commissioners, as Tupelo led the Lee County farmers into the twentieth century.[39] Bonds were issued within the week and by midsummer the Tupelo to Fulton road was being improved.[40]

While the Fulton road project was being developed, Tupelo itself was moving ahead in the paving of its own streets. In a vote on a bond issue only 13 people voted against the issuance of $50,000 in bonds to be used for street paving, a city hall, and some improvements on the electric plant.[41] Early in 1912, the newly organized Businessmen's League placed itself behind a program that encouraged the issuance of an additional $50,000 in bonds to macadamize more streets.[42] The bond issue passed with only 67 dissenting votes and 264 in favor of the project.[43]

For the next three years the construction of streets, curbs, and gutters was a continual topic in the newspaper and the minutes of the board of aldermen. Early in the construction of sidewalks and curb drains, the city paid for all work necessary to establish the proper grade for the sidewalks and curbs and the individual property owners were responsible for completing the job. By 1915, enough citizens had petitioned the city to do all work and assess the property owners for the costs.[44]

Tupelo had led the way and set the mood for much of the county. The newspaper hammered away week after week with its front-page editorials favoring more and better roads. The "Good Roads Train" of the Frisco railroad stirred still more excitement and attracted large audiences.[45] By 1912, ten miles of macadam road had been completed in the county and Tupelo was paving its own streets. The county's interest in good roads was now ready to be translated into action. District One in the county followed the example of the third district in voting to issue $50,000 in bonds for road improvements.[46]

As the number of automobiles increased, the pressure for more hard-surfaced roads mounted accordingly. Registered automobiles in the state had grown from 20 in 1900 to 24,000 in 1916.[47] Tupelo was still glorying in its good roads and each visiting tour of the county's good road system added to its pride.[48] The town and county were determined to remain at the vanguard in road development. Tupelo's experience in paving its own streets led directly to the next stage of development. In the process of laying the curb and gutters for the town, contractor Frank Goodlett of the Tupelo firm of Leake and Goodlett became interested in the possibility of building concrete highways in the county.[49]

The prospect of concrete roads, once it had been raised, remained front-page news. The contents of presentation varied from the themes of the low maintenance cost of concrete roads to more esoteric details of the actual construction procedure.[50] A delegation composed of four members of the board of supervisors, the mayor and road commissioner Will Robins, the county attorney Guy W. Mitchell, Frank Goodlett, and newspaper editor Frank L. Kincannon all traveled to Detroit for the purpose of investigating the practicality of building concrete roads on the lines that had been surveyed and adopted in the county.[51] Thus, in July 1914, the contract for forty-nine miles of hard-surface road including eleven-and-a-half miles of concrete road was let.[52] Upon completion of this road, the county could point with pride to the first concrete road in the state and one of the first in the South.[53]

The efforts of Tupelo's leaders in the construction of the good roads were guided by the same commitment to efficiency and technology that characterized a major wing of progressivism.[54] William Anderson directed the legislation with the touch of a master. Will Robins' flair for technological matters had already been revealed in his handling of the drainage program. His passion for basic engineering was further excited by the road project and he gave it his full attention. By completion time, he was regarded as the state's foremost expert in highway construction.[55] Frank Goodlett, a construction engineer whose first love was poetry, contributed experience and sound judgment as well as the initial idea of using concrete for the road's surface.

The consequences of the completed roads, streets, and sidewalks mark the years 1909 to 1912 as one of the major stages in the development of the town. Jane Jacobs has suggested the "streets and their sidewalks . . . are its (the city's) most vital organs."[56] Tupelo's response to the improvements lends support to this argument. The freshly paved streets were like a transfusion bringing more life and activity to the community. The construction of the good roads altered the daily routines of the community in a positive fashion.

The paved streets that replaced the muddy thoroughfares added an immediate neatness to the town. This rapid transformation seemed to spark a concern with the town's appearance.[57] In time, attractive parkways divided the broad streets and brought a degree of charm to the community. Tupelo citizens seized the oft-used phrase, "the city beautiful" from the Columbian Exposition in Chicago.[58] For the next 20 years, the expression "city beautiful" was the favorite way of describing this small city.

Tupelo's roads caught the attention of the *Memphis Commercial Appeal,* which featured the town's accomplishments in a full-page tribute. The article described the Lee County road system as being among the finest in the region and the most conspicuous feature of the community. The writer was struck by the beauty of the town. "The broad clean streets, well paved and well kept, with their white ways and pretty little parkways, its handsome homes and commodious stores and business houses, all go to make up a community, which would be the pride of any section."[59]

The presence of the new roads not only brought an improved appearance to the landscape; it also helped to promote an improved mental image of the town and county as well. There quickly emerged a glow of self-confidence that was even more apparent than the self-congratulatory attitude following the establishment of the cotton mill and other industries. Occasionally, the enhanced confidence shaded over into brashness as it did in a *Journal* editorial. "Only a few years back, Tupelo was nothing but an unimportant village. Today she is as modern a little city as you will find. Her people are ultra-progressive. What the town wants she goes after — and usually gets."[60] The convenience of the good roads led the state's two leading colleges to select Tupelo as the site of their annual football game for the years 1915 and 1916.[61]

Even more important was the way in which the sidewalks added convenience to town life and enlarged Tupelo's commercial activities. Churches and courts could expect to have their meetings at the appointed schedule. Merchants could conduct business on a routine basis. Moreover, the improved roads increased the volume of trade by making the town more accessible to the rural areas. Good roads and general prosperity were credited with bringing an increase in bank deposits of 25 percent between 1912 and 1914.[62] Merchants reveled in their newly achieved prosperity, gleefully acknowledging that business had never been better.[63] A three-story department store, or mercantile building as it was called, was soon built to capitalize on the expanding business traffic. This new structure was a part of an enlarged business district that was shifting away from the close physical proximity to the railroad to a pattern determined by the improved roads.

Shortly before the new concrete highway was constructed, the potentialities of the road were prompting changes. Two of the wholesale grocery companies announced that they were purchasing trucks that could be used profitably with the improved roads.[64] Soon even more trucks and traveling salesmen were to roll and bounce over these roads as Tupelo began to establish a flourishing trade with other parts of the country and communities in nearby counties. By 1923, the wholesale grocery business alone amounted to three million dollars annually. [65]

The status of the growing number of traveling salesmen is noteworthy. When the *Tupelo Journal* issued its special edition marking its fiftieth anniversary in 1923, it paid tribute to its leading citizens. The newspaper gave special recognition to four groups of professionals: physicians, attorneys, ministers, and traveling salesmen. The 47 salesmen featured received more space than any of the other professionals and one article suggested that the drummers were the major representatives of Tupelo to the surrounding area.[66]

The good roads soon played a vital role in the town's industrial development. The wives and daughters of farmers could be easily and quickly transported to the textile mill where they provided the labor. With an enlarged labor supply, the cotton mill expanded its own operation to include the manufacturing of shirts in the early twenties.[67] In 1923, manufacturing potential was increased again.[68] By the late twenties the county's school buses were doing double duty, transporting not only children to school but also women to the factories. Branches of the garment company were constructed in smaller towns along the route to shorten the travel distance and to tap a larger labor pool.[69]

Faster transportation also permitted the development of processing plants for perishable products. The dairy industry was the first to take advantage of the opportunity and a long-sought creamery was established in 1915.[70] This was an important step toward encouraging dairying in the hinterland and making Tupelo the center of the dairy industry in the state.

The coup of having built the first concrete highway in the region became incorporated almost immediately into what Richard Wohl and Theodore Brown call the "usable past."[71] The visiting tours of the good roads system, which continued for years after the roads were completed stood as a statement that Tupelo was different — a leader among Mississippi communities. By telling and retelling the story of the building of the road, the Tupelo citizens were able to transform the roads into a monument honoring the cooperation, diligence, and progressivism of the community. George McLean, who became one of the city's most progressive citizens, remembers his first contact with Tupelo. As he and his father rode on the smooth roads, the father commented to the young son that this was a progressive community as evidenced by its roads and an ambitious man should think seriously about living in such a community.[72] McLean never forgot those good roads and frequently reminded Tupelo citizens and visitors alike of the heritage of Tupelo and its history of cooperation and achievement.[73] This same man headed a delegation, of eight Greyhound buses, that descended on the state capital over a half-century after the construction of the concrete highways to present a plan for bringing an extensive system of four-lane highways to the state.[74] It was no accident that Tupelo was once again on the cutting edge of the highway movement in the state.

Tupelo's leadership in the development of the good roads suggests its importance to the county as an idea center. The completion of the transportation system enhanced that role. If trade and industry symbolized bread to the town, ideas can be considered the yeast that gave life to the whole community. From the beginning of the development of cities perhaps their most outstanding characteristic has been the organized style of life that has permitted the city to be the center of ideas.[75] In the give-and-take relationship between town and country, Tupelo was able to exert a disproportionate amount of influence on the rural areas. The new roads gave Tupelo an even greater opportunity to affect changes throughout the county as described in Chapters 6 and 7.

The significance of the roads has continued to grow over the years. As other students of urban life have observed, the automobile and improved transportation affected the rural areas and country even more drastically than they affected the highly urban areas.[76] "Providing every village and almost every farmstead with rapid transportation (automobiles and modern highways) helped to convert almost the entire country into an urban pattern of home and service center distribution."[77] In this way the new transportation and improved roads were doing for small towns what streetcars had done for the larger cities at an earlier period.

Summary and Conclusions

As the twentieth century began, Tupelo's physical dimensions and trade area were restricted by inadequate overland transportation. The town's leadership pulled itself together as an effective team, addressed that problem, and helped to provide a "good road" system. Once the system of town streets and good roads were in place, the town had many economic and psychological advantages.

The impetus for the initial action came from an outside agency, the postal authority. The post office called for better quality of roads in order to provide rural mail service. Local leaders saw this as an opportunity to fulfill a longtime goal of improving the roads and thereby improving both the quality of life in town and increasing the town's commerce. By adhering to postal requests, the leaders felt they could remove some of the objection to an increase in taxes to provide better roads. Or at least they could refocus the blame for a tax increase.

The leadership team consisted of Mayor Will Robins; former mayor, now State Senator William D. Anderson; businessman/engineer Frank Goodlett; the editor of the newspaper; and other business figures. These men were able to perform the technical tasks of passing special state legislation, mastering the art of road construction, as well as becoming social architects who brought the town together in support of the roads' programs.

The payoff was significant. The freshly paved streets produced an attractiveness to the town that had heretofore been missing. It increased business opportunities by making the town the retail and wholesale hub for the subregion. It pulled the town together and strengthened a sense of community. It provided the town with a usable past. Towns that are able to address their own problems are more likely to continue that behavior in the future. Tupelo had the skills, experience, and confidence to continue its community development in subsequent challenges.

The road system and the community effort that brought it to fruition became part of the storytelling and cultural legends of the town. It was evidence that success was possible through cooperative effort. The town had taken a major step toward becoming a community.

CHAPTER 6

Community Development
And the Agricultural Transition

Although Tupelo had expanded its economic base by adding manufacturing and enlarging its trade area through the "good road" efforts, the town's existence on the eve of World War I was still bound to agriculture. More than 80 percent of Lee County's population was dependent on agriculture for their livelihood.[1] Consequently, Tupelo's cash registers were good barometers of farming conditions.

Fortunately for the farmers and the town that served them, the early part of the twentieth century was a good time for agriculture. Financing the good roads would have been almost impossible had it been otherwise. It was especially good for cotton farmers. There was an expanding local and world market for the South's main staple. The growth of textile factories in the region had further increased the demand for lint. With new uses and increased demand for the derivatives of cotton seed, the future of the southern yeoman had never looked brighter.[2] In the words of an eminent agricultural historian, "the early years of the century, if not a golden age, seemed to herald one."[3]

The news from the marketplace fell on the ears of the South's farmers like music from the sirens. Lured by the prospect of prosperity at last, the region became even more firmly attached to the fleecy staple. Not only did cotton acreage increase, but the yield per acre climbed as well.[4] But the economic good times did not last and just as the second railroad could not offset agricultural depression, neither could the good roads. At the height of the prosperity and with its defense lowered, Lee County and the South was floored by a vicious one-two punch — World War I and the boll weevil.

Hit first by the effects of World War I, the region was caught with a bumper crop yield in 1914 only to see a major curtailment in the European market when deliveries could not be made.[5] The year before, more than 60 percent of the American cotton crop was shipped abroad. Almost as soon as the war began, the cotton industry went into a sharp decline.[6] Lint that sold for twelve cents a pound in August dropped to six cents a pound by December.[7]

Panic struck the Tupelo merchants and Lee County farmers almost simultaneously. Elements from both groups urged growers to abandon the nonmarketable staple in the field and at least spare themselves the expense of the harvest.[8] A more acceptable national plan called for every local person to buy a bale of cotton if he could possibly do so.[9] In this way the bale would be held off the market until conditions improved. Persons who were willing to make such an investment had their names published on an honor roll in the local paper.[10] Considerable excitement was generated by the program that even included having President Woodrow Wilson enter the campaign.[11] It is not clear from available data whether the attempts gave any relief to the situation, but clearly it was not a cure.

The first blow to the cotton industry shocked the system; the subsequent attack by the boll weevil sent the entire agricultural body into a trauma. Dr. L. O. Howard, entomologist of the Department of Agriculture, in testifying before the House Agricultural Committee described the situation as "absolutely the most difficult problem in economic entomology that the whole world has ever had to handle."[12] The Department of Agriculture estimated annual direct damage to cotton at $300 million and indicated that the indirect costs could not be estimated.[13] Lee County's crop in 1916 was only about half what it had been two years before.[14]

It was clear that strong and positive action was necessary and plans sprouted like weeds only to wilt in the harsh realities of the times. Almost all proposals called for organized efforts, and it was generally agreed that there was no hope of success unless the people involved could work together. Floyd Hunter, writing almost 40 years later, voiced the sentiments of Tupelo leaders when he suggested, "southern leaders . . . are convinced that organized efforts on a large scale are necessary to improve agricultural methods."[15] As in previous cotton crises the most popular projects were those calling for diversification.

The leaders threw themselves into the effort as though it were a holy cause. Many of the editorials possessed the same impassioned pleas of an enthusiastic evangelist as they called on farmers to save themselves by turning from the narrow path of one-crop farming to the broader highway of diversification.[16] Churches included prayer for the farmers as a common part of their worship services. Speakers and the newspaper were fond of describing the activities as a "crusade."[17]

But the situation called for action and not speeches. In this, or any situation it is not technically correct to say that communities act. Individuals take action, and by linking their own action to others it becomes community action.[18] In this case the prime mover was Samuel James (Jim) High, the vice president of The Peoples Bank.

Jim High was a local man whose family had been among the first settlers in the area. The original S. J. High was one of the earliest merchants in Pontotoc after purchasing land from the Chickasaws.[19] Jim High was born in Lee County in 1872. There he was educated and grew to manhood. He prepared himself for a banking career by attending Eastman's Business College in Poughkeepsie, New

York. He was appointed assistant cashier at the Bank of Tupelo in 1896. The next year he married into one of Lee County's most prominent families when he was wed to Anne Bell Allen, the daughter of Congressman John Mills Allen.[20] Seven years later, High joined with his father-in-law, John Allen, and J. J. Rogers to form The Peoples Bank in 1904.[21]

High was one of the businessmen who felt the crunch of the cotton disaster. Bank deposits in his own bank dropped 50 percent in less than a year after the boll weevil hit in force in 1916.[22] Years later, an elderly Jim High recalled those hard times. "We had neither cotton nor corn nor feed in 1916. Bankers like myself found their note cases full of notes, which farmers could not pay. Merchants who had carried farmers on credit could not collect their accounts. That boll weevil convinced us that it was folly to depend on a one-crop system. It was too much of a gamble."[23]

High, a pleasant looking man with a hint of a twinkle behind his gold-rimmed glasses, seemed an unlikely agent of agricultural change. He even joked about his own ignorance of the techniques of farming. He liked to tell the story about a farmer who, after receiving a loan, asked the banker about the depth of planting his seed. "Plant deep," High spoke authoritatively and without hesitation. After the farmer had left his office and before High could get back to the business at hand, the thought occurred to him that the yeoman might actually take his advice. Rushing from his desk and into the street he shouted to the departing farmer, "But not too deep."[24]

The course that Jim High followed in addressing the agriculture crisis demonstrates a network approach to community development. High, in addition to his position at the bank, was also the president of the Progressive League, Tupelo's organization to promote diversification in agriculture. Through his association with the Progressive League, High routinely received leaflets on agricultural diversification from Bradford Knapp.

Bradford Knapp, who had succeeded his father, Seaman, as one of the nation's most ardent promoters of diversification, had perceived that without the aid of towns and cities, even the best designed diversification schemes might fail. His address, "Diversified Agriculture and the Relation of the Banker to the Farmer," delivered before a receptive audience in Dallas, Texas, was most useful in bringing High's own ideas into sharper focus.[25] In the speech Knapp warned that unless the towns and cities worked closely with the surrounding agricultural areas both would suffer disastrous consequences.[26] Moreover, he continued, the banks through the use of credit were in the best position to bring about diversification. Knapp gave the community an additional clue when he cited a bank in the Pacific Northwest that had employed a livestock specialist to help the farmers in the surrounding territory.[27]

Armed with this information, Jim High began to utilize two different lines of his network: his personal ties to his father-in-law and his business ties through the Progressive League and Lee County Bankers' Association. He began with his father-in-law, Congressman John Allen. Allen had become involved with raising

Jersey cattle through his law school mentor and lifelong friend, L. Q. C. Lamar. While Allen was studying law with Lamar, Lamar was deeply involved with an experiment in raising some of the finest Jersey cattle in the South. So intent was Lamar, that he not only refused to grow any cotton, he also denied his manager an acre of the staple for himself. He made up the loss of the manager's income by increasing his wages.[28] Allen was so impressed with Lamar's dedication that he himself became caught up in the project and offered Lamar a registered heifer as a gift. When Lamar refused the gift, Allen kept her for the beginning of his own herd.[29]

In his freshman years as a congressman, John Allen retained his interest in his now growing Jersey herd. He encouraged a number of major businessmen-farmers in Tupelo to form the county's first Jersey Cattle Association.[30] The organization hired an experienced dairyman from the Midwest and predictions of a prosperous milk industry gushed forward. When the forecasts were not fulfilled immediately, the association sold its livestock and disbanded the short-lived operation.

High sought to revise the effort of diversifying Lee County's agriculture through dairying. The Progressive League, a critical part of High's network came on board eagerly as did another dimension of High's network, the Lee County Bankers' Association, which also became a sponsor of the program to diversify agriculture.[31]

The Lee County Bankers' Association reached out through its network and added another degree of legitimacy to the efforts by involving the public sector. In 1916 the association sent Mayor Will Robins, county agent J. E. Ruff, and a leading farmer, A. P. Smith, to Oklahoma to purchase 30 registered Hereford bulls and 5 Holstein bulls.[32] The same organization negotiated for a carload of breeding sheep to be sold at cost to Lee County farmers.[33] A year later, the bankers brought in two more carloads of registered Jersey heifers.[34]

The network extended to the town's businessmen. They actively participated in the diversification efforts by providing prize money to the agricultural clubs that promoted diversification plans.[35]

The diversification efforts bore tangible results. The number of cattle increased in Lee County by almost 50 percent between 1910 and 1920. The amount of hay and corn had tripled and doubled, respectively, during the decade. The number of pigs doubled and poultry increased by 50 percent. Cotton acreage decreased by 50 percent during the ten-year span.[36]

There were other tangible gains as well. Bank deposits tripled between those bleak times in 1916 and 1923. In 1923, *The Wall Street Journal* turned the national spotlight on the Lee County effort. The newspaper cited The Peoples Bank and Lee County as a national model. "While Congress, mistaking irrelevant and superficial symptoms for disease, is attempting to legislate prosperity to the farmers. . . . The Peoples Bank of Tupelo, Mississippi, has got down to fundamentals. It is leading the farmers of Lee County into ways of prosperity and contentment."[37]

It was a flattering column, but not entirely accurate. The Lee County experience demonstrated that for at least this county, community development works. Unfortunately, efforts at the community level cannot overcome the greater national economy. Lee County local programs were able to buffer the community from some of the worst economic blows but there were no miracles. Consequently, the decade of the twenties was a period of economic fluctuation that followed the national trends.

At the very beginning of the decade full prosperity seemed in sight. Cotton prices rose to 38.5 cents a pound, the highest since the Civil War, in April 1920. In 1921 the price was down to 9.8 cents a pound. Moreover, the cotton yield was down in 1920 and for the next four years the entire state of Mississippi produced less than one million bales.[38]

Tupelo's businessmen were more convinced than ever that it must diversify its agriculture. The Lee County Bankers' Association hired a dairy specialist, Sam Durham. Durham provided the technical assistance to Lee County's farmers. He gave community demonstrations in the care, feeding, and breeding of dairy cattle. Durham also gave advice in the purchasing of stock. As part of his duties he wrote a weekly column for the *Tupelo Journal*.[39]

Jim High remained active in promoting dairying and captured the imagination of the public through his perpetual use of slogans. His first was one of his favorites, "a cow, a sow, and a hen, a factory on every farm."[40] He kept a placard on his desk, which depicted the unlikely heroines of his plan as "The three mortgage lifters."[41] The Peoples Bank bought front-page advertisements in which it pressed hard on the diversification theme changing only the slogan. Finally the bank's focus was narrowed primarily to milk production and it offered the optimistic hope, "Prosperity Follows the Dairy Cow." High gave substance to his slogans through a credit system that encouraged diversification.[42]

While The Peoples Bank was unquestionably a major leader, the development efforts were supported strongly by the newspaper and merchants. Maintaining the tradition of the *Journal* in its endorsement of farming improvement, the editor threw himself behind the cause. Whole issues were devoted to husbandry, and diversification was the dominant topic for over a decade.[43] Moreover, the local paper received added incentive through the persistent urging of new adaptations by the mid-South's foremost champion of diversification, C. P. J. Mooney, editor of the *Memphis Commercial Appeal*.[44] In particular, the *Journal* passed along ideas from the Memphis paper as well as making use of the cartoons and following the *Commercial Appeal* in printing a front-page column for practical advice to farmers.[45]

The town's businessmen actively participated in the diversification efforts by providing prize money to the agricultural clubs, which promoted diversification plans.[46] Many of the merchants sponsored a promotional program that gave away Jersey cattle to local farmers in an open lottery.[47] The town's leading department store, R. W. Reed Company, developed a complete home orchard with the aid of Mississippi A. and M. and gave away 100 packaged home orchards.[48]

The whole town seemed to be swept up in the diversification mania of the twenties. When the county's dairy program, headed by Sam Durham, ran into financial difficulty, some of Tupelo's most active citizens came before the city government rather than the county board to request the necessary funds. One councilman questioned the legality of the city spending the money. Nevertheless, a motion was made and passed, which provided the financial support to keep the dairy program alive.[49]

The two railroads were also active in Lee County's drive for farm changes. Beginning in 1927, the Mobile and Ohio Railroad promoted the raising of strawberries and tomatoes in several parts of the country.[50] That same year, the Frisco Railroad was instrumental in bringing a Carnation Milk condensery to Tupelo. Durham's program had been successful to the point that the industrial agent of the Frisco Railroad brought Tupelo to the attention of the Carnation Company as an excellent location for a condensery.[51] After the initial contact was made, the Lee County Bankers' Association acted as the spokesman for the town in presenting the case to Carnation. Following a series of meetings, Tupelo had gained an all-important market for its milk.[52]

The announcement of the coming industry was hailed in the largest headlines since the end of the World War.[53] The news sent the community into a flurry of excitement. The Tupelo Oil and Ice Company announced that it would begin immediately to manufacture dairy feed. The county's dairy specialist called all dairymen together to set in motion the production of milk for Carnation.[54] The Bankers' Association brought in the dairy expert from the state's agricultural school to help in the development of pastures.[55] The *Journal* published rather specific instructions on how to buy a dairy herd and followed this with a special edition welcoming the Carnation Milk Company.[56] The festive mood was capped off with one of the biggest parades in the town's history.[57]

The success of the Lee County diversification program brought the area and its participants another round of applause. C. P. J. Mooney praised Jim High in his work, *The Mid-South and Its Builders.*

"It is doubtful if there be in the Mid-South any man who has been more efficient than he [S. J. High] for the development of his home city, his country, and his section of the state in all that makes for good. The material progress of Tupelo and Lee County during the past 15 years has been such that any community might take justifiable pride in it."[58]

Dunbar Rowland, one of Mississippi's leading historians, repeated essentially the same tribute.[59]

Jim High, The Peoples Bank, his fellow bankers and businessmen had worked hard to keep the beast of economic depression from their door, but the economic forces were too powerful. The economy of small towns like Tupelo had been sick for most of the decade of the twenties. The community programs had sheltered the local economy as much as possible. Most of the nation's rural trade centers with their small banks had not fared as well. Between 1922 and 1929 almost 20 percent of the banks in the United States failed. Most were the small country banks.[60]

The final collapse came in the new decade of the thirties. Between March 1930 and September 1931 bank deposits in Mississippi fell by 47 percent. Of the 127 Mississippi banks that closed, 7 were in Lee County. On Christmas Eve 1930, even The Peoples Bank closed its doors.[61]

Not until April 28, 1933, did the stockholders agree to reopen the restructured Peoples Bank. Seven former depositors opposed the reopening and sought to block it through the courts. Not until April 1, 1935, did the United States Supreme Court affirm the original order to allow the bank to reopen.[62]

It was evident that local bootstrap efforts were not sufficient to provide prosperity for the rural South. The region, so lacking in basic infrastructure, capital, and technical assistance gained an extra boost with the creation of the Tennessee Valley Authority in 1933. T.V.A. was created not only to produce cheap electricity, but to spearhead the economic renaissance of the region. One of the South's strongest supporters of T.V.A. was John Rankin, congressman from District One and Tupelo native.

Because of Lee County's efforts at community development and John Rankin's influence, Tupelo was selected to become the nation's first T.V.A. City in October 1933.[63] One student of this new power program suggested that this particular town was selected for the honor as a direct result of the diversification program during the preceding decade. Because of its achievements, Tupelo had gained a head start over neighboring communities. The town was almost certain to be an asset to T.V.A. promoters who could point to Tupelo achievements and claim credit for not only the results of electrification but diversification as well, without making the proper distinction between the two.[64]

The news that T.V.A. was coming to Tupelo and that the President himself was going to be on hand for the festivities brought a ray of light to the community, which temporarily pushed aside most of the darkness of the depression. The town was beside itself with joy and self-congratulations as a crowd estimated to be in excess of 75,000 turned out to see and listen to President Roosevelt return their greetings and applaud their efforts.[65] The setting seemed reminiscent more of a fairy tale with the accompanying celebration of the hero marrying the heroine than a poor Mississippi community striving to improve itself. The occasion was not simply a breather from the heartache of a prolonged depression, it was an event that most of those 75,000 would remember for the rest of their lives — the President of the United States had come to pay his respects to small-town Mississippians.

Tupelo had its moment in the sun and the cheap electricity it had long coveted. The federal government had added an enormous dimension to the agricultural transition that seemed once again in motion. This was only the beginning of a series of changes that would completely alter the relationship of the town to the country.

An important element in the altered relations in Lee County was the change in leadership structure. Arriving on the scene at almost the same time as T.V.A.

was the new owner of the *Tupelo Journal,* George Alonzo McLean. He was a native Mississippian, born and reared in Winona, Mississippi, about 100 miles south-west of Tupelo, on the edge of the Mississippi Delta. McLean was a young man, not quite 30-years' old when he arrived in Lee County. He had received some of the finest academic training in the nation. He earned his baccalaureate from the University of Mississippi. He had taken graduate courses in sociology at the University of Chicago where he had begun writing his doctoral dissertation. Prior to that, he had studied psychology at Stanford and philosophy and religion at Boston University.[66]

Originally he had planned a career in the Presbyterian ministry, but his social views were considered too progressive and out of step with more traditional thought. He turned instead to academics. He taught sociology and philosophy at Adrian College in Michigan before returning to his native South as an instructor at Southwestern (now Rhodes) College in Memphis.

While at Southwestern, McLean's efforts to work with tenant farmers and day laborers in the surrounding area brought him into conflict with Edward Hull (Boss) Crump, Memphis' strongest political figure. Ignoring Crump's demands to cease these extracurricular activities, the nontenured McLean was forced from his teaching position and out of the city.

Driven from the Bluff City, McLean had his first encounter with newspaper work in a brief stint with a newspaper in Grenada, Mississippi. Independent and determined to work to improve conditions for the common man in his home state of Mississippi, McLean wanted his own newspaper. A close friend, knowing of McLean's ambitions, suggested that he consider purchasing the *Tupelo Journal,* which had fallen victim to the depression. With little delay, he bought the bankrupt *Tupelo Journal* from the financially troubled Peoples Bank and Trust and threw himself immediately into the role of community developer.

McLean, though born into a prominent family in Winona, was primarily concerned with the plight of the common man. He was a complex man, but the trait that best identified him was his deeply held set of religious principles. He understood and practiced the social gospel. He believed that Christians should minister to physical and social needs as an extension of their concern for the spiritual condition. In his words, "men are God's methods." Those religious convictions were to undergird all of McLean's efforts for the next half-century.

McLean was a small man with a firm square jaw and bright alert blue eyes that were accentuated by wirerim glasses. When he first came to Tupelo in 1934, his premature baldness detracted from an otherwise boyish face but enhanced his image of maturity and scholarly wisdom. His erect posture while addressing audiences of all types became a familiar sight. With both hands clutching the lapels of his suit coat, he seemed a composite of teacher, stump politician, and evangelist. Eschewing all hints of profanity, he spoke so emphatically and positively that any attempt at stronger language would have seemed superfluous. The message was always the same. He called for dedicated hard work and a form of pragmatic self-reliance that emphasized the need for local people to solve local problems by borrowing and implementing ideas and programs.

From the outset, he had a clear vision of what the county could be and a general idea of how to achieve the vision. He was soon to learn that having a clear vision and being well educated were not sufficient to be accepted as a leader. He was a newcomer whose progressive views seemed unrealistic, idealistic, or just plain wrong.

Unlike earlier community leaders, such as Jim High, who was a part of the leadership network, McLean was clearly the outsider with neither the support nor trust of farmers nor the ear of the town leaders.

Through a painstaking process, McLean would have to make three achievements. He had to become linked to the existing leadership network as well as be accepted by farmers. He had to establish a power base from which to work, and he had to sharpen his vision to gain a specific focus and starting point for the community development process.

He accomplished the first of these goals by earning the trust and respect of key leaders through the Presbyterian Church. McLean and his wife, Anna Keirsey, were hosts to the Bible study class in their home. Among the individuals who visited there were Phil Nanney, the town's mayor and president of the Bank of Tupelo and C. Richard (Dick) Bolton, an attorney, and key member and later president of the board of directors of The Peoples Bank. Nanney was one of the central leaders in the public and private sector. Bolton was a business leader and was from one of the oldest families in the area. It was his grandfather, Richard Bolton, who was among the original town builders in northeast Mississippi.

As in many southern towns, the Presbyterian Church was a critical link in the leadership network of the community. Through the influence of Nanney and Bolton, McLean was much more quickly in touch with other community leaders. Many businessmen, however, were troubled by McLean's hard-hitting editorials on behalf of workers. Some businessmen even boycotted his newspaper and his editorials remained a point of contention between the editor and other businessmen for almost a decade.

While McLean was seeking to gain a voice among the power structure, he faced the equally daunting task of breathing life into the moribund newspaper. McLean was a novice in newspaper work. As a way of maintaining his own perspective, McLean painted the inside of the *Journal* office green, as he said, "to remind myself that I was just as green as grass and had to learn how to run a newspaper."

Always a proponent of team leadership — McLean had to build his own team at the *Journal.* His alter ego, University of Missouri-trained Harry Rutherford from nearby Union County, walked into the *Journal* office looking for a job — any newspaper job — in those lean depression days of 1936. In time he became the editor, with McLean continuing as publisher. Shy and brilliant, one of the quietest and brightest men to serve as editor in the *Journal's* proud history of talented editors, Rutherford was content to stay in the office and work toward the same goals of his employer, while McLean dashed about in search of ideas and audiences to absorb those thoughts. The team was complete when William (Bill)

Stroud, whose own California-based newspaper had gone under in those hard times, took over as the business manager. Tough, unyielding in his insistence on a well-run newspaper, Stroud helped to set the business on an even keel from which it has not swayed.[67]

Even before his news team was begun, McLean had trekked to the University of Wisconsin in 1936 to learn more about dairy farming from the university experts.[68] The community leadership chose to build on the work of the Jim High era.[69] It was already in place and had been successful. The dairying program received a major boost when Rex Reed threw his support behind the endeavor. Reed, a wealthy businessman with multiple interests including a large garment factory, was generally regarded as one of the most influential men in town.[70] His special love was his Jersey cattle herd, unquestionably the finest in the county.[71] His influence and knowledge of the cattle industry marked him for a central position in the program.

All plans were temporarily thrown off course in April 1936, when Tupelo suffered a damaging blow from one of the worst killer tornadoes on record.[72] The destructiveness of the tornado made it all the more imperative that action be taken to brace up the economy. Two days before the terrible storm, McLean, in his characteristically optimistic fashion, had written an editorial titled, "It Can Be Done!" referring to the economic and social advances he cited.[73] The first issue after the havoc, he remained positive. His editorial was titled, "Tupelo Will Build on This Wreckage a Better and Greater City."[74]

Characteristically, McLean was hard at work promoting his master plan for regional economic development shortly after the rubble from the disaster was cleared away. McLean understood that the problems of Lee County were common in all the area. He was interested in addressing these broad problems and felt it could best be done by a multicounty consortium. This would allow a pooling of resources and would raise the economic level of the whole region. The project called for an organization of all counties in northeast Mississippi by means of which these areas could pool their ideas, talents, and resources in a common effort to improve farming and promote industrial development. Farm organizations would concentrate on establishing new markets and the improvement of agricultural techniques. The organization would be financed by a self-imposed taxation on profits of the electrical power associations and natural gas companies. These companies could expect a return on their investment in the form of increased use of power by industries brought to the area and the improved prosperity within the counties.[75]

The first step in the implementation of the idea came with the organization of the Northeast Mississippi Poultry Council in 1936. It was hoped that the council would stimulate the development of the poultry business in the counties and would assist poultrymen in marketing their products. There was nothing original in this organization. It was modeled after a similar council on the Mississippi coast.[76] Nonpoultryman George McLean was elected the first chairman.[77]

This infant wing of the program had come out of the starting gate quickly, but the race proved longer and more hazardous than any steeplechase imaginable. The remainder of the program lagged far behind. The jealousy and rivalry among the towns stifled the efforts to cooperate. For almost five years, the towns did not develop local sponsoring agencies with the strength to support agricultural development on a unified basis. Finally, the overall Northeast Mississippi Council was formed in 1941.[78] Two years later, the major project of the council remained the promotion of poultry.[79] This effort had been successful to the extent that poultry dressing plants had been established in Oxford, Houston, Corinth, and Tupelo, which provided both a ready market and also gave employment to more than 100 persons.[80] However, when George McLean departed for the U.S. Navy later that year, it was apparent that this particular association would never bear the anticipated fruits. The coordination of the farmers in such a broad area proved an overwhelming task and a bitter labor strike in Tupelo had virtually undermined the attempts to build an industrial base.[81]

Paralleling the attempts at a regional council were the efforts to build a county dairy association. This county livestock association, which began in 1938, was designed to benefit the poorest farmers in the county. Unfortunately, many of the farmers who could not afford quality stock had been touched only tangentially by the previous project. The goal was to use artificial insemination to assist farmers to upgrade their stock without the expense of having to purchase a high-quality bull. Sixteen Tupelo businessmen agreed to hire and pay the salary of dairy expert Gale Carr.

Carr had been establishing world records with dairy herds at the Shelby County Penal Farm near Memphis.[82] Carr, a self-educated man with the mind of a first-rate scientist and the pragmatic insight of a midwestern farmer, had already pioneered in artificial insemination as an inexpensive and practical way of establishing a superior dairy herd.[83]

Upon his arrival in the community, Carr's first order of business was to register all the cattle brought in under the first dairy expert a decade earlier. Following this, it was necessary to establish a broad-based association of cattlemen in the county as a means of dispersing information to the largest number of people possible.[84] The efforts were rewarded after the first full year of activity with the Jersey Bulletin Accomplishment Award for the most complete program of any association in the United States.[85] The Lee County Association became the first association to repeat that achievement the following year.[86]

In 1941, the Tupelo Area Artificial Insemination Association was officially organized.[87] This was a significant breakthrough when compared with earlier attempts to get quality livestock into the hands of the common farmer. Initially, the association started with one full-time technician and three bulls valued at $10,000.[88] The service program was provided to farmers within a 33-mile radius of Tupelo. For a service fee of five dollars per cow, farmers built an excellent herd and without the expense of maintaining a bull of their own.[89] By the end of the decade, over 7,000 cattle a year were being bred in this manner and it was estimated that a single bull had added over $1 million to the wealth of the area.[90]

Tupelo merchants returned to a version of an earlier promotional arrangement to provide registered heifers to Lee County farmers. The merchants gave their customers "bull money" to be used much in the same way that trading stamps from grocery stores came to be used. In this case, the "bull money" and only "bull money" could be used to purchase some of the registered stock that would go on sale in a special auction.[91]

The dairy program was a success. By the end of the 1940s, Lee County led the state in milk processing. The local Jersey Club won the national Jersey Bulletin Accomplishment Award five times during the decade of the forties. Most important, the program had reached the common farmer in a substantial way. The value of the cattle of the average farmer had been increased by an estimated 25 percent.[92] Moreover, a spirit of cooperation among farmers and between town and country had been augmented.

The project's success had also established George McLean's credibility with businessmen and farmers alike. While many remained skeptical of many of his positions on social matters, most agreed that he was a man of vision. He did his homework, understood the craft of community development, was concerned with the best interest of the community and was not a self-promoter. In short, he could be trusted.

In the midst of the initial success, McLean volunteered for naval service during World War II. Upon his return in 1945, local businessmen, demonstrating their support for his community development skills, asked McLean to serve as president and manager of the local Chamber of Commerce. McLean not only agreed but committed himself as a nonsalaried manager, while still serving as the owner and publisher of the *Journal*. McLean was still concerned that the community development projects had not involved the poorest half of the population. As usual, he turned to a reputable source for technical assistance. The *Journal*, not the Chamber of Commerce, put up $5,000 in 1945 to commission a study of Lee County for the purpose of developing a long-range plan. He hired the Doane Agricultural Service, the largest agricultural management service in the nation.

Rural Community Development Councils

The ultimate product or recommendation of the Doane Agricultural Service was the development of the Rural Community Development Councils.

The Rural Community Development Councils (RCDCs) and the cooperation that they spawned are the genius and the driving force behind the Tupelo Model.

They constitute the headwaters from which all the success of Tupelo and Lee County would flow. It is not an overstatement to write that the RCDCs represent the Holy Grail of community development that still draws hundreds of town leaders from around the nation in search of the "Tupelo Secret" for community development. Unfortunately, what these seekers find at the end of the twentieth century are the products of more than 50 years of community development. And without an understanding of the Rural Community Development Councils, one cannot understand the Tupelo Model.

The Tennessee Valley Authority had urged the development of such programs in the area surrounding its home base of Knoxville, Tennessee. At the war's end in 1946, George McLean and True D. Morse, the president of the Doane Agricultural Service were looking for such a model. McLean's brief experience as the manager of the Chamber of Commerce had convinced him that the traditional Chamber of Commerce was too narrow in its approach. It served the interests of some of the town's businessmen, but only incidentally the full community. It did not command interest or respect of rural citizens. Even within Tupelo it was seen as an organization for enriching businessmen.

Armed with the results of the Doane Study, which, among other things, documented the need to build on the successful dairy program, McLean urged businessmen to help develop an entirely new organization that would unite town and country in an even stronger way. This organization would mobilize farmers and get them involved in the development of their own communities.

The first order of business was to gain the commitment and engagement of local people. This process began by stressing the "at stakeness," a term that was used by McLean and Morse, to demonstrate the economic threat that faced rural communities. Morse and McLean had done their homework. In conversation after conversation with people in the rural areas, they presented the economic projections for agriculture, particularly agriculture in the South and especially northeast Mississippi. They were small farmers, trying to scratch out a living on small nonmechanized farms at a time when they would soon face the competition of well-capitalized farmers using the latest machinery on more productive lands that were better suited to mechanized farming. Their entire futures were at risk. The signs were clear: adapt or lose everything they had.

McLean had private conversations with opinion leaders in all rural areas. He stressed three dimensions of the problem. First, there were the economic figures that told of a region already poor and which would be left farther behind if they did not continue the economic transformation begun with the dairy/artificial insemination program. Second, McLean spoke compassionately about the personal and social consequences of poverty. He talked about the companion problems of health, housing, and limited opportunities, especially for the children. Third, he bemoaned the sense of fatalism and resignation that accompanied poverty. McLean reminded the rural leaders that a poverty mentality often isolated one person from another and destroyed community. This failure to work together was eroding the fabric of democracy. "It is unfortunately true," McLean wrote in a leaflet distributed to every family in the county, "that in many parts of America the people have stopped coming together, discussing their mutual problems; assuming their common responsibilities; and taking necessary **group action**. [emphasis his] Such practices constitute the very **essence of democracy** [emphasis his] and unless we return to these fundamentals we shall further endanger our democratic freedom. Maybe **we** can't revive such practices 'in the nation' — but we can make a start in **our local community.**"[93]

This same language was used in conversations with townspeople. Moreover, he warned that if the agriculture of the region collapsed, businessmen, whose customers were farmers or even linked to agriculture indirectly, would feel the economic implosion. Their life-styles would be imperiled. Local citizens were cautioned by daily editorials and articles that, if the rural population were dislodged by economic pressures, customers would be lost, prospective labor for factories not yet built would be gone, and the hope for a transformation to an industrial economy would be stillborn. It was imperative to hold the population in place or risk a subsequent labor shortage that would imperil a transition to industry. Clearly this challenge affected town and country and, ultimately, meant potential economic ruin for both.

With the problem framed in such a way, the self-interest, indeed the very survival of rural and townspeople converged. There could be no doubt. But the problem was not presented without an alternative proposal that would counteract the macroeconomic forces.

McLean, like all good leaders, understood that the key to consolidated action is to bring the common interests of otherwise divergent groups into alignment. The details for the rural development project evolved over a decade. Conversations between McLean and True Morse, as well as with agricultural specialists of T.V.A., helped shape the final product. However the plan was so complete by 1946 that the only remaining step was implementation.

Changing the Culture

The resulting Tupelo Model, and its prime ingredient, the Rural Community Development Councils, is not merely about problem solving, as important as that was. This effort is concerned with extraordinary outcomes with no hint of "business as usual." The program sought to change fundamentally the way people relate to one another. It is an excellent example of what Thomas Kuhn calls a paradigm or model shift.

The vision was simple, but bold and engaging. "There Is No Limit To What An Organized Community Can Do — If It Wants To!" While this language focused on the community, McLean had learned the lesson that other successful community developers understand. Community development must address individual problems first and foremost. Indeed, McLean reminded others that community development is a means of solving individual problems by working together. He knew that most people were too busy wrestling with their personal problems to have time or interest in community concerns. Like other successful community development, the Tupelo Model is a means of solving personal problems by working together.

Step one in that process was in framing the economic, social, and political problems in a way that those affected could recognize their own suffering, i.e., acknowledge their own "at stakeness." Step two was to construct a realistic, mean-ingful solution to those problems. McLean's model was appealing in its simplic-ity and wholeness. The plan was simple enough to be detailed in an eight-page leaflet that McLean provided for every citizen in the county. For those who heard the message, there was common agreement. "It made sense."

The model ultimately called for every rural community in a seven-county area to organize a Rural Community Development Council. Such a council would function roughly like a New England town meeting as a way of drawing together all citizens in the community. Initially, however, rather than undertake such a massive coordination of communities, McLean consciously selected three pilot communities in three separate counties: Blackland, Brewer, and Dorsey in Prentiss, Lee, and Itawamba counties. Each of these communities had demon-strated the greatest interest in such a program and seemed the most likely to orga-nize themselves. McLean spent countless hours communicating with the local opinion leaders to be sure that they grasped the program with all of its richness and subtleties. Only when McLean was sure that the opinion leaders shared his enthusiasm and passion did he want them as partners in the movement. Any fail-ure would likely undermine the credibility of the process. He understood that these councils must succeed in a way that would bring dramatic results, if these beacon communities were to provide the guiding light for other communities.

McLean found the right leaders. They exuded a contagious sense of almost unwarranted optimism. Their behavior modeled the "can do" spirit that was always a hallmark of McLean. They threw themselves into the community devel-opment projects with the sobering realization of the consequences of failure or more particularly of failure to act. McLean personally trained them in the process of highlighting the self-interest of fellow citizens. He urged his fellow communi-ty leaders to "arouse the desire of self-improvement" in their neighbors. McLean further suggested "this should lead to an organization through which the people can gain information, express their group desires, and marshal their group efforts."[94]

Each of these councils was provided technical assistance by Doane Agricultural Service, T.V.A., the School of Agriculture of Mississippi State College, and a wide variety of technical associates hired by Tupelo businessmen. Nevertheless, the focus was on local self-help. "Each Community must develop a Leaven of Leadership from Within the Community and Seek to Strengthen It in every pos-sible manner so that it will grow strong enough to do the required job. This is the basic conviction of the Rural Community Development Council Program." McLean would remind fellow citizens for the next 36 years that "there is no Santa Claus at the State Capitol, State College, or Washington. If you want the job done, you will have to do it yourself."

Just as McLean stressed that community development always addresses indi-vidual problems, he also emphasized that all action begins with individuals. Each person in the community has a role to play by maximizing his/her own produc-tivity. "Increased Production Per Person, Per Acre, Per Animal Unit is the Master

Key That Will Unlock the Door to Increased Prosperity and Better Living in the South."[95]

The need to enhance the capacity of each individual grows from one of the most basic tenets of the Tupelo Model. Everyone, each and every person, white, black, young, or old is a potential resource. The most fundamental goal of community leaders, Tupelo leaders would argue, is to release the resource that is locked within each individual. In McLean's words, "It should be obvious to any person that the greatest asset Mississippi has is Mississippians." He also would add that uneducated, unorganized people are often a liability. Only through the conscious effort of increasing the productivity of each person can a community expect a fundamental improvement. Tupelo leaders, even today, note that just as the objective of many businesses is to add value to raw material, so too, community development seeks to maximize the value in its basic resource, humans.

The Rural Community Development Councils were structured around the principles of local people addressing their problems by the maximum use of human resources. This structure and networks themselves have helped to achieve community development. The organizations build from the top down and bottom up. At the top levels, nearly 100 percent of the business people in Tupelo were active participants in the development process. Almost to a person, each agreed that their economic prosperity was dependent on a complex partnership among businessmen and between the town and county. Businesspeople were expected to generate the necessary fiscal capital to finance the whole process. Each businessperson was asked to make a three-year commitment to the funding of the program. This reflected something of the degree of commitment and allowed the fledgling organization ample time to prove itself. As noted earlier, very little financial assistance came from outside Lee County.

Businesspeople were also expected to contribute their time as volunteers.

This expectation or norm of volunteerism raises an essential point about community development. How do community leaders manage their own lives in a way that permits free time for community development? Here, too, the issue is a personal one that must be resolved by the individuals. George McLean devoted 50 to 75 percent of his time to community development, while still serving as the publisher of the newspaper. Over the years, many of the key leaders have made a similar commitment of time. McLean and others "found" the time in two ways. They became leaders, rather than managers in their business. They developed effective work teams that relieved them of some of the most mundane or routine work. Secondly, they changed their perception of community development. Community development was and is seen as a way of increasing profitability and thus enhancing the bottom line. Community development is seen as part of the way of doing business in Tupelo.

Consequently, community leaders like McLean, and there are many of them in Tupelo, learn to lead their own work organization before they can become effective community leaders. This means maximizing the human resources within the workplace. Part of the incentive or motivation to become a more effective business leader is the necessity to create "free time" to do community development, which is also necessary for the prosperity of business. The two are intertwined. Such a perspective is another example of the paradigm shift that has occurred. Yet this shift is explained as a way of maximizing self-interest. Tupelo leaders know that they can increase their profitability through community development.

This underscores another principle of the Tupelo Model. Everyone needs some type of development or training including and, especially, the leaders. Businesses, they know, are more likely to fail as a result of poor management rather than the shortcomings of laborers. Business leaders often need training to become community leaders.

The business leaders in 1946 remained engaged in community development through the remnants of the Chamber of Commerce and after 1948 through the Community Development Foundation that replaced the Chamber of Commerce. They also worked through the overarching Rural Community Council that was housed in Tupelo. The Rural Community Development Councils predate the Community Development Foundation. It was realistically and figuratively the foundation of all the agencies and organizations that followed. After the establishment of the Community Development Foundation, the Rural Community Development Councils came under CDF administration.

All RCDCs were structured to create dense social networks. Each had a board of directors composed of local ministers, school administrators, vocational education teachers, farmers, and officers from the women's home demonstration clubs. Each council had five officers: the president, who was normally a respected farmer; a junior president, usually a member of the Future Farmers of America (FFA), in order to engage the youth in the community and to prepare them for future leadership roles; a vice president, normally a woman who was active in a home demonstration club, although some presidents were women; a treasurer of either sex, and a song leader, also of either sex.

The board of directors was to establish strong neighborhood groups, normally composed of 10 to 12 families. Groups of this size allowed maximum involvement by almost everyone in the community. Each neighborhood group elected one of their members for a place on the board of directors. Each neighborhood group had at least one technical agriculture advisor.

All of the civic clubs in the nearby towns participated in a program entitled "Partnership for the Mutual Development of Towns and Rural Communities." Through this organization each of the clubs became a partner with the RCDCs. Each neighborhood group had at least one partner from a town civic club. McLean explained the purpose of this partnership as a means of expressing "friendship and sincere respect." One of the stated goals or objectives of this partnership was to "stimulate all parties to our best endeavors." With so many neighborhood groups, it meant that almost 100 percent of the membership of the civic clubs served as a neighborhood partner. Each civic club member was to attend a minimum of four monthly meetings, at least once a quarter. Specific dates were suggested and these programs often celebrated the partnership between town and country.

As noted earlier, each rural council was linked to Doane Agricultural Service, T.V.A., Mississippi State College, and a large contingency of agricultural technical advisors. Representatives from each of those groups attended most of the RCDC monthly meetings. The primary link between the Community Development Foundation and the RCDCs was Sam Marshall, the director of the Rural Community Development Council. Marshall was a graduate of the School of Agriculture of Virginia Tech and a former military officer. Technically, he was an employee of the newspaper, the *Daily Journal,* which shouldered the expense of this position for the first three years of its life. A vital contact was M.C. "Pat" Dougherty, a volunteer in this effort. Dougherty, as the president of a production credit association, which loaned money to farmers, had perhaps more rural contact than any man in Lee County. He and his wife attended perhaps more meetings than any single volunteer with the possible exception of George McLean.

The monthly meetings were a lively mixture of business and social activities. Members often revisited or continued conversations begun after church the previous Sunday. There were always comments about weather, farming, and market conditions. Members sometimes played games and there were always such activities for the children. Food, cakes, pies, and other desserts were an added appeal of the meetings and seemed to make each meeting a celebration. Songs, often church hymns and other favorites were sung with gusto, though not always well. They were among friends and sour notes only added to the merriment.

The business segment of the meeting was a time for discussion and deliberation. Today, David Mathews, president of the Kettering Foundation, makes clear the nature of deliberation. "It is process attached to action." And so it was here at the RCDCs. The programs and meetings provided for total inclusion. It was a means of engaging the public in deliberation and action without an intermediary agency.

There were no boundaries on the topics or issues. When George McLean described the plan, the Rural Community Development Councils would be "concerned with the improvement of all phases of life. Education, farm management, homes [housing and family concerns], religion, and government **must** [emphasis his] receive appropriate attention at one time or another."[96]

By 1947, there were 41 RCDC units in 5 counties. During the first three years of their existence all RCDCs had a common theme. The initial projects were designed to be relatively simple but with high visibility. Highest priority was given to the increase of productivity of each person, each farm animal, and each acre of land. Concurrently, however, emphasis in 1947 was on improving the physical appearance of each of the communities. Total attention was given to increasing farm production in 1948. In 1949, all councils conducted a yearlong leadership program with assistance from the technical advisors. The program proved pivotal. Everyone had access to the training. By the year's close, every community had reached a critical mass of leadership and there was a common understanding that almost everyone could and should exercise leadership at one time or another. It was commonly agreed among members that the success of the RCDC units seemed to explode after that.

Each council undertook communitywide projects. All had clean-up projects. Litter was removed from the roadsides. Churches and schools were repainted and refurbished. Community and church cemeteries were frequent targets of Saturday afternoon cleanups. Men, women, and children worked alongside each other. Food and song were often integral parts of these workdays. The women would pool cooking activities and provide dinner on the grounds.

With less fanfare and celebrations, private homes were also being painted or in some cases painted for the first time. The outbuildings were repaired and cleaned, sometimes whitewashed. These rural Mississippi neighborhoods began to take on a neatness more frequently associated with New England. But it was Mississippi, poor Mississippi, but no longer the downtrodden Mississippi made famous by the earlier magnificent photographs of Walker Evans. There was newfound pride. The neighborhoods were beginning to look loved.

I visited some of these rural neighborhoods as a young boy and contrasted them with the communities where my grandparents lived less than 50 miles away. While my own grandparents, the Swiss and German heritage still evident, were meticulously neat, their neighbors and the broader community had much less commitment to aesthetic beauty. The people in Lee County seemed more lively and animated. These normally reticent Mississippians were eager to "show off" their neighborhoods and tell of the transformation.

The partners, those civic club members who lived in towns, often participated in the projects. However, all had been cautioned and instructed by McLean and others that they were not there to offer advice, but as a gesture of friendship. In a one-sentence stand-alone paragraph, McLean provided direction. "It should be clearly pointed out that the civic club members are not going to come out to the farms and try to give advice on how to farm." In a subsequent statement, directed both to rural and town citizens, McLean added, "Neither are the civic club members going to attempt to 'lead' the rural community. The basic principle is the development of leadership 'within' the rural community itself."

The focus was always on helping rural communities help themselves. Even Sam Marshall, the director of the Rural Community Development Council, was urged to go to the meetings, sit in the back of the room and admonished, "keep your mouth shut unless addressed by the members."

These town partners were, of course, much more than decoration. They were part of the critical network and boundary-spanning functions of the rural councils. The councils obviously brought the rural participants together in ways that strengthened community. Because of all the interconnection of the intertwined organizations and agencies of schools, churches, vocational programs, and agricultural programs, the rural areas became more closely knit than ever before. They were also linked to other rural communities within their own county and to communities in other counties. Coordinated action was becoming a regular and expected occurrence.

The culture itself was being transformed. Community collaboration was the norm. Cooperation between rural and towns was ongoing. The technical experts provided a critical component in increasing productivity. As the area made economic gains, the increases went directly to the rural people.

To further stimulate community and individual improvement, the business leaders sponsored a competition between communities. The Rural Community Contest was open to every rural community in Chickasaw, Itawamba, Lee, Monroe, Pontotoc, Prentiss, and Union counties. The contest was between communities. There was no reward for individuals, "except the reward that comes to the individual as a result of increasing his farm production or the satisfaction that comes from helping create the best rural community in northeast Mississippi."[97]

Northeast Mississippi is basketball territory and the rivalry between these communities is deep. The creators of the rural programs had hoped to eliminate or reduce much of this competition, but when their early efforts did not work, the decision was made to take advantage of the competitive spirit in a way that would add more excitement to community development by means of the Rural Community Contest.

The contest scoring was divided into two parts. The first gave credits or points for improvements made by the community as organized groups. The second awarded points or credits to individual farm families for work that its members did to improve farm production or home improvement. For the former, councils would establish projects, many of which might require a full year to complete or implement. Points could be earned by doing the various cleanups. A common practice was for the whole community to come together to create a model demonstration farm. The community would usually select the farm of an elderly member of the community or one who had suffered some personal difficulties or tragedy. Everyone would meet at the farm with tools, tractors, etc., then, with the technical assistance of the agricultural experts including university faculty, renovate the farm until it was a model farm including terraced fields, a necessary component on many hillside farms of the surrounding areas. Farmers would learn the best practices while creating this model farm. It was important to engage the young people so that they, too, could learn and then continue these "best practices."

The community received points if all of the family members kept detailed farm records on productivity. They got points or credits if they had perfect attendance at meetings and the biggest payoff came if the community got 100 percent of the community involved as members of the RCDC process. This provided added incentive or pressure to get everyone in the community involved.

The second means of acquiring points was through the efforts of individual families to improve their own productivity and quality of life. Here, one can see clearly a means of doing community development while addressing personal problems. The Family Score Card targeted specific activities that would earn points for the community. If any member of the family adapted more productive farm practices, they received points. If any family kept detailed farm records including such things as the pounds of feed given a cow and the pounds of milk produced. If any members took courses that increased their skills such as literacy training or vocational education courses, the family received points. Painting one's house or making other substantive improvements earned points for the community. Having all the children inoculated against childhood diseases produced credits. If children had perfect school attendance or strong grades, credits were given to the community. In short, any effort to improve one's quality of life carried its own reward and provided extra credits to the community.

At the end of the year, outside judges would visit all the communities to evaluate their projects and make the final tally of points. Such judges would be drawn from the faculty of universities and colleges in the area. Professors of sociology would sometimes come as judges and bring classes along to see the Tupelo Model firsthand. Prominent leaders from other towns in the South would be invited to serve as judges. Often they would carry ideas and insights back to their home communities and this way the model was deliberately disseminated.

The winning communities would be announced at the Mississippi-Alabama Fair and Dairy Show held annually in Tupelo. There, the community achievements of all the communities, not just the prize winners, were center stage as each community depicted its accomplishments. It was a time for celebration, not merely for the winners, though these winning communities still display their awards 40 to 50 years later. The celebration was for the progress of the whole area.

The number of RCDCs grew quickly from the original three pilot councils. By the mid-1950s there were 56 RCDC units. Every rural community in Lee County, both white and black had formed RCDC programs. Almost every council had 100 percent membership from its citizens. The annual meetings were drawing almost 6,000 persons. Six thousand people doing community development and then attending the annual meeting! The fruits of the efforts were on display everywhere.

The Tupelo newspaper, which soon changed its name to the *Tupelo Area Journal* and then to the *Northeast Mississippi Daily Journal*, gave daily attention to the activities in the rural communities. Virtually every community project was featured in the paper. The "can do" spirit was captured in picture and printed word. The self-conscious pride continued to sweep through the area.

Coverage by the *Journal* was an ongoing celebration of the advantages of cooperation. It documented the power of the partnerships. It helped ingrain this new approach as routine behavior of the area. New norms were being crafted and social capital was on parade. The successes, and their daily documentation, paved the way to making rural people receptive to new ideas and progressive thinking.

Not surprising, the high visibility given rural areas increased the newspaper circulation in the hinterland enormously. By the mid-1950s, the Tupelo newspaper had the largest circulation of any nonmetropolitan newspaper in the nation. The importance of this should not be overlooked. It increased the influence of the newspaper by reaching into almost every home in the area. The newspaper and George McLean turned much of the profit back into financing still more community development projects. The financial success of the *Journal* was helping to fuel the community development process.

The partnerships forged in the 1940s helped unify the whole area as it moved into industrialization. It made it easier for the county and city to work together to build an industrial base. County and city governments' cooperation has been routine for the past 50 years. Farmers-turned-industrial workers identified themselves as Lee County citizens, rather than as laborers. Labor-management relations were often cooperative. Labor unions did not emerge, but neither would town leaders, especially prolabor George McLean permit any hint of exploitation of labor. Factory wages remained well above that in the remainder of the area.

After the RCDC was established, McLean urged the members of the Chamber of Commerce to disband this traditional business organization and form a new community organization. The new group would have a much broader base of participation and would concern itself with a more general range of community issues. McLean reminded his fellow businessmen that they had all learned the necessity of investing in their businesses to have any hope for a profit. The same was true of the community. A monetary commitment should be viewed as an investment in the community.[98] If their customers were poor, their earning power, to say nothing of their own self-development, was limited. By increasing the quality of life and earning potential, the businessmen would increase their own earning potential.

The town's three banks and the *Journal* were the foundation contributors. Each was asked to make a pledge to invest $1,000 a year for three years. Key businesses were asked for the same commitment. Below the top echelon, other businesses were asked to pledge $750, $500, and $250, down to the smallest amount of $100.[99]

There was widespread support for such an organization. Eighty-eight Tupelo businessmen met in the Hotel Tupelo on October 8, 1948, to form the Community Development Foundation (CDF). In its initial year, 1948, the newly formed Community Development Foundation raised more than $25,000. The old Chamber of Commerce had never had a budget of more than $8,000. The fledgling organization began with 151 charter members.[100]

The Community Development Foundation coordinated nine other organizations under its umbrella. The CDF was now a true coordinating association as it brought together the Rural Community Development Council, the Tupelo Marketing Company, the North Mississippi Livestock Association, the Tupelo Area Artificial Insemination Association, the Lee County Jersey Cattle Club, the Lee County Animal Health Program, Industrial Committee, Merchants Committee, and Agricultural Committee.

The star in the CDF crown was the Rural Community Development Council. The program captured the imagination of agricultural leaders across the South. In 1948, the Federal Reserve Bank of St. Louis made the Tupelo Plan, as it was soon called, the model in its own agricultural and rural development promotions.[101] The national headquarters of the American Legion urged its more than 4,000 posts to encourage the adoption of the "Tupelo Plan."[102] Paul Chapman, the dean of the College of Agriculture at the University of Georgia, gave the program added confidence when he hailed it as the most complete program of rural development of which he had knowledge.[103] Between 1950 and 1970 more than 25 foreign nations sent delegations to Tupelo to examine at first-hand the progress of this Mississippi community.[104] In 1967 Orville Freeman, then secretary of the Department of Agriculture, referred to the RCDC as "by all odds the best program of rural development I have been exposed to anywhere around the country."[105]

The organization maintained its focus on improving life for the small, low-income farmer. The agricultural technicians geared their approach toward such individuals.[106] Unfortunately, even this special emphasis was unable to go against the tide of mechanized farming. By 1948, thousands of tenant farmers throughout Lee County and the South were being displaced by laborsaving machinery. Small farm owners whose limited operations negated the use of large expensive machinery were similarly squeezed from their lifelong occupation. In 1950, the average farm size in Lee County was 61 acres, too small to gain optimum use from much of the new equipment.[107] Moreover, tighter health regulations imposed on dairy farmers necessitated major expenditures in order to achieve minimum health standards. For some farmers the capital was not available; still others feared that the expense would erase their profit margins. They, too, chose to find other employment.[108]

More than 20 percent of Mississippi's population migrated from the state between 1950 and 1960.[109] The six counties contiguous to Lee County experienced a similar gross loss.[110] Lee County's population decline beyond Tupelo's city limits was not as severe as surrounding counties. However, it declined from 26,710 to 23,368 for a 14 percent net population loss.[111] The RCDC units had stabilized the communities. Complementing these efforts, the industrial program of Tupelo's Community Development Foundation had geared itself toward accommodating this displaced population from 1948 forward. Between 1950 and 1960, Tupelo's population increased 49 percent from 11,527 to 17,221.[112]

The essence of the rural transition is captured in the experience of the Brewer community, one of the three original RCDC communities. In 1947, the first full year of the RCDC program, Brewer had 105 families. Eighty-five percent were farm families. Only 20 percent had any member of the family employed in industry. In a little over a decade, by 1960, there were still 105 families, but only 15 percent were farm families and 80 percent of the families had a member working in an industry.[113]

The transition was, of course countywide and over the course of almost a half-century, Lee County was transformed from a rural county to an industrial one. In 1945, there were 4,507 farms in Lee County.[114] By 1990, of the 31,178 employed persons in the county, only 494 were employed in agriculture.[115]

Even with the transition, the Community Development Foundation maintains its ties to agriculture. The RCDC is administered under the Private/Public

Partnership Division of CDF. During the decade of the 1980s CDF promoted two major agricultural projects. Working with other counties in northeast Mississippi, it has successfully completed a large swine production program to provide needed pork for the area's meat packing plants, particularly Bryan Foods in West Point, Mississippi. In 1993, it brought to fruition the creation of an Agri-Center, which will promote livestock shows, a farmer's market, and provide a vehicle for involving more youth in agriculture as a future career.

Despite the transformation of the county's economy, the RCDC units remained vibrant for over three decades. Fifteen RCDC units were still functioning in 1986.[116] They were a stabilizing force within the communities and prevented the deterioration of the community. Many of the communities prospered during this transition. Moreover, the internal sense of community and the cooperation and goodwill between town and country helped to facilitate the transition to an industrialized community. The spirit of cooperation was evident as the town and country worked together to secure industrial jobs. Town leaders were more conscious of rural needs as they assisted in the industrialization of the county's economy. This cooperative spirit tended to permeate the industrialization stage discussed in Chapter 7.

Summary and Conclusions

The relationship between Tupelo and the rural population changed during World War I. The economies of the two areas remained intertwined, but town and country became partners in a search to bring economic stability, if not prosperity, to the farm. The crisis began with the collapse of the cotton trade caused by the disruption of European markets and the boll weevil infestation. The town businessmen, especially bankers who had outstanding loans to farmers, faced the same disaster as their rural customers. One of those bankers, Jim High of The Peoples Bank, was the catalyst for a widespread diversification program. The basic plan was modeled after a diversification success story in the Pacific Northwest. Working through his business and personal networks, High helped to coordinate the county's first successful diversification effort.

The initial success was reversed when the cotton market took a second plunge at the beginning of the 1920s. Undaunted, the town's businessmen and farmers increased their effort to balance cotton farming with dairying. Bankers, working through their local association, united to hire a dairying specialist. Other businessmen joined the effort as town businesses understood the need to invest a portion of their profits in a community project aimed at improving the economy for the whole county.

Not even the successful diversification efforts were sufficient to thwart the depression of rural America. There were, however, short-term gains in that the area was more prosperous than it would have been otherwise. More important were the unplanned longer-term gains of community-building. Businessmen had become more adept at working together. Investing in the community and coordinating the public and private sector became more standard. Boundaries between town and country were being redefined.

The diversification program of the twenties built the foundation for a more extensive effort in the succeeding decades.

One sees in this experience that community development is not simply achieving goals. Community development is a process by which elements in the community are coordinated so that channels of cooperation and communication are opened. Networks and organizations are created and barriers to cooperation are lowered or circumvented.

The renewed efforts at diversification utilized some of the same community structure, especially the cooperative efforts of banks, to develop a more complete diversification program. The catalyst in this effort was George McLean, a newcomer to the community. Interestingly, McLean offered a plan of development that would later receive national acclaim, but was not acted on until he had proven himself personally as an individual who could be trusted. McLean himself learned that leadership often begins by listening and then acting as a servant-leader to help the people help themselves.

This second phase attempted regional organization with very limited success. There were not sufficient ties to hold the counties together. The greatest success came when the Lee County Livestock Association hired dairy specialist Gale Carr to provide technical assistance to Lee County farmers. Through his technical expertise, the county developed an artificial insemination program that made it possible to service the cattle of even the poorest farmers and thereby bring them into the development process.

McLean was convinced that the key to community development was to begin at the grassroots level. He argued that citizenship was a privilege and that if given the proper tools, common people, acting as good citizens could best address their own economic social problems.

Acting on that assumption, McLean helped to establish grassroots community development organizations, which he called Rural Community Development Councils, in rural communities in five counties. Citizens in these communities were taught team building by working together on common yearlong community improvement projects. The process strengthened the horizontal ties in the community and enhanced community identity.

The rural units were linked to the town through civic clubs, which served as partners with the rural communities. In this way the community boundaries were again being redefined, as town and country were learning to work together as standard behavior.

Even with massive rural migration in the 1950s and 1960s, Lee County retained a higher percentage of its rural population than its neighboring counties. The community development efforts stabilized the community, enhanced cooperative efforts, and became the scaffolding for the industrial development a generation later.

When George McLean first unveiled what became known as "The Tupelo Plan," he titled his editorial, "It Can Be Done!" His short-range goal was to raise the quality of life for the poorest segment of the population by providing them with the organizational structure, the basic skills, and access to resources. His long-range goal was to consciously construct a model that would demonstrate the possibility for other communities to achieve these same goals.

He hoped to establish a model that would begin with the development of human resources, then combine these individual skills into an effective organization that could work as a team so that the variety of talents would complement the whole.

For the wealthier segment of the population, he appealed to their own self-interest by arguing that financially poor customers are a drain on business. By investing in the skills of ordinary citizens, their earning and purchasing power increases. Investment in community development was good business that paid dividends.

It was a win/win arrangement that marked the style of this community leader who had first learned community development through the conflict approach.

CHAPTER 7

The Industrial Transition

The efforts to bring industry into the community prior to the 1940s were sporadic and short-lived. Moreover, there was no real continuity in the factors that triggered interest in industrialization. The first attempt was born in those enterprising days of unbounded enthusiasm that followed the coming of the second railroad in 1887. Problems of limited local capital augmented by a prolonged depression crushed the individual endeavors. However, the economic crisis of the 1890s brought greater havoc to farms and prompted a cooperative attempt to build industry as a viable supplement to the ailing agriculture. Unfortunately, this fruitful flirtation with factories was not sustained after its prelude. By contrast, the agrarian difficulties subsequent to World War I and the boll weevil infestation motivated agricultural innovations but no systematic industrialization. No organization, new or old, gave consistent attention to manufacturing as a potential solution to the problem.

By the mid-thirties, the South as a whole agonized over its economic plight.[1] President Roosevelt referred to the South as "the Nation's No. 1 economic problem."[2] This assertion was further documented in the remainder of the report which argued in part that the South, "lacking industries of its own . . . has been forced to trade the richness of its soil, its minerals and forests, and the labor of its people for goods manufactured elsewhere."[3] Mississippi lagged behind its sister states economically and the northeastern section of the state was considered the poorest area in the poorest state in the Union.[4]

Even this does not go far enough in describing Tupelo's specific situation. The town was severely damaged by a terrible tornado in 1936. More than 800 homes were destroyed. Two hundred-thirty persons were killed and another 2,000 were injured. Many people lost their life's possessions. What little capital there was in town had to be used for rebuilding purposes.[5]

Despite the sorrow produced by the tornado and the lingering depression, the times were not without hope. Mississippi towns were alive with the prospect that industrialization would chase away their economic woes. To that end, the state chose its best known proponent of industry, Hugh White, as its governor in 1935. White vaulted into prominence when he was credited with reversing the slumping conditions in his hometown, Columbia. Subsequent to the closing of his own lumber company, White devoted himself to building a strong Chamber of Commerce that raised the subsidy necessary to lure a garment factory to town. Shortly thereafter, two more textile mills joined the first. Most Mississippi communities took little cognizance of the low wages of Columbia's garment factories but saw only the town's growing payrolls and the rising retail sales. Consequently, they were delighted with White's plan to use the "Columbia Method" as the basis for his statewide program to Balance Agriculture with Industry.[6]

Similar plans were implemented in towns and cities throughout the South. A major focus was on municipal and state organizations that offered tax exemptions as well as other advantages to prospective industries.[7] A second point of attention was the cheap abundant labor that was often the real bait in the competition for factories. These were the main ingredients in the industrial transformation of small cities in the Southeast.[8]

The transition called for unity of action as a means of mobilizing people and resources.[9] Labor, however, was not willing to be grist in the South's industrial mills. By early 1937, strikes had spread to garment factories throughout Mississippi. Spurred by depressed economic conditions and C.I.O. labor organizers, the state's workers were stirring as never before.[10]

The strikes were similar to the labor disputes that had occurred earlier in other parts of the South. Workers were not organized in labor unions and in most cases, the leaders of the strikes spoke against union affiliation.[11] Strikers gained a welcome champion in the *Tupelo Journal* whose editorials and on-the-scene reports by Harry Rutherford hammered away at the injustice of their wages and conditions.[12]

George McLean rankled industrialists across the state by accusing them of betraying Mississippi's workers. He argued that businessmen had lured "starvation-wage outfits" to the state under the guise of progress. Once the factories were established, McLean charged, the industrialists had blocked improved conditions in the name of state's rights.[13] The editor stopped short of urging laborers in the local textile mills to assert themselves, but when a sit-down strike began on April 7, 1937, management placed the blame at McLean's door. Most of the town's merchants initiated a boycott against the newspaper, but McLean continued to report the position of the workers.[14]

The strikers were equally intransigent. They refused to compromise their demands for a 15 percent wage increase over the existing ten dollars a week and a reduction of the work time from 46 to 40 hours per week. Support among employees of the Tupelo Cotton Mill grew steadily, but the strain produced by a week without pay made the setting a tinder box.[15] When the local unit of the national guard appeared on the grounds adjacent to the cotton mill to "practice" artillery fire, the stage was set for a potentially dangerous confrontation. The firing of the heavy weapons brought strikers from the factory like angry wasps from their nests. Armed with wrenches and other pieces of loose metal, they swarmed across the open field prepared to do battle on the spot. No explanation by the commander of the unit could convince the strikers that these events were anything but an attempt at direct intimidation.[16] The unit pulled back but the labor leaders acted almost immediately to form an alliance with the C.I.O.[17]

The union affiliation never had time to develop. Following this encounter, vicious rumors involving the activities of the other side flowed freely through each of the camps. Not even a personal visit by the governor could ease the tensions. Two weeks into the strike both of the opposing groups were divided among themselves. Discouraged by their own infighting and fearful that there might be truth in the rumor that the owners planned to burn the factory and blame the strikers, the workers finally abandoned the mill and strike after 15 unsettling days.[18]

Both sides had lost, but Tupelo's workers had stood up to their former bosses in an unparalleled fashion and for a time threatened the social structure. Some of Tupelo's leaders were not prepared to let this action go unchallenged. The leader of the strike, Jimmy Cox, was abducted from the streets of Tupelo and taken to a secluded spot. A rope was tied around his neck and the other end attached to the car axle. Only disagreement among the cowardly participants prevented his brutal murder. Instead, he was tied facedown to a log and severely beaten with belts.[19] Returning to town, some of the same men went to the hotel room of Ida Sledge, who was seeking to organize the factory women in the International Ladies' Garment Workers' Union. The threats against her were sufficient to drive her from town.[20]

It would be difficult to exaggerate the tension and division within Tupelo. Few towns were so deeply divided as Tupelo was at this point. Labor felt betrayed by management. Many workers had lost confidence in the community power structure that offered no sympathy for their economic plight. Businessmen had been shaken. The spirit of cooperation of which they boasted appeared to be a myth. They were shocked by the depths of anger of the workers and the difficulty of reconciling the differences between management and labor. Many of them despised George McLean and saw him as the catalyst for the protracted strike. Some of these men never forgave McLean.

By autumn, matters had normalized to the point that differences were being settled in legal channels. Twenty women who had been fired from the Tupelo Garment Factory because of their membership in the International Ladies' Garment Workers' Union were ordered to be reinstated by the Labor Board.[21] The town government, like the political bodies of other small towns, tried to remain aloof from controversy and failed to act during the tension of the spring.[22] Six months after the strike ended, the Board of Aldermen sought to prevent the rise of future labor trouble by a city ordinance. Henceforth, the town acknowledged the right of workers to organize but made it illegal to solicit membership for labor unions during working hours or one hour before or after the work day.[23]

No amount of effort by any of the town's agencies could heal the deep schisms within the community. Nor did a common recognition of the economic problems draw the diverse units together. Each of the major elements sought to organize itself in order to increase its strength. Laborers formed company unions in the late spring of 1937, but the infighting and fear of reprisal by management rendered them helpless from the outset. Their actual demise came when they were ordered to be dissolved at the same legal hearing that reinstated the women in the garment factory.[24] No subsequent labor organizations were generated.

Businessmen faced a similar problem. They found neither organization nor program that could muster widespread support. The Chamber of Commerce was revived in 1938 with the hope that it would become a rallying point for townsmen. It promised to work toward industrial development but was greeted by an unenthusiastic response from many businessmen. Some of the prominent citizens were cool to the idea of bringing in new industry in light of the recent turmoil. Perhaps they were also reluctant to dilute further their own position by sharing power with extra-local industrialists.[25] James M. Savery, the new president of the Chamber of Commerce, headed a short-lived movement to reopen the cotton mill on a cooperative basis. The workers would own a majority of the stock in a plan modeled after a hosiery mill in Kenosha, Wisconsin. There was never much support for the idea. It smacked too much of socialism for many business leaders and the workers could not find the capital for the initial investment. In less than a month the venture was abandoned.[26]

The most eminent townsmen, like their counterparts at the turn of the century, had large agricultural investments and preferred to support efforts that would improve farming conditions. They vigorously joined with George McLean in sponsoring Gale Carr and his promotion of dairy cattle in the county. Their endorsement of agriculture consistently exceeded their interest in industry throughout the late thirties and World War II.

Other businessmen favored industrial growth but never became active in the community's efforts to enlarge the economic base. Just as leaders in other towns relied on their communities' "natural advantages" these men placed their hope in T.V.A.'s cheap power and Governor Hugh White's industrial programs to bring industry to the area.[27] This course, too, brought disagreement. George McLean opposed White's efforts on the grounds that they had been used to exploit Mississippi's labor.[28]

As an alternative to the governor's Balance Agriculture with Industry Program (BAWI), McLean attempted to regenerate the Northeast Mississippi Council. In its earlier form, this organization had promoted agricultural diversification. The revised version called on towns in the northeastern corner of the state to eschew petty jealousies and pool their talents and resources toward gaining major factories for the area. After the war began in Europe, McLean urged the council to seek a munitions factory.[29] Unfortunately, the fledgling organization was no more successful in uniting the towns than Tupelo had been at pulling its divergent parts together.[30]

The war, for all its tragedies, served to snatch Tupelo from its wheelspinning industrial endeavors and set it on a more solid course. Perhaps more than anything else, World War II was one of the crises that united the members of the community.[31] The solidarity of the times was described in part in Chapter 6. Dairymen worked together in a manner sufficient to merit national attention. Workers invested a large percentage of their earnings in United States War Bonds to show their involvement. The newspaper, churches, and businesses focused daily attention on the war.

Farmers, many of whom would become workers in the subsequent factories, had come to trust McLean's leadership in light of the dairying success.[32] Tupelo's economy was badly depressed at the beginning of the forties, but once the dairy benefits were manifested in the town's cash registers, some businessmen, too, became committed to McLean's ideas. By the war's end, Tupelo reversed its failures of the early forties.[33]

Because McLean's earlier efforts were now paying dividends and time had healed earlier disagreements, McLean was warmly greeted when he returned in 1945 from his service as a naval officer. Most of the community leaders recognized that a new economic structure would emerge in the wake of the war, and they wanted to be as close to the leading edge as possible. They had collected 30,000 dollars during the closing period of the war and wanted to invest in the economic development of the community. They approached McLean and asked him to serve as an unpaid manager and president of the local Chamber of Commerce. He was to use the newly collected funds as the initial community investment.[34]

McLean accepted the offer and at their suggestion set out to locate an "industrial expert" who could bring industries to northeast Mississippi. After extensive travel and extended conversations with economic developers he concluded, "that if there were such an 'industrial medicine man,' he was already at work in some community that could afford to pay him ten times as much as we could." After hearing his report, the local leaders concurred. The responsibility for local development should fall to "the local community and those who love it." Their task was to improve the community and enhance its ability to attract industry. In years to follow, local volunteers left their own work in order to travel throughout the nation telling the advantages of locating in the area.[35]

As matters stood in 1945, there was no doubt that the economy would change. Agricultural jobs had declined from 7,144 in 1930 to 6,216 in 1940. Ten years later, the county had lost an additional 600 farm jobs.[36] The dislocation was traumatic to farmers whose livelihoods were forever transformed. Moreover, it is estimated that for every five farms that disappeared, one retail store was eliminated.[37] The economy was in a nosedive. As one local leader expressed it, "we were in a hole and there was a snake in there with us. We had to get out."[38]

None of the local leaders in Lee County had experience in attracting industry. The last outside industry to relocate to Lee County was the Carnation plant in 1927, 18 years earlier. The county had its successful dairy program and through the Tupelo Area Artificial Insemination Association, Tupelo leaders had contact with many area farmers. Since farmers constituted a majority of the county's population, it seemed logical that the county further diversify the economy by producing vegetables and fruits.

The leaders did their research. They worked with the economic development program of T.V.A. and discussed vegetable production with agricultural universities. They visited successful vegetable programs in west Tennessee. They learned that it was not sufficient merely to increase production. This could have disastrous economic consequences if the goods could not be marketed. Therefore, local leaders established a marketing association for sweet potatoes, strawberries, and blackberries. Going further, local leaders contributed $30,000, most of which they had committed for the economic development of the area.

The marketing association was carefully constructed for efficiency and to maximize the returns to the farmers. The corporation focused on warehousing, curing, processing, and marketing these truck crops. The corporation was limited to a 6 percent return to the investors and no officer could receive any compensation for his work in the corporation. Clearly, the purpose was to guarantee that the profit would go to the farmer and to the marketing facility for the farmers' benefit.[39]

This grand plan failed!

Farmers were never consulted and involved in the formation of the project. Too few were interested in making the transition to truck farming. All participants, or would-be participants agreed that it was a good plan, but this well-conceived plan did not attract the involvement of the farmers.

Within a year the plan was shelved. Decades later, those who had lost money in the project could smile and even laugh about "their marvelous marketing plan." They had learned a valuable lesson. Good plans begin by listening to the people involved. What are their hopes? In what activities are they willing to invest their time and money?

With the creation of the Rural Community Development Councils, the town and county established the channels of communication, which if used properly would prevent similar fiascos in the future. For the next several decades, the RCDCs served the county well. Local people were engaged in the economic transformation of the county.

There seems to have been no bitterness about the failure of the marketing association. The lesson was well learned, that people matter even in the best of plans or especially in the best of plans.

The collapse of the marketing association was such a profound experience that its primary lesson that people come first was quickly incorporated in the community's basic principles of community development. McLean, as the publisher of the newspaper, had the strongest voice in this matter. He insisted that in these hard economic times, the greatest asset for the county was its labor force, which was becoming uncoupled from agriculture. This labor force, if it could be retained and retrained, would be the foundation of industrial development. But the labor force must not be betrayed by those who would develop the county.

McLean stated this position in almost every speech and editorial relating to economic development. Perhaps his most articulate statement came in 1947 in the keynote address to Omicron Delta Kappa, a national leadership fraternity. "Mississippi needs industry, but it needs the highest type of industry. Not the lowest type. We do not want to be the dumping ground for labor exploiters. That type of industry will harm our people and our existing industrialists. Frankly we [Lee County] do not want a manufacturer unless he has a record of fair play with his employees and is interested in paying as good of a wage as possible. Selling her people short is the poorest practice ever engaged in by the South. We have real advantages to offer industry and cheap labor should not be one of them."[40]

In this speech, McLean specifically noted that the state and its communities must be concerned with all of its people, not simply those who would go on to college. Moreover, Mississippi needed to turn its thinking process on its head. No longer should blacks be viewed as "a problem," as had been traditionally done. Blacks, along with the white population, should receive the best education possible. The state must begin to invest in all its people if it were to realize the potential that was locked within each individual. The economic future of the state depended on this change of policy.[41]

It was a central premise in much of McLean's efforts for the remainder of his life. People, organized and working on behalf of the community and their own interests, were at the heart of the "Tupelo Plan," as it was subsequently called.

While the role of organized people was the linchpin in the scheme, there were other principles that also formed the framework of the development strategy. Second only to the tenet that such development begins with people is the understanding that local citizens must be responsible for the improvement of their own community and local citizens must accept the responsibility of investing their own time, money, and other resources.

The question is how to get businessmen to commit a part of their profit for community development. In the early years whenever this query was posed, McLean would tell the same story to explain how and why businessmen invested in the community. "I feel that some businessmen are like some farmers. Have you ever seen a farmer on a cold winter day trying to milk a scrub cow? He pulls and strains trying to get a teacup of milk. He hasn't put very much in the front end and he doesn't get very much out of the back end. We are convinced that both businessmen and farmers have got to put their time, their talents, their money, and their enthusiasm into their community effort if they hope to get something out of it."[42]

This principle has not varied. Speaking 30 years later McLean characteristically sounded the same theme. "We know that this is our community and we have the responsibility of doing whatever is necessary to promote the well-being of our people. . . . There is no Santa Claus at the state capitol, at the federal capitol, and not even at Tupelo. The job of developing your community is your job. It is your responsibility, your highest privilege."[43]

This sense of "responsibility" has religious overtones and Lee County leaders draw heavily on the strong religious values of their culture. They consistently stress their own responsibility as "servant-leaders." The servant-leader is an ongo-

ing theme for all of the last half-century. McLean, drawing on his religious training was often the most likely to quote biblical scripture in his speeches. He was
especially fond of quoting Luke 6:38: "Give and it shall be given unto you." The
servant-leader, he reminded the community, would be rewarded, perhaps not
materially but a reward would be forthcoming.

There are four additional principles that have directed the economic development for the last half of the twentieth century: (1) Attract smaller industries; (2)
Scatter the industries throughout the area; (3) Form partnerships with governmental and technical agencies; and (4) Maintain a focus on the economic development goals while remaining flexible with the method of reaching the goals. The
first of these has been to attract smaller industries as opposed to large employers.
By so doing, the county hoped to achieve two fundamental objectives. The first
was to avoid having an industry with such extraordinary size and clout that it
could dictate or dominate the community. The second objective has been to diversify the industry so that an economic slump in a specific industry would not crip-
ple the community.

From the beginning, Lee County leaders have insisted that their program be an
area development scheme. This meant in part that it was not actually the Tupelo
Plan, but the Lee County Plan because all of the county was to benefit. While Lee
County is the focal point of much of the activity, all of the area is directly and
indirectly affected.

Because this was an area development project, the plan sought to distribute factories throughout the area rather than clustering them in Tupelo. Tupelo would
function as the service center of the region. Since the majority of the county's population lived in the rural sections, it was projected that farmers would make the
transition from agriculture to industry, but continue to live in the rural area and
make only a short commute to factories located in the surrounding rural area. In
addition to the added convenience of bringing the jobs to the labor, the industrial base would bring new tax revenue sources to the county government and make
it more enticing for county government to become a full partner in the development process.

An additional axiom was Tupelo's willingness and eagerness to engage federal
agencies as technical assistants and partners in the development. While this idea
may not receive notice in the decade of the nineties, it was relatively unusual for
southern communities in a time of racial unrest to seek federal assistance. Key
Tupelo leaders, however, had already made the commitment to social justice for
all its people.

The concluding principle was to recognize the need for flexibility in achieving
the goals within these other principles. In very practical terms, this meant that the
county would have to build on its own success and that it could not rest at any
level of achievement. The county must continually find new and better ways of
strengthening itself. To underscore this objective, McLean frequently quoted
Oliver Cromwell. "He who ceases to get better, ceases to be good."[44]

The principles behind the economic development evolved over a ten-year span of thinking about economic and community development. During that period, various leaders had contributed to an unstructured laundry list of ideas. These principles gained focus around the Doane Agricultural Report commissioned by George McLean.

As noted in Chapter 6, McLean, assisted by local accountant M. M. Winkler, approached True D. Morse and the Doane Agricultural Service in September 1945, to make a yearlong study of Lee County which, in turn, would provide the raw material to establish a program of development for the area.[45]

The final report had three parts. There was a survey of all physical, biological, social, and economic factors affecting the area. Most of this data were drawn from the 1940 census. Part two was the draft of a community plan. Part three suggested a mechanism for administering the program.[46]

The report proposed a good basic plan. Interestingly, however, there was little in the proposal that McLean had not advocated almost ten years earlier. There were two vital contributions of this external study. First, the Doane's report served as a rallying point to pull together different elements of the community. The Doane name provided credibility that McLean did not have when he first unveiled his ideas. Second, Doane Agricultural Service became an important link in Lee County's network. In later years it contributed to identifying Lee County as a national model while True D. Morse was the undersecretary of Agriculture in the Eisenhower administration.

As described in Chapter 6, the first step in implementing the plan was the pilot effort of establishing Rural Community Development Councils in three agricultural communities in three different counties. The success and rapid dissemination of the program to fifty-six communities in five counties enhanced the quality of life. Even more important, it provided a feeling of empowerment.

The RCDC project was a means of making it possible for the whole county to become an active partner in the community development process. The rural-based organizations helped people to help themselves. In addition, it aided in retaining the labor base in the area. Moreover, it improved their skills as farmers. Demonstration farms were established, and better farming techniques were incorporated in the daily farming operations including better managerial proficiency.[47]

The Rural Community Development Councils, however, could not alter the economic system and offset the loss of farm jobs with new job opportunities. This required strengthening the manufacturing base. The weakness in the industrial foundation was apparent. The number of manufacturing jobs had decreased from 1,492 in 1930 to only 956 in 1940 after the closing of the Tupelo cotton mill. Three-fourths of the manufacturing jobs in 1940 employed women.[48] There were too few employment opportunities for men. Therefore, the highest priority was to create jobs for men.

The breakthrough came quickly. In February 1946, the industrial team led by men like James M. (Ikey) Savery, Josh Whitesides, and Phil Nanney of The Peoples Bank and Bank of Tupelo respectively, working with George McLean reached an agreement with Daybrite to establish a branch factory in Tupelo.

Daybrite, the St. Louis-based corporation noted earlier, produces flourescent light fixtures. The company projected an opening in the summer of 1947 with an expected employment of approximately 200 men.[49]

Daybrite was secured under the terms of the state's BAWI plan. This scheme allowed the town to issue bonds to assist with the financial support to recruitment. The solidarity of the community was reflected in the bond issue election. The bond issue passed by a vote of 744 to 14, a 98 percent positive vote.[50] Tupelo was becoming unified.

Success in attracting a male-employing industry, the first nonlocally owned industry in almost 20 years buoyed spirits. This triumph combined with the unbridled local support for the Rural Community Development Councils gave the leaders the confidence for still bolder action. The leaders wanted a central coordinating agency that would better represent the economic and social changes that were stirring in the community. Thus in 1948, two years after the initiation of RCDC, the town leaders decided to abandon its traditional Chamber of Commerce in favor of a totally new Community Development Foundation (CDF).

The successor to the Chamber was quite distinct from its predecessor. Its focus was on the entire county, not the town with its traditional corporate limits. Within a short time, Tupelo bore the unoriginal label of being "the city without city limits." By coordinating the RCDC and Tupelo Area Artificial Insemination Association (TAAIA), the organization had immediate grassroot ties to the rural area. The Community Development Foundation, as implied by its name, accepted the premise that community development was a necessary forerunner to economic development. By strengthening the horizontal ties or human infrastructure, the county felt it could address any community problem, including economic development. Because it took this broad approach, CDF was concerned with every phase of community life including industrial development, agriculture, transportation, housing, recreation, education, and religious life. By the early 1950s, CDF had committees to work on 17 different facets of life in Lee County.[51]

The Community Development Foundation has certain defining characteristics. CDF casts a wide net since it is concerned with every aspect of community, not simply retail, industry, or other commercial ventures. Therefore, it seeks a broad membership. In time, over one-fourth of the membership was drawn from outside Tupelo and 10 percent from outside Lee County. Its membership eventually exceeded 1,200 members. Originally it had a very small professional staff and relied primarily on volunteer efforts of its members. As industrial development became more sophisticated its professional staff grew.

Much of the strength of the Community Development Foundation is its coordination of the public and private sector. Thus, a representative from the office of the mayor and the president of the county's board of supervisors are guaranteed positions on the executive board of directors. The county invests large sums of money in the annual budget of CDF, and has been a loyal and staunch supporter of the organization.

The public sector has been a full partner in every aspect of the program. Over the next 35 years, mayors such as James Ballard, Clyde Whitaker, Jimmy Caldwell, Jack Marshal, and Glen McCullough worked in tandem with CDF.

The private sector is represented by members from the business community. Each of the three main banks and the newspaper, the *Journal,* which have always been the major financial supporters are guaranteed positions on the executive board.

The full board rotates membership on an ongoing basis in order to provide new blood and new ideas, CDF has an annual orientation to assist new members and is constantly seeking a broader support base.

As noted above, CDF operates through a number of committees that cover all aspects of community life. The specific committees' structure may vary over the course of time to increase efficiency of operation. These members and the staff are extremely efficient. Attention to detail is routine. Nothing is left to chance. The members believe that luck is spelled "W-O-R-K."

CDF expects and insists on the investment of time and money to the organization. Proxies may not be sent to board meetings. Moreover, big ideas require substantial funding, and major contributions from the members are expected. One of the original founders, Julius Berry, phrased this aspect best: "Everything given to the Community Development is an investment in our future prosperity . . . not a donation on which no return is expected."[52] In addition to local investments, CDF established vertical ties to external funding agencies that have served it well and lucratively.

Although it was not planned, CDF has had stability at the top of its program. Its first three executives, Sam Marshall, Cecil White, and Truman Brooks, served from 1948 to 1956. Harry Martin became the chief executive in 1956 where he has remained to this date in 1999. In time he became recognized as one of the nation's leading community and economic developers. Over the years, his tireless energy has symbolized the work of the Community Development Foundation.

The Community Development Foundation adopted a team approach from the outset. McLean served as a catalyst and spokesperson but the workload was spread among a broad number of members. The cornerstones were: the Bank of Tupelo (which after mergers was renamed the Bank of Mississippi); The Peoples Bank; the Citizens Bank (which subsequently merged with Deposit Guaranty); and the *Daily Journal.* These four organizations were the major financial supporters and, as noted, were assured places on the executive board.

Tupelo's banks, especially the Bank of Tupelo and The Peoples Bank, have had a long history of involvement in community development. The effort of these banks has been pivotal in the success of the Community Development Foundation. Not only have they been strong financial supporters, but their presidents and officers have been central participants in almost every community development project during the last half-century. The consistent engagement by the banks has helped to involve the bank directors who are among the most influential members of the business community.

When these bank directors combine with other key business leaders and elected officials at a typical monthly CDF board meeting, they represent most of the county's most influential organizations. For that reason, CDF with the unflagging support of the banks, the newspaper, business people, and public figures has been the primary driving force in the county for the last half-century.

With this strong leadership base in place in 1951, the county was able to attract its second major industry, Rockwell, which makes Delta power tools.[53] This time the community did not work through the BAWI, but handled all arrangements locally. It provided land, transportation needs, and assisted with financing and training labor. In return, Rockwell later contributed capital for an airport expansion and building a Youth Center. It was the kind of partnership that has characterized the relationship between industry and the county throughout the past 40 years.

Even with its Community Development Foundation, Lee County, like any other place, has major divisions. The industrial efforts in the 1950s encountered the same basic opposition that had challenged the industrialization at the turn of the century. Large farmers were opposed to the drain on their labor with the new industries. They mounted a concerted effort to halt or redirect industrialization. The CDF membership was too strong and it turned back the challenge.[54]

A second confrontation came from an unexpected source. As Lee County's economy grew, it attracted the attention of organized crime operating out of Phenix City, Alabama. For a brief period, the group gained a toehold in the county. This was met by a unified response in which the local leaders did not blink. Once again the solid front prevailed and the syndicate left the area.[55]

Meanwhile, Lee County leadership was continuing to build the human infrastructure to improve its economic position. The county reinforced its own strength as well as buttressing the economic efforts of neighboring counties when it took the lead to form a regional economic development organization that involved all north Mississippi counties.

The North Mississippi Industrial Association was modeled essentially along the lines proposed for the old Northeast Mississippi Council. It was to promote the entire area for economic development. Just as planned earlier, the industrial organization received its financial support from the area's power companies. The electrical and gas distributors set aside a specified percentage of their profits for the sponsorship of the association. The power companies could expect a return on their investment in the form of new industrial customers who would be high energy users. All participating communities were eligible to make relevant claims on the service of the development agency.[56]

Within five years of this achievement, Lee County was able to capitalize on the area's flourishing furniture industry. Lee County leaders, Ikey Savery, James Ballard, W. E. McClure, George McLean, and Harry Rutherford had been instrumental in establishing the initial furniture factory in northeast Mississippi in the late 1940s.

Tupelo's experience with the furniture industry provides some interesting insights and hopefully some lessons for communities seeking to broaden their industrial base.

Initially, Lee County was in competition with neighboring Union County as the site of the area's first furniture factory. After Tupelo leaders understood that the new furniture factory would be located in Union County, they offered their assistance to be sure that the factory would go to Union County. Lee County even offered some financial aid to assure the success of the new factory. What these Lee County leaders understood is that if this new industry came to a neighboring county, it would open several economic development opportunities. One possibility is that other businesses could be created, which would be suppliers to the original organization. A second possibility, not initially seen, was the likelihood that workers in this factory might someday start their own competing furniture factories. By 1999, there were more than 200 furniture factories within 60 miles of Tupelo. More than 180 of these factory owners gained their furniture experience working in the original Union County company, or working for someone who did. Moreover, Tupelo has become the central supplier for the furniture industry in ten counties. It was the model of a win/win situation.

As early as 1955, the upholstered furniture industry was a significant part of the economy. Lee County sought to be the hub of this production by becoming the supply center to the furniture industry. In that year it successfully lured Super Sagless, which makes internal mechanisms for chair recliners and bed davenport construction. Shortly thereafter, National Springs Corporation also relocated in Tupelo. They were later followed by polyurethane producers whose products are used as cushioning, padding, and stuffing.[57]

The industrial growth of the 1950s had been good for Tupelo's economy. Bank deposits had risen from $20 million in 1950 to $52 million ten years later. Retail sales had moved at a similar pace going from $26 to $51 million in that span, and automobile registrations in the county had doubled from the 7,400 in 1951 to more than 15,000 in 1961. Tupelo's population had grown from 11,527 in 1950 to 17,221, more than 49 percent.[58] By the late fifties, it was obvious that industries were attracted to the area because of its large pool of unorganized unskilled labor. It was equally apparent that this labor in its present vulnerable state would receive minimum wages and that labor and the trade they generated would tend to stagnate around low wages. Labor unions, it was feared, would frighten away industries since even as late as the 1990s almost 80 percent of relocation destinations occur where there are no unions.[59]

The challenges were to sustain that growth, to build on those gains, and to spread the rewards throughout the area.

Lee County prided itself on a good business climate. According to spokesperson George McLean, a good business climate consisted of three components. The most basic component is workers who provide a good day's work for a good day's pay. Second, there must be sound management that respects the quality of its work force and its product. Third, the community must seek the best working conditions for labor and management.[60]

In a concerted effort the community worked for three years, from 1959 to 1962, to establish a means of assuring a good business climate. It began with the creation of the Community Relations Agency, which operated to protect labor without the necessity of a union. The agency held meetings with management to assist with any labor problems. In its original form, the agency was also to receive complaints from labor and conduct a behind-the-scenes study to determine the validity of the complaint. If the grievance proved worthy, the industry would be instructed to correct the problem. The real teeth of this approach was the knowledge that the prolabor *Tupelo Journal* would expose the situation and bring pressure on the offending company. On several occasions, such companies were forced to change policies and managers. In extreme cases, the factories were forced to leave town.[61]

A second major effort to improve the business climate was to upgrade the skill of workers by vocational training. The CDF and the *Journal* had established a privately funded vocational development center in the 1950s. This was no longer adequate by the 1960s. Consequently, the community leadership established a branch of Itawamba Community College in Tupelo. Over the course of the next 30 years, this branch far outgrew the original campus in the number of students and has become a center for basic and advanced industrial skills.[62]

The third action occurred during 1961-1962 when CDF, working closely with the Lee County Board of Supervisors, built a large industrial park in Verona, seven miles south of downtown Tupelo. In 1990, this park was recognized by *Site Selection Magazine* as one of the ten most outstanding industrial parks in the nation.[63] The park provided a setting for the burgeoning industries and fulfilled the promise to disburse industry throughout the county.

With this additional economic infrastructure in place the industrial growth accelerated. The newspaper, the *Daily Journal* renewed its commitment to help spread the benefits to the whole county. As a symbol of that dedication, the newspaper changed its name to the *Tupelo Area Daily Journal* in 1961 after 90 years of the same name. As an additional statement of its concern for rural development, the *Journal* privately funded a pilot day care center to provide for the children of working parents in the village of Palmetto. Working with CDF it also took the lead in establishing an areawide anti-poverty agency, LIFT, Inc., with the philosophy of providing resources to help people help themselves. Going beyond the commitment of money, George McLean agreed to serve as LIFT's president. He remained as a board member for the next ten years.[64]

It was this spirit of volunteerism and willingness to invest time and money, which characterized what was now being called "The Tupelo Spirit." Men like Ikey Savery, who owned the county's oldest insurance agency often neglected his own business to work on the CDF: industrial committee J. C. Whitehead, who became president of the Bank of Tupelo in 1960, restated the bank's eagerness to fulfill its responsibility of community service. As president of the bank, Whitehead served on almost all major community committees.[65] The Reed family, among the county's most prominent members, continued its community activity. Jack Reed, later to be the Republican gubernatorial candidate and educational advisor to President George Bush, routinely budgeted more than 50 percent of his time to community projects.[66] CDF depended primarily on volunteer effort. As noted earlier, the CDF board of directors did not allow proxies, and thus many of the town's most prominent citizens gave many hours a week to committee and task assignments as a regular part of their civic responsibility.

Certainly not all of the community leaders liked one another. There were the normal jealousies and rivalries, but while they argued behind closed doors, and some disagreements were fierce, the group learned the skills of reaching consensus. Sometimes that came from the wit and charm of various participants or sound reflective judgment, but in all cases there were those consensus builders who, working one-on-one over coffee or in boardrooms, hammered out agreements outside the public vision.[67]

Those who were the best at consensus-building were those individuals whose constancy on behalf of the community had earned the trust of fellow leaders. Individuals who by their action clearly placed community interests above personal gain were the best consensus builders. Even a man like George McLean, whose personal views and public statements were often controversial, was a consensus builder. He was consistently seen as putting the good of the community first and because he could always use the persuasiveness power of the newspaper.[68]

This consensus-building was a hallmark during the decade of the sixties. There were many issues in the 1960s that could have ripped the town apart. Most prominent of these was the racial turmoil that came to be focused on the state of Mississippi. The racial unrest was the sternest test of the community's horizontal ties. The town formed biracial committees. The most influential of these committees were headed by Amos Reece, as a spokesperson for the black population, and George McLean. Reece and McLean were longtime friends who had built trust over the course of a lifetime. Taking advantage of these avenues of dialogue, the committees met literally day and night with a primary goal of opening even more means of discussion and thereby addressing grievances and finding common ways of working together.[69]

The city government attempted a reconciliation between the state and federal governments. Unlike the Mississippi legislature, which was fighting against federal money as well as "federal intervention," Lee County had forged a variety of partnership efforts between local government and federal agencies.[70]

Tupelo business leaders worked with other state business leaders to help bring calm in the midst of controversy.[71] Within Lee County the concerns for community development provided a common focus and basis for cooperation across racial and ideological lines. Community leaders reminded one another and the community that the county's progress had been possible only through cooperative efforts. The county had to continue to build consensus for the good of all.[72]

It was a challenge far greater than that posed by the disgruntled farmers or even the mobsters of the fifties. The community held together. At times the industrial development efforts struggled as it swam against the tide of the state's national image. The same people who worked to maintain racial harmony continued to do industrial development. The workload reached a crescendo of activity. Only a community effort could have accomplished so much. The resulting industrial growth was taken as proof that community development, building strong community ties, was the prime ingredient in economic expansion.

In 1967 and 1968, Lee County gained more manufacturing jobs than the remaining 81 counties of the state combined![73] If the state's business leaders had doubted the value of community development as a prologue to economic growth, those doubts could be erased. In two decades, the county had been transformed from one of the state's poorest to one of its most successful.

In 1950, Lee County had 1,740 manufacturing jobs; by 1969 it had 9,600. The annual manufacturing payroll had increased more than tenfold from $4 million in 1950 to $42 million in 1960. The number of manufacturing jobs had elevated Lee County from eleventh to third in the state. Lee County had 88 industries. It had met its goal of diversification. Of the 19 major categories of manufacturing, Lee County had 15. The county had been true to its principle of seeking smaller industries. None of the factories employed more than 700 persons. The largest manufacturing employer was the locally owned Reed Manufacturing with just under 700 employees.[74]

The whole county had benefited. The population loss in rural Lee County had been halted and reversed. After respective losses of 17 percent of the open-country (outside municipalities) population during the 1940s and 20 percent of the open-country population during the following decade, even the open-country population had grown. Every small municipality in the county increased its population. Verona, the site of the county's first industrial park, gained almost 128 percent. Plantersville and Saltillo grew by 59 percent and 56 percent respectively.[75]

The town's community development efforts, even in the midst of the turmoil, earned it national recognition. Moreover, it has distinguished itself with its willingness to address racial issues. Thus in 1967, the National Civic League awarded Tupelo the status of an All-America City. It was the first southern city to win the award.[76]

Naturally, Tupelo and Lee County celebrated its distinctive honor. Tupelo and Lee County do not take their accomplishments for granted and celebration is an integral part of their activities. They do it annually at the CDF closing banquet and for other special occasions, but it is usually accompanied with plans for future work.

Therefore, it was not surprising that as the decade of the sixties drew to a close and Tupelo came closer to its centennial celebration, the theme chosen was "The Second Hundred Years." Leadership took their preparation seriously and invested thousands of man-hours in planning for the future at least one decade at a time.[77]

Included in the construction of those plans was assessment by external consultants, deemed to be at the vanguard of economic development. After considering the outside perspective, the CDF Board of Directors prepared ten-year-objectives and then identified annual projects that would move the community toward its long-range goals. This method of planning has subsequently become incorporated in the operations of CDF. At the beginning of each decade, a team of evaluators spend a week examining a vital aspect of economic development and prepare an elaborate report. The CDF Board of Directors then sets the annual goals and the professional CDF staff prepares the projects to achieve the goals.

In 1970, major changes had already occurred which demanded that Tupelo rethink its relationship to the county. As noted above, the economic changes had brought prosperity and population growth to the other municipalities in the county. It was the largest population gain that any of these municipalities outside Tupelo had ever experienced. They were now in a position to work as more active partners in future development.

Recognizing this reality, one of the first actions was to form the Lee County Council of Governments (COG) that drew all of the county's municipalities into a working unit. One of the first activities of the Council of Governments was to establish an Industrial Development Assistance Commission. Its areas of operation were: (1) site location surveys, (2) site analysis surveys, (3) industrial related research, (4) industrial promotion and (5) industrial support systems. In addition, COG conducted an analysis of the labor market in the council area. The Council of Governments set job creation as its number one priority.[78]

There was no question that Lee County's plans for the new century would begin with job creation. The task was twofold. The community would continue to enhance its role as a manufacturing center. It would also create the human infrastructure to create jobs in the service sector.

As a manufacturing center, Lee County needed major improvements in the transportation system that served it. The county had become a hub for manufacturing despite the fact that it was more than 70 miles from the nearest four-lane Interstate. It was a sore point, that this community that had pioneered in good roads had subsequently been unable to develop or influence the building of a solid transportation system.

Lee County leaders, therefore, took the initiative to create a grassroots groundswell for a massive four-lane highway program for the state. It began by involving most of the prime movers in northeast Mississippi. They formed an organization with the acronym H.O.P.E. (Highways Our Pressing Emergency). By June 1971, the group was ready for its first concerted action. More than 800 leaders from 14 counties rode chartered buses to the state capitol in Jackson. There they sought to rally the legislators behind their cause. Legislators offered sympathetic words, but nothing substantial.[79]

It would be a long hard battle. Over the next half-decade, George McLean would spend much of his time as a transportation advisor to the governor and president of H.O.P.E. In these roles, he coordinated support for highways both at the local and state level. Unfortunately, the legislation was not approved until 1987.

Meanwhile in Tupelo a manufacturing milestone was reached, though it could not have been recognized at the time. A. E. "Bo" Bland and Wilbert G. "Mickey" Holliman, who had learned the furniture business while working for Morris Futorian, broke from Futorian in 1970 to form their own furniture company, Action Industries. It was a modest beginning with only 40 employees. In 1972, however, Action Industries merged with Lane Furniture Company.[80] During the course of the next 20 years, Action became the largest single manufacturing employer in the county.

Even more important, their success seemed to trigger a succession of entrepreneurs who departed Futorian and began their own companies, some in barns, some in equally modest barnlike structures.

The whole area was abuzz as bright, hardworking individuals saw their chance and seized it. Hasell Franklin in Houston, Gerald Washington in Pontotoc, Hugh McClarty in Blue Mountain, and later Jim Muffi in Nettleton all built companies worth millions of dollars each in a relatively short time. These small communities, unable to attract outside capital for industries were now benefiting from local investment.

Not since the original settlers had the area been so alive with entrepreneurial activity. The work was hard but the rewards could be great. Moreover, furniture construction required limited initial capital. The basic skills could be learned quickly. The raw materials and supplies were readily available. Some of the companies that in time were to do millions of dollars in business began by hauling their finished product to furniture stores in the back of pickup trucks. Bold entrepreneurs, in some cases with less than a high school diploma, raised themselves to annual net earnings in the seven figures.[81]

Lee County was on its way to becoming the center of the upholstered furniture industry. With Tupelo as the supplier hub, the furniture factories were clustered in the ten counties within 60 miles of Tupelo. Some of them were located in little more than open fields, far from an established industrial park.

The furniture they produced had common features. Almost all was upholstered. Much was motion furniture, reclining chairs, sectional pieces that could be easily rearranged, and some sleeper couches. It was targeted for the lower end of the market, what is called "promotional furniture" in the trade. Only a limited number of the early factories produced goods for the moderate to higher-end market.[82]

The rush toward the furniture industry further helped to unite the economy of all of northeast Mississippi though only a few visionaries and the furniture manufacturers understood the interconnectedness of the area's economy. Nevertheless, cooperative efforts, such as the H.O.P.E. expedition gave evidence of increasing regional identity.

Equally important, the burgeoning furniture industry provided the area with a manufacturing base that was certain to extend into the next century. Even with the automation of many industries that would reduce jobs, northeast Mississippi was for the foreseeable future an industrial area. From this point forward, northeast Mississippi regularly paced the state in the creation of manufacturing jobs.

For this reason, CDF's long-range plans were certain to begin with strengthening its manufacturing base. In 1971, it began work on two industrial parks, one north of town to complement its park south of town. During the next two years, CDF and local governments invested $1.2 million in the two centers.[83]

By the mid-seventies Lee County began to attract industries at the mid-to-higher technology level. These were industries that required extensive computerization and robotics. Tecumseh, which makes refrigeration compressors for air-conditioners and other cooling appliances, was the first of this newer breed.

The home plant in Tecumseh, Michigan, was in the midst of a labor strike when the company began to look for an alternative site. The original attraction to Lee County was the availability of the right-sized building which had been abandoned by Panellyte. Tecumseh officials had strong reservations about the quality of the work force.[84]

This gave CDF a chance to demonstrate its coordinating abilities. Working with Larry Otis, the director of Tupelo's Itawamba Junior College, CDF committed to help prepare the labor. Otis traveled to Michigan to study the company's existing plant and training program. Returning to Mississippi, he quickly established a system to prepare the labor force. This effort grew into an ongoing training program that is still functioning in 1993. It is typical of CDF's work. CDF spends most of its time assisting existing businesses and maintaining its high quality of community services.[85]

This type of effort has become routine for CDF and its professional staff. As operations have become increasingly sophisticated and specialized, a professional staff of approximately 15 individuals evolved to maintain the high-quality programs. They initiate projects such as the labor training programs, infrastructure improvement, creation of industrial parks, conducting labor analyses, and generating and maintaining current accurate data that is used in industrialization development.

A microcosm of the work of CDF is apparent in the preparation and facilitation of the annual CDF banquet. The staff handles all coordinating activities including the preparation of elaborate and appropriate industrial displays and decorations. On the evening of the banquet, they will serve and feed more than 1,500 people. The program will include a carefully orchestrated expression of gratitude to the hundreds of people who have assisted with the previous year's activities, including technical assistants from across the nation. There will be four speakers, including a summary of the previous year's accomplishments, plans for the new year, speeches by the executives of the newest industries, the introduction of new board members and a plaque to the out-going chairman of the board.

The punctuality of the program is so precise that when the program begins, one could set her timepiece at 6:00 p.m. When the first speaker moves to the platform, she can check the accuracy of that timepiece because it will be 7:00 p.m.; this, after serving and feeding 1,500 people. She can make a second check of that timepiece when the meeting is adjourned and it will be 8:00 p.m. Distinguished and honored guests will be transported to the country club for a more relaxed reception, while the staff remains to clean up. All of this will occur with calmness and deliberateness. It will include all of the proper decorum. One of the most startling aspects of the whole affair is that almost none of the 1,500 guests are amazed at the professional proficiency with which they have been surrounded. It is all taken as a matter of course. Almost everyone expects this type of performance from the CDF staff. The most remarkable feature is that these professionals have worked at this level of efficiency almost every day of the year for over four decades. It is a tribute to the staff and its president, Harry Martin.

Neither the professional staff nor the 1,100 dues-paying members of CDF can relax, however. The ultimate challenge for any economic development program is to adjust to the external economic and social shifts. The most visionary leaders understood in 1970 that manufacturing would undergo major shifts away from low-skilled labor and toward more capital intensive industries. They understood that service jobs would surpass those in the manufacturing sector, probably within the decade of the seventies.

As such transitions occur, jobs are bound to be lost as well as created. It is estimated that even healthy economies will often lose 7 to 8 percent of its jobs in a year.[86] Thus all economic development programs must consistently work toward job replacement. One can argue that job replacement has become the central task of economic development. There can be no resting on past achievements.

With that understanding, Lee County leaders began to rethink the human infrastructure necessary for future economic development. Education, it was determined, would form the centerpiece of that infrastructure. Consequently, Tupelo and Lee County turned its attention to strengthening its educational system.

Tupelo leaders understood that reinvestment of a portion of the economic gains was essential for any subsequent growth. Consequently, the town and county working jointly proposed to spend $700,000 for a new vocational technical center, which would serve both the Tupelo and Lee County school systems. Voters concurred with their vote of 777 to 198.[87] This training could help provide the growing need for workers in the factories.

The *Journal* kept the community's focus on education and the community effort required to build a good educational system. McLean, the visionary, always planning for the future, ever the social architect, erecting organizations and constructing social bridges, again generated yet another social edifice. He knew that the long-range plans being formulated would require large pools of money. For that reason, in 1972 he established a community foundation that would serve as a reservoir to collect funds. The acronym for this organization was CREATE, (Christian, Research, Education, Action, Technical Enterprise).[88] His expectation was for the community to take advantage of tax laws and contribute to a locally controlled, tax-exempt foundation. Per usual, McLean was the largest contributor. Eventually, he willed the *Journal* and its holdings to CREATE.

Tupelo's leaders, never ones to think small, knew that much of the nation's future economic growth would center around universities. With that in mind, they gained local support to call for legislation that would allow a branch of The University of Mississippi to be built in Tupelo.[89]

By 1974, that dream was realized with the opening of the Tupelo branch of The University of Mississippi. It was built on property belonging to the City of Tupelo adjacent to Itawamba Junior College (later Itawamba Community College) and leased to the university. Funds for a Resource Center, which served both campuses were channeled through the newly established CREATE, Inc.

Two years later in 1976, McLean, still concerned that a greater share of the economic gains should go to the poorest people in the community, made a public pledge. He called for more support and investment in the county schools whose budgets were far below those of the city system. For his part he stated, "Mrs. McLean and I and the *Daily Journal* pledge to you that we shall do our full part. We ask each of you to join us in this pledge."[90]

As always George and Anna Keirsey McLean, his wife, delivered on their pledge. Working with the School of Education at Mississippi State University, they developed a Reading Aide program that eventually placed a reading aide in each of the classes in grades one through three in all of Lee County schools. To fund the program, the McLeans spent $150,000 a year of their own money for the next ten years.

At the beginning of the experiment the students were reading at only the twenty-third percentile level, near the bottom of the nation's average. Within five years they had progressed to the sixty-eighth percentile and eventually approached the ninetieth percentile. The program was so successful that it helped promote Mississippi's first publicly funded statewide kindergarten in 1982.[91]

Concurrent to the educational experiment in Lee County, the Tupelo Public Schools selected Dr. Julian Prince in 1976 as the new superintendent of schools.[92] Prince was an ideal team member in Tupelo's development program. Prince, too, thought big. He knew schools. He knew the educational literature and he was a visionary. The new superintendent saw in Tupelo's community development effort an opportunity to build a good school that could help blaze the way to a stronger community. As part of his self-assigned responsibilities he wrote a weekly education column in the *Journal*. In time it became the single most frequently read column in the newspaper. His efforts complemented those of other community leaders who understood the vital role of education in subsequent development.

By the time he left the system to become dean of education at Sanford College, he had helped mold one of the best schools in the state. A year after he left, the Ford Foundation and Harvard's Kennedy School of Government recognized the town and school as having one of the ten best public-private efforts in the nation.[93]

The focus on education, like a giant avalanche, spilled over into the 1980s where it gained even more momentum. CDF maintained its emphasis on education as the basic infrastructure in economic development. To that end, CDF continued its annual industry-education day. On that day almost 1,000 teachers, school administrators, and businessmen meet for the entire day to better articulate the link between education and industry.[94]

CDF formed a partnership with T.V.A. to establish the National Model for Career Technical Education. This program integrated the activities of the public school's vocational technical program with the vocational programs at Itawamba Junior College. By beginning training in high school and continuing it in junior college, young laborers could bring strong labor skills to the marketplace. The program also strengthened both the public school and junior college by eliminating turf battles of earlier years.[95]

Four years later, in 1986, CDF built on the success of this program by once again linking with T.V.A., Itawamba Junior College, and IBM to establish a model literacy lab for the Southeastern United States. The program, titled Principles of the Alphabet Literacy System (PALS), had been pioneered by IBM. The technology employed interactive animated video with a computer stored voice that enabled nonreaders to associate sounds with letters, letters with words, and to use words to create sentences. It was a major first step in assisting school dropouts who were virtually untrainable without at least minimal literacy skills.[96]

CDF is currently working to improve the facilities for vocational education. The organization has already raised $2.5 million. It continues its affiliations with T.V.A. and has added liaisons with the State Department of Public Education, CREATE, and the State Community College Commission. All are forming a partnership with the vocational programs at Northeast Mississippi Community College and Itawamba Community College to promote this Northeast Mississippi Technology Initiative.[97]

Not even the death of one of the area's education champions, George McLean, in 1983, slowed the community's resolve to improve its schools. In the year that McLean died, Lewis Whitfield, a bank president with Deposit Guaranty, founded a grassroots movement to promote private donations to the Tupelo Public Schools. Whitfield's organization, the Association for Excellence in Education, attracted 400 families who combined their support and contributions. The program now provides approximately $150,000 per year for school use.[98]

This strong bedrock support complemented efforts by CDF, the *Journal*, and Julian Prince. It captured the town's attention with the same zealous spirit that marked the initial RCDC movement. It had the buoyant optimism that characterized the infant years of individual development. It has been an infectious effort in which local individuals at all levels can participate, unlike the more sophisticated and professional process of industrial development of the 1980s. What had begun as the community's effort to make education the infrastructure of industrial growth had now been transformed to make education the infrastructure of the horizontal ties within the community. The school system was becoming the community's pet project, its jewel in the crown of economic development. The town now had enough wealth, thanks to the jobs' program, and it could afford a good school system.

Support for the school has continued to grow. The city appropriated over $1.25 million to the Quality Leap Forward to reduce the teacher-student ratio.[99]

Later, a local businessman, L. D. Hancock, gave the school $3.5 million dollars in property to fund a Learning Center for the teachers. Using these funds, the school can spend between one and two thousand dollars per teacher to improve their teaching skills or allow them to develop teaching projects.[100]

The whole community demonstrated its support for the school when the town passed the largest school bond issue in the state's history, $17 million. And in 1990, at a time when school bonds are being defeated across the nation, the school bond issue passed with an 88 percent approval.[101]

Such local efforts, given the proper vertical ties can have consequences for a much broader audience. In this case they did. Jack Reed's involvement with local schools led him to chair the state's board of education. His success at that level catapulted him into the gubernatorial race and eventually to the chairmanship of the National Advisory Council on Education Research and Improvement. The same visibility led the state to select Tupelo's school superintendent, Richard Thompson, to be the state's superintendent of education. These same vertical ties have fed new information and resources back to the local level. As this has occurred, the momentum for school reform has mounted.

For many in Tupelo, the school has become the central showpiece. The public-private cooperation manifested in Association for Excellence in Education won a national award. The Ford Foundation and Harvard's Kennedy School of Government identified the town's work as one of the ten best public-private cooperative efforts in the nation. The same program was cited by the selection committee of the National Civic League when it named the city an All-America City for the second time in 1989.[102]

The school's academic program is acknowledged to be one of the best in the state. Its academic decathlon team has won the state's academic decathlon every one of the eight years of its existence. Led by local student Mit Robertson, who placed second in the nation in 1992 and fifth in 1993, the decathlon team also finished as one of the top teams in the nation. These and other achievements have prompted local leaders to think in terms of making the school one of the best in the nation.[103]

Not only does the school perform well in academics but in athletics as well. Its athletic program has been rated the best in the state for six consecutive years. During that time, Tupelo has won state titles in football, baseball (twice), soccer, and cross-country track.[104]

CDF's economic development program followed a parallel course of the educational program including being named as one of the ten best economic development programs in the nation in 1987 by the Industrial Development Research Council.[105] Education and economic development followed similar courses because the same spirit of community that sparked economic growth was the driving force for the school support. As noted frequently, education and economic development were also united by design. CDF leaders had championed education as a means of raising the quality of the labor force and thereby making the area more attractive to industry. Good schools also added to the overall attractiveness to new business. Lastly, the educational vibrance was fueled by the town's economic gains and from the deeply held belief that the community's wealth should be used to improve the quality of life, especially by providing opportunities for the children.

Investment in the educational infrastructure was now the central component in community development. These efforts, combined with improved transportation, enlarged industrial parks, and the extensive services provided through the Community Development Foundation helped make Lee County even more attractive to industry. In a very real sense, the jobs were the fruit of community development. Jobs were created in even-greater numbers during the 1980s despite a national economy in which most nonmetropolitan towns were losing ground economically.[106]

During a nine-year span from 1983 to 1991, Lee County averaged 1,033 new manufacturing jobs per year for a gross total of 9,297. There were, of course, the accompanying job deaths, but the county managed a net gain of 3,120 jobs for the 1980s.[107] CDF continued its ability at job replacement and even had succeeded in replacing the defunct Pennsylvania Tire Company with Cooper Tire Company that employed even more people than its predecessor. Moreover, Cooper was another midlevel technology industry which required higher labor skills and paid higher wages.

One of the major accomplishments of the community and CDF was its ability to come to the aid of its existing companies that were being buffeted by the tides of international competition. CDF provided labor training and other support to assist the companies through a transition period. Managers of some factories confided that they would not have survived had it not been for the efforts of the community.[108]

During that same period Lee County attracted international companies from the Netherlands, Canada, Australia, and Switzerland. In the 1990s, CDF could boast of "The Tupelo Area's Global Connection" as part of its annual theme.[109]

Manufacturing employment had increased from less than 2,000 jobs in 1950 to more than 17,000 in 1992, more than an eightfold increase. During that time the manufacturing payroll grew from $3.95 million to $339 million, almost a tenfold increase. (See Tables 7.2 and 7.3) Thus wages per job were also accelerating and producing greater individual wealth.[110] In 1989, Lee County boasted of 29 Fortune 500 companies. It had more than 15,000 employees in manufacturing, which constituted 40 percent of its employment base. By the end of 1992, the county had 17,033 manufacturing jobs, the most manufacturing jobs in its history.[111]

Table 7.2

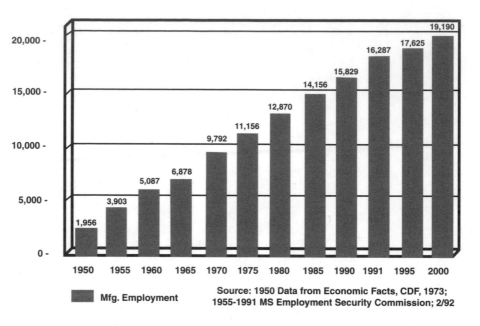

Manufacturing Employment
With Projections to the Year 2000
1950-2000

Mfg. Employment

Source: 1950 Data from Economic Facts, CDF, 1973;
1955-1991 MS Employment Security Commission; 2/92

Table 7.3

Manufacturing Payrolls
Lee County, MS
1950-1992

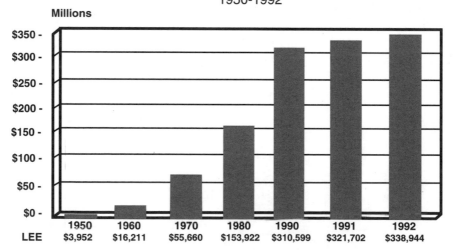

	1950	1960	1970	1980	1990	1991	1992
LEE	$3,952	$16,211	$55,660	$153,922	$310,599	$321,702	$338,944

Source: 1950 Data from 1973 CDF Econ. Facts, 1990-1991 MS Emp.
Security Comm. 1992 estimate using 3rd quarter of 1992

There were other important changes in the manufacturing base. Lee County had achieved the industrial diversification it sought. Of the 19 manufacturing categories, Lee County had employees in 18. The only category missing was the manufacture of tobacco and related products. (See Tables 7.4 and 7.5)

Table 7.4

Lee County
Number of firms by Standard Industrial Classifications (SIC)
1962-1990

Data not available for 1966 & 1988

Number of Firms

SIC	1962	1964	1968	1970	1972	1974	1976	1978	1980	1982	1984	1986	1990
20	16	22	20	19	17	14	13	12	10	8	8	8	9
21	0	0	0	0	0	0	0	0	0	0	0	0	0
22	1	0	0	0	0	0	1	1	3	3	3	3	2
23	5	8	9	9	10	11	14	14	13	12	11	11	11
24	2	3	4	4	5	6	5	6	5	6	6	6	3
25	6	7	8	11	11	11	12	17	16	14	19	19	22
26	2	2	3	2	2	3	4	5	6	6	5	5	5
27	8	7	7	5	4	4	4	4	4	4	5	5	6
28	4	2	3	3	4	5	4	5	5	5	5	5	5
29	1	1	1	0	0	0	0	1	2	1	1	1	0
30	3	2	4	6	5	6	9	9	13	13	14	14	19
31	0	0	1	1	1	1	1	1	1	1	0	0	0
32	4	6	8	7	7	6	8	8	8	8	7	7	7
33	0	0	0	0	0	0	0	0	1	1	1	1	1
34	2	5	5	5	3	4	11	13	12	10	14	14	9
35	2	4	6	5	4	5	7	10	10	9	7	7	8
36	1	1	2	2	2	2	3	3	3	3	2	2	1
37	0	0	1	1	0	0	0	0	1	1	1	1	4
38	0	0	0	0	0	0	0	0	1	1	1	1	1
39	1	0	1	0	0	0	1	0	1	0	0	0	0

Source: 1950 Data from CDF Econ Facts, 1990-1991 MS Emp.
Security Comm. 1992 estimate using 3rd quarter of 1992

Table 7.5

Standard Industrial Classifications (SIC)

20 - Food & Kindred Products
21 - Tobacco Products
22 - Textile Mill Products
23 - Apparel & Other Finished Products Made from
      Fabrics & Similar Materials
24 - Lumber & Wood Products, except Furniture
25 - Furniture & Fixtures
26 - Paper & Allied Products
27 - Printing, Publishing, & Allied Industries
28 - Chemicals & Allied Products
29 - Petroleum & Coal Products
30 - Rubber & Miscellaneous Plastic Products
31 - Leather & Leather Products
32 - Stone, Clay, Glass, & Concrete Products
33 - Primary Metal Industries
34 - Fabricated Metal Products, except Machinery &
      Transportation Equipment
35 - Machinery, except Electrical
36 - Electrical & Electronic Machinery, Equipment, &
      Supplies
37 - Transportation Equipment
38 - Measuring, Analyzing, & Controlling Instruments;
      Photographic, Medical & Optical Goods; Watches & Clocks
39 - Miscellaneous Manufacturing Industries

**Source: 1950 Data from CDF Econ Facts, 1990-1991 MS Emp. Security
Comm. 1992 estimate using 3rd quarter of 1992**

Despite Lee County's stated preference for diversification, many industries do tend to cluster in order to have the critical mass necessary to function efficiently. The furniture industry is one of these. In the process of becoming the central supplier to area furniture factories, Lee County had become the hub of the nation's upholstered furniture industry. By the late 1980s, furniture had become a billion dollar industry in northeast Mississippi. Lee County alone had 39 furniture suppliers and 41 furniture manufacturers. In the 10-county area there were 104 suppliers and 177 furniture manufacturers.[112] (See Table 7.6)

Table 7.6

Northeast Mississippi Furniture Suppliers & Manufacturers

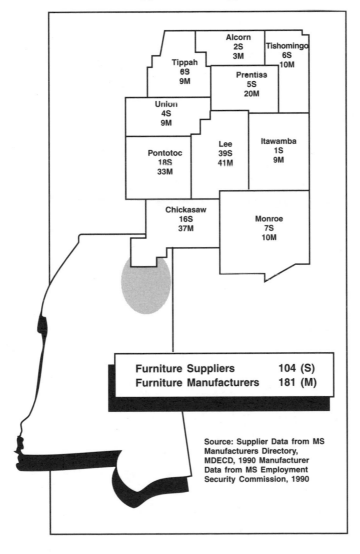

The majority of Lee County's new jobs during the 1980s came in the furniture industry. Of the 3,120 net additional jobs, 1,857 or 59 percent were accounted for in the furniture industry. Furniture production had grown faster than any other segment of the county's manufacturing economy over the past two decades. In 1970, Lee County had 1,162 workers in the furniture industry, which account-ed for 11.9 percent of the manufacturing jobs. By 1990, the county had 4,279 furniture-related jobs, accounting for 26.8 percent of the manufacturing employ-ment.[113] (See Table 7.7)

Table 7.7

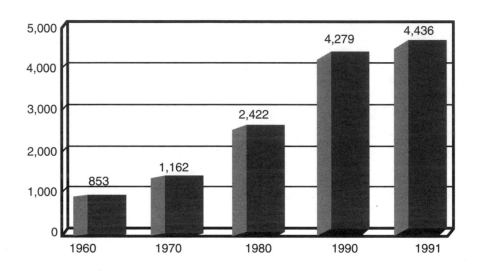

Lee County's Furniture Industry Employment

Source: MS Emp. Security Comm. Year-End
Reports, 1960, 1970, 1980, 1990, 1991

This large mass of furniture manufacturers had its own multiplier effect, by which these manufacturing jobs generated additional jobs in the area. The most obvious was the emergence of furniture markets to assist with the outlet of the products. Because many of these furniture operations were of modest size and with limited resources, it was difficult for them to display their products in the larger regional markets of High Point, North Carolina, or Atlanta. Into this niche came Ed Meek and V. M. Cleveland, who boldly challenged the larger markets by establishing a Tupelo furniture market that opened in September 1987.

By almost any standard their effort was a success. The first year they displayed in 70,000 square feet of space and attracted 88 exhibitors and more than 4,000 buyers, many of whom were area furniture retailers. A rival market soon appeared. After the two merged, Tupelo's market expanded rapidly. By 1993, the exhibition space was almost one million square feet. There were more than 6,000 exhibitors and approximately 15,000 buyers.[114]

There was an immediate impact on the local economy with a large influx of external money. The market also increased outlets and sales that benefited the area manufacturers. The presence of the market helps to complete the furniture industry's base and to better define the place and role of northeast Mississippi in the industry. It is also an important linkage in establishing a regional identity among the manufacturers and the market which, combined with the supplier base, provide tangible bonds within the region.

The furniture industry is one of the most apparent examples of the regional nature of the economy. But just as Tupelo stepped beyond its corporate boundaries after World War I, so now its economy has gone far beyond county boundaries. The newspaper, as noted earlier, had altered its name to the *Tupelo Area Journal*. By 1974, it had dropped that name in favor of the more descriptive *Northeast Mississippi Daily Journal*. Its circulation rose to 40,000 in a 15-county area, and the *Journal* had become an important area communication component. CDF affects that regionalization by publishing data under the heading of both Lee County and "Tupelo Area" or "Tupelo Trade Area."[115]

Tupelo's trade area, which covered a small region in the 1970s, expanded greatly in the 1980s. Additional retail expansion came in 1990 with a new regional mall called the Mall at Barnes Crossing. Its very presence and location bespoke its regional outreach. It was placed far north of the city in an open field at the intersection of U.S. Highways 78 and 45.

The banks also expanded their trade area with mergers that made them even more dominant. As the regional financial center they have established branches in many of the surrounding towns.

The North Mississippi Medical Center is a prime example of Tupelo's role as a regional service center. It is also an example of the fruits and reciprocal nature of community development. Tupelo's original hospital had a modest beginning. In 1920, several local physicians worked in tandem to gain use of the abandoned Y.M.C.A. building near the downtown section. This facility was soon determined to be too small. For almost a decade a local physician, L. C. Feemster, led the effort to establish a completely new hospital. Dr. Feemster and others attracted the attention of the Commonwealth Fund, which had assisted other rural areas to build hospitals. After a courtship of almost eight years, the Commonwealth Fund agreed to a coupling of the fund and Tupelo. A basic condition of the agreement called for local residents to raise $50,000 of the required $300,000 cost of the hospital.

Raising the money was a test of the area's commitment to development in the community. It was also an endeavor that helped unify the community. Between 1935 and 1936, local leaders generated $48,000. Then came the disastrous tornado in April 1936. The town was decimated. Officials from the Commonwealth Fund toured the devastation and concluded that the hospital was needed immediately and moved to eliminate the necessity of raising an additional $2,000. Construction began soon thereafter. In October 1937, the town completed an attractive hospital set on a hill overlooking the town.

The success of the effort buoyed the community's confidence and brought community and hospital together for what proved to be a strong union. Following World War II, local initiatives attracted still more funds from the Hill-Burton Hospital Program. The use of the federal monies almost doubled the number of hospital beds from 50 in 1937 to 95 when the addition opened in 1950. The North Mississippi Community Hospital, as it was then named, became an important regional resource when it added a large mental health complex. To reflect its enlarged services and regional mission, the name was changed to its current one, the North Mississippi Medical Center (NMMC) in that same year of 1967.

Within a decade, in 1977 the medical center undertook the largest hospital construction and renovation project in the state's history. The North Mississippi Medical Center began a capital campaign that raised $3,100,000 from local contributors between January 1977 and August 1979. The feat underscored the community's policy of reinvesting the money earned through economic development. These initial monies were leveraged to initiate a $26 million construction effort. As a memorial to the project, a local artist, Ke Francis, worked with local citizens to celebrate the community project with a dedication story, which was enshrined in a time capsule. Francis described the time capsule and its contents as a "symbol of the strength and unity between North Mississippi Medical Center and the community served." He added that the time capsule was created as a "monument to that feeling of community which is present here in Lee County. It is a way of showing the human concerns of the people employed at the Medical Center are an outgrowth of the concerns of this community for its people."

Community leaders understood that the medical center was a means of meeting community and regional health needs while strengthening the economy. The community and the medical center have continued to extend the regional services of the medical center by establishing community hospitals, family medical clinics, and mobile technology and home care in its 22-county service area.

In 1990, NMMC began its first family medical clinic in neighboring Pontotoc County. By 1993, it had established family medical clinics in 11 of the 22 counties served. At present, North Mississippi Health Services has 17 clinics and a hospital that emanate from the main hub of the 644-bed North Medical Center. The center has developed a health program that covers more than 66,000 clients.

The center is a direct participant in the county's job creation effort. As noted earlier, it is the county's largest employer with a total payroll of 4,100 employees. In addition, it makes the county even more attractive in seeking new and expanded industry. Among its numerous medical centers, which includes a Woman's Hospital, a Wellness Center, Same Day Surgery Center, Behavioral Health Center, and Cancer Center, the NMMC has also added a Center for Business Health, and an Industrial Work Center. The Center for Business Health provides occupational health services to the area's industries and businesses. The Industrial Work Center offers functional capacity evaluations and other programs to help injured workers regain some or all of their capabilities.

NMMC can boast that it contributes directly and indirectly to the profits of local industries. It provides direct health care that prevents injuries and illnesses. Therefore, there is less loss of job time. The medical center has rehabilitative programs for those who are ill or injured, which helps them to return to work more quickly. The medical center has been able to keep medical costs at a lower level of increase, 3.4 percent per year over a three-year period, as compared to the national average of 8.1 percent per year during that same span from 1990-1993. In 1993, NMMC's budget had a remarkably impressive 0 percent increase.

The September 27 cover story of a 1993 *U.S. News & World Report* cites the parent corporation North Mississippi Health Services and the North Mississippi Medical Center as one of the model health maintenance organizations (HMOs) in the nation. The article suggests that local success stories such as that achieved by NMMC can serve as an effective model for the national health reform movement.

The medical center, the banks, and regional mall also symbolize the gradual shift toward service jobs. Even with the ongoing increase in manufacturing jobs, the number of service positions in the county now constitute the majority. [116]

Nevertheless, the growth of service jobs reduces only slightly Lee County's dependence on manufacturing because the multiplier effect of those manufacturing jobs continues to support many of the jobs in the service industry in a way similar to the way that agriculture once dominated the retail trade in the town. By 1992, Lee County's 17,033 manufacturing jobs accounted for approximately 39 percent of the county's overall employment of 43,744. This is quite different from the job distribution in the state and nation. In Mississippi as a whole, 28 percent of the workers are employed in manufacturing and only 17 percent of the nation's work force is employed in manufacturing.[117] (See Table 7.8.)

Table 7.8

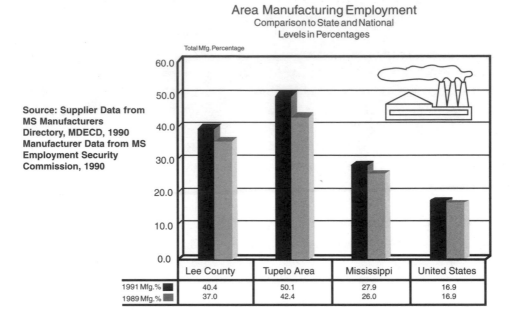

Source: Supplier Data from
MS Manufacturers
Directory, MDECD, 1990
Manufacturer Data from MS
Employment Security
Commission, 1990

Area Manufacturing Employment
Comparison to State and National
Levels in Percentages

Total Mfg. Percentage

	Lee County	Tupelo Area	Mississippi	United States
1991 Mfg.%	40.4	50.1	27.9	16.9
1989 Mfg.%	37.0	42.4	26.0	16.9

Lee County's growing service-based economy, as in other towns and cities, has influenced the emergence of the arts by providing the critical mass that can support such endeavors. Consequently, Tupelo has a symphony with more than 1,000 dues-paying patrons. The theater group has a similar number of supporters. The town's art gallery has a Main Street address in the prestigious old Peoples Bank Building.[118] The enhancement of the quality of life also has commercial consequences for manufacturing. Industrial managers confide that these amenities contribute to attracting new industries and help retain existing industries when they consider expansion.

The growth and transition have also brought crises and new tests to the area. Local merchants must now compete with chain stores eager to make a profit without having made the same investments in the community that local businessmen have made. In a second crisis, the town outgrew its water supply but with its characteristically strong team effort, local leaders reached out to area leaders to form the Northeast Mississippi Regional Water Supply District. They utilized the best technical assistance available and financed the effort with a 96 percent positive vote on the water bond issue.[119] The county moved through a crisis that could have halted its growth and did so with almost no wasted motion. The leaders have become adept at problem solving.

Perhaps the most severe test in the 1980s came with the death of George McLean. Many observers, from both inside and outside the community, were certain that his death would curtail the community's progress. But while his vibrant style and contributions were missed, the progress continued.

McLean received many honors in life: *Nation* magazine's Man of the Year (1937), *Progressive Farmer's* Man of the Year (1948), T.V.A.'s first Distinguished Citizen Award (1981), and hundreds of other citations. Yet the most lasting tribute may be that the work he helped initiate continued after his lifetime. It has been suggested that the real test of a leader's effectiveness is found in the achievements of the constituents.[120] Measured by that and almost any standard McLean was a successful leader.

Lee County's success has never depended on one individual, though its achievements in the postwar period were hinged to organizations such as CDF, the *Journal,* and local banks. During this period, Tupelo developed strong leadership teams who could disagree personally but maintain focus on community interest. They have had an effective coordinating agency that has encouraged and facilitated teamwork and team building.

Tupelo and Lee County's success is rooted in leaders who are generalists, that is, leaders who are actively involved with many phases of community life as opposed to specialized leaders who work on single issues. In a study conducted by Harold Kaufman more than a quarter of a century ago, Kaufman found that Tupelo's strength was not in having more leaders than do other towns, but in having more generalist leaders.[121] Subsequent studies in other towns have also concluded that generalist leadership is critical to community development.[122]

These generalist leaders work as social architects. They create service agencies that implement projects and programs. They build organizations that enhance potential. They construct vibrant horizontal ties within the community and durable effective vertical links to external agencies. They continually encourage and develop new leadership.

Thus when George McLean died, his widow, Anna Keirsey, took charge of a young *Journal* staff, maintained its concentration on community issues, and increased the paper's circulation and its profitability. She was a board member of AHEAD, a grassroots support group for highways. This group concluded the work begun by George McLean with his highway group HOPE. Mrs. McLean sponsored educational programs and helped found a leadership development program for all of northeast Mississippi.

Similarly, J. C. Whitehead, while serving as president and CEO of the Bank of Mississippi also chaired the Northeast Mississippi Regional Water Supply District that resolved the water crisis, chaired the board of North Mississippi Medical Center, served on the executive board of CDF and countless other community boards. Jack Reed has continued to work on projects ranging from Boy Scouts, to downtown associations, local, state, and national educational advisory boards. Lewis Whitfield's community services range from chairing the CDF's executive board, founding educational support groups, helping to develop a free medical clinic, and numerous other community services. Billy Crews, McLean's successor as publisher of the *Journal* coordinated area legislators to bring added clout for the area, helped establish Habitat for Humanity in Northeast Mississippi, worked on the Reading Aide program, and developed one of the area's best day care centers, all as a volunteer beyond his duties at the newspaper.

The community continues to work through existing agencies and constructs new ones as the need arises. Through the effort of CREATE that contributes almost a million dollars a year, the community invests time and money to raise the quality of life of all its citizens.[123] In an intrepid move, CREATE has sponsored a free medical clinic with more than 100 citizen volunteers and a volunteer medical staff of 75.

CREATE and its director William Parham are currently funding an area development plan as the community continues its outreach program to the entire region.

CHAPTER 8

The Last to Organize:
The Black Experience in Tupelo/Lee County

The black experience in Tupelo and Lee County has many of the characteristics of black history in other parts of the region and nation. In one sense, African-Americans play a central role in the county's economy. They are a major source of cheap labor in an economic system built on low-paying jobs. Yet in the broader perspective they have been almost invisible to much of the white community. In Tupelo, they have always occupied only a small, residential area that is out of sight of much of the white community. For almost all of the county's history, these biracial communities intersect only at a limited number of points.

Most observers of Tupelo and Lee County describe the community as a model for "good race relations." Tupelo/Lee County, unlike many other small southern towns has almost always followed a moderate path that avoids polarization and confrontation. The overwhelming majority of the white population believes strongly in the principles of fair play. The community prides itself in trying to "do the right thing for all of its people." But also like most towns and cities in the United States, the white population has not been fully sensitive of the barriers faced by the minority population nor the role, often unintended, of the white population in the placement of those barriers. For any community leader who views his own community as immune to racial strife, Tupelo's experience can be an important teaching tool.

For much of the county's history, the folkways governing race relations have almost always been rigid. In "respectable" white society, black people were not disliked, and were never to be consciously mistreated, but the matter of segregation was not debatable. The two communities were to remain separate and clearly defined roles regulated the behavior of each race. These views, like strong southern kudzu vines, wrapped themselves around all they touched and covered the whole landscape of the society. Sometimes these engulfing views have been almost suffocating in their intensity and pervasiveness.

Despite the reality of a biracial society, blacks and whites shared a common dream. They all wanted a good life for themselves and a better life for their children. Unfortunately, the means of achieving those goals were never the same.

One needs to go back to the beginning to understand how far blacks have come and the obstacles they have had to surmount. In 1870, only 14 families of the 58 black families in Tupelo listed any personal or real estate in the town's first census. With the exception of the town's two negro blacksmiths, none of these property owners reported assets of as much as $100. There were no black professionals; even the ministers toiled as common laborers during the week.[1]

More than three-fourths of the black population ten years of age or older were illiterate. In 1870, only 52 minority children in the entire county were listed in the census as attending school.[2] Within Tupelo the only black students were the children of the black property owners.[3] None of the ministers had any formal training and many were themselves illiterate, having gained their knowledge of the Bible from listening to other preachers.[4]

In the early years, blacks had no political clout. During the 1870s, the Democratic Party controlled all town and county offices and whites controlled the Democratic Party. At election time, the Ku Klux Klan became better organized and more visible. If threats by hooded horsemen were not sufficient to intimidate local blacks, other types of intimidation were employed. On election day, all the cannons in the county were hauled near polling places where they were fired at regular intervals. Pistols were blatantly displayed by roving bands of white men. As a final precaution against black success, clerks at the ballot box had a pocket filled with marked ballots. These would be substituted for the blacks' ballots, which were thrust into a separate pocket.[5]

For the past 125 years blacks have sought to improve their lot by following one or more of four primary courses. They could commit a kind of lemming suicide by hurling themselves into the face of oppression; manipulate the system with a B'rer Rabbit-type cunning; organize and make gains for the larger group; or they could move and hope for a better life in a distant land. There have been very few who followed the first of these possibilities; a heavy amount of the second, especially since blacks have always been in the minority. At their largest, the black population was only 30 percent of the total in the nineteenth century. This ratio shrank to 21 percent midway through the twentieth century. Organization as an instrument of improvement has varied throughout history. Migration has been a constant means of social improvement.

Migration began shortly after the end of the Civil War. Vernon Wharton, writing about former slaves throughout the South, concluded that "there was enough moving about in the summer and fall of 1865 to give the impression that a large part of the population was on the march."[6] Carl Schurz described freedmen who "walked away merely for the purpose of leaving the places on which they had been held in slavery."[7]

Within Tupelo, there were 58 separate black households in 1870. By 1880 only

24 of the original households had representatives still living in the town of Tupelo.[8] It is estimated that no more than six of the families could have disappeared entirely from the survey as a result of death.[9] This would mean that at least 54 percent of the black population migrated from there during the decade of the seventies.

Such a mobility rate would not be unusually high for the period. One study of migration found that 49 percent of the former slaves from small plantations in the deep South had relocated in a new area within a decade after the end of the Civil War.[10] Tupelo's black outmigration was similar also to non-southern rural communities of the period. Trempealeau County, Wisconsin, had an outmigration of 71 percent, while Roseburg, Oregon, and two agricultural sections in Kansas experienced outward movements of 66, 56, and 41 percent.[11] Nor were such high mobility rates restricted to rural settlements. Cities as diverse in region and size as Waltham, Massachusetts; Poughkeepsie, New York; Atlanta, Georgia; San Francisco, California; and San Antonio, Texas, had at least half their populations to move during the 1870s.[12]

For the next century, migration for blacks, as for other Americans, was a common means of improving one's social position. It was a selective migration. Those blacks who owned their homes or who had skilled positions were much less likely to migrate. Thus, migration served as a safety valve by which those individuals with the fewest horizontal ties tended to move to other parts of the nation. This may explain why the frustration of poverty rarely caused a social explosion. There was always the possibility of migration with the expectation of a better life.

For those who remained, there have been individual blacks who have achieved wealth, power, and status both within the black community and in the broader community as a whole. Blacks, like other Americans, have pursued the same sense of privatism that has marked the search for the good life. But Lee County's black population, like its white counterpart, has also found strength in organization.

Lee County's blacks first found the power of organization in the 1880s. Initial leverage came from the high rate of mobility and the threat to move. Whites who were dependent on black labor were concerned that unless life improved for their workers in Lee County, almost all that labor force might leave the area. After the 1880 census confirmed the outmigration, the local newspaper editor called for improved conditions for the county's blacks as an inducement to remain in the area.

The editor wrote that black laborers were leaving the area because their wages were simply too low to permit them to survive economically.[13] Encouraged by a sympathetic rendering of their plight, blacks began to stir for the first time since the Civil War. Black farm laborers from Tupelo were at the vanguard of a Negro Farmer's Aid Society formed in 1883 to unite blacks to improve conditions.[14] Perhaps inspired by the determination of the farmers, Tupelo's black teachers followed suit by organizing the "Colored Teachers of Lee County" in the summer of the same year. Painfully aware of their own meager training, they requested that a normal school or institute be established to prepare other teachers.[15]

Strong black resolve continued to gain improvements into autumn. Shortly before election time, a group of bold black leaders called for a political rally. Approximately 100 persons gathered on a Saturday morning on the courthouse lawn to nominate a ticket for county offices. The local newspaper and no doubt many of the white townsmen attempted to pass off the group as the pawns of "some designing and unscrupulous person or persons."[16] Prominent whites, alerted to the presence and purpose of the caucus, used a familiar formula. They approached well-known, though no doubt vulnerable, blacks and "advised them in a calm and dispassionate way [of] . . . the indiscretion and bad policy of the course they proposed to pursue."[17]

Blacks held their own. The data are not clear as to the success of this specific encounter, but the black ability to organize helped to redress some of the ills of earlier decades. The decade of the 1880s was one of the best periods for blacks. They had the right to vote despite their inability to put together a political machine. The construction of the second railroad provided new job opportunities during the mid-eighties.[18] Major social events in the black neighborhoods were reported regularly in the newspapers and courtesy titles were used before the surnames of blacks in the news items. By the end of the decade, blacks achieved a major goal of having one of their own hired as a policeman in the community.[19] Concurrently hope for a viable farmer organization was still alive as blacks were swept up in the wave of Farmer Alliance movements.[20]

The unrest among farmers held out the promise of a new and brighter day for blacks in the community, many of whom were farmers themselves even though they lived within the town limits. If poor whites and blacks could become aligned in their discontent, the promised land would be in sight. The ironic turn of events described in Chapter 4 saw blacks become instead the whipping boy of frustrated white farmers and opportunistic political conservatives. The threat of organized black voters was the chief weapon used by conservatives to thwart the Populist attacks on the existing system.

Blacks came under some of the same intense pressure in the nineties that they had known in the early seventies. Politicians used the racial issue to stir their audiences into a frenzy of excitement.[21] The local newspaper printed stories designed to place blacks in a bad light. Stories of black crime or rumors of black coalitions were increasingly frequent.[22] No longer were their social events, including marriages, reported in the local news as they had been in the eighties. The practice of using courtesy titles before the surnames of blacks disappeared entirely. Pressure on them could also be direct and en masse. In the heat of the controversy, financing for additional rooms at the black school was cancelled.[23] A group of local black men had to build the rooms through their personal efforts.[24] On a state level, the Constitution of 1890 almost completely disenfranchised blacks.[25]

Expressions of frustration by blacks made little impact on the events of the emotionally turbulent nineties. The blacks had clearly lost the political encounters of the decade. The Populist Party was not able to sweep the field but the white small farmers were on the verge of controlling the elections in the state. V. O. Key refers to the Civil War as the first political crisis for the black man and the rise of populism as "the second great crisis whose influence persists."[26] Blacks in Tupelo had actually lost ground. Harold Faulkner depicted the quandary of blacks in all the "Tupelos" across the South when he wrote, "Though the white society of the South was in a better position than it had been in many years, the Negro race ... entered the most discouraging period since the emancipation in 1865."[27]

Deprived of the power of the vote, blacks continued to lose ground during the next two decades. However, the downward skid was reversed in a most curious way. The agricultural problems associated with the infestation of the boll weevil served to dislodge farm laborers, white and black. In this agricultural crisis, workers desperately needed new jobs. Employment opportunities were to be found in the factories in the Midwest and the East, many of which were operating at full speed to provide goods and materials for World War I.

The war itself brought an estimated decrease of 870,000 European immigrants and hence a reduction in the supply of cheap labor.[28] The labor shortage was compounded by the loss of workers to the armed services and the demand for additional materials created by the conflict. Labor agents scoured the South promising good jobs, better housing and schools, and less discrimination. One report described these recruiters as "carrying free [railroad] tickets in their pockets and always glowing promises on their tongues."[29] The *Chicago Defender*, like the mythical Sirens, urged southern blacks to heed the "call."[30]

All of these factors served as "pulls" in the push-pull scenario of migration. At home, the cotton disaster resulting from the invasion of the boll weevil was perhaps more critical than any other "push" factor.[31] Additionally, labor recruiters and copies of the *Chicago Defender* were in the Tupelo area to take advantage of this crisis.[32] It is generally agreed that economic motives were the most compelling in the migration. The poor housing, inadequate schools, and discrimination were also major contributors to the outflow of migrants.[33]

The mass exodus during the 1910s drew over 300,000 blacks from the southeastern United States, 130,000 of whom were from Mississippi alone.[34] Lee County lost approximately 2,000 blacks as a result of the migration.[35] Moreover, the pattern and channels of mobility were established for the next half-century.[36] Such a sweeping shift of the population had the immediate effect of reducing the labor supply in the South and offered a challenge to the existing racial patterns. So significant were the changes emanating from the population shifts of the period that a leading figure in black history has referred to the experience as "the great watershed in American Negro history," following emancipation.[37]

The sharp curtailment of labor shackled the Tupelo economy for a time. One news report in 1918 told of 80 freight cars of cotton that could not be unloaded because of a labor shortage.[38] The Board of Aldermen adopted an ordinance requiring employers to issue a work card to all employees to assure that all able-bodied men were actually working. The card was to indicate the number of days the laborers worked per week. The ordinance read in part, "that all persons shall carry a card showing that they work six days in the week."[39] Persons without such a card would be brought into Police Court.[40]

The outward migration once again provided local remaining blacks with leverage. Just as in the 1880s, employers were willing to improve black living conditions as an inducement to remain in the area. This time it came in the form of improved schools. As late as 1920, almost 30 percent of the town's black population ten years of age or older was illiterate.[41] The ten-grade system had been without distinction since its inception. Heretofore, the educational program for blacks in Tupelo had never had a teacher who was a graduate of an accredited college.

Tupelo's black teachers were employed six months a year and were paid only $250 for that half-year's work. Consequently, all teachers could never be more than part-time educators.[42] These features offered little or no incentive for trained personnel. Moreover, the students themselves were poorly motivated. A majority of the black children attended school infrequently.[43]

Finally in 1923, in an attempt to remedy this problem and at the same time shore up the sagging agricultural situation, Tupelo hired A. M. Strange on a 12-month contract to serve as principal of the school and agricultural advisor to black farmers.[44] Almost immediately, Strange gained the attention and cooperation of the male students by involving them in agricultural education with a monetary payoff. Students raised crops as a part of their education and shared the profit. By the end of the year, 30 boys in his class shared a net profit of $1,825.30 for the year's work.[45]

The young educator set about gaining the involvement of adults as well as students to work toward improved physical facilities and a strengthened program. Following a visit to the school, the editor of the newspaper referred to the progress as "remarkable" after little more than a year's effort. The editor urged whites in the community to take note of the achievements and commended the cooperative spirit, which had brought the changes.[46]

It appeared for a time that the success would be short-lived. After Strange failed to secure a pledge of support from the mayor, who seemed to resent the galvanic young teacher, he left the system for a position in Clarksdale, Mississippi. A year had not passed when the normally intractable Mayor Will Robbins relented and drove to Clarksdale to urge the prodigal educator to return.[47]

In a burst of creative energy, Strange renewed his task with enhanced enthusiasm, and like the good leader that he was, he again involved the student body. Each student was urged to bring a brick to school every morning as a rather unusual entry fee. When enough bricks had been collected the students began on-the-job training in construction as they built structures for the school.[48] Without receiving a penny from the city, Strange and his students completed six buildings on the campus.[49] Concurrently, he expanded the number of grades from 10 to 12.[50] Successful programs such as the one in agriculture were continued and new ventures were launched. As a result of the school's music program, all of the churches were able to expand their musical offerings now that they had trained pianists. For years thereafter, graduates of the school formed the backbone of musical programs in all the black churches and civic clubs. The town's first symphony orchestra also resulted from the efforts of the school. It was this black symphony, which performed for President and Mrs. Roosevelt in 1933.[51]

Never before had a black-engineered endeavor received so much positive attention within the town. Blacks were stirred to a greater sense of pride and self-respect.[52] Strange was accorded a sign of deference, unique in the town's treatment of blacks, when in 1930 he was asked to address the local Rotary Club.[53] Forty years later, A. M. Strange was identified by longtime residents as one of the three most outstanding figures in the history of the black community.[54] In recognition of his contributions, the library in the predominantly black section of town was named in his honor.

Strange was able to work with a degree of autonomy that was rare for blacks in Tupelo. The community recognized that unlike some of the local black ministers, this educator was essentially his own man.[55] In ten years, the school budget provided no money for construction or maintenance and yet he built the entire school without city aid. Moreover, he brought in outstanding teachers from regions outside the South who, in turn, introduced new ideas.[56]

Tupelo's competition with other communities has been acute in maintaining men of Strange's competence. In 1933, he accepted a better offer from a nearby town and left.[57] (Interestingly, this was the year just prior to the beginning of George McLean's career in Tupelo.) The black community was never quite able to fill the void caused by his departure and the school ceased to be the rallying organization for blacks.

Strange had served as a catalyst in other efforts in the black community. During the period of his influence, Tupelo's black men moved from the background shadows to form a local chapter of the Elks Club, which in time became a center of black efforts at self-improvement.[58]

During the tenure of A. M. Strange, the school became the central source of pride and bonding point for the black community, just as the school would be for the whole community during the 1980s and early 1990s. Unfortunately however, neither Strange nor the broader community could halt completely the black out-migration. Even more unfortunately, the school lost its binding power after the departure of Strange.

Even after World War II, when civil rights issues were bubbling to the surface nationally, the black community was tentative. Black property owners were especially cautious. Years later many confided that they had expected old barriers posed by segregation and discrimination to wither through an inevitable evolutionary process that would flow naturally from the changes initiated by World War II.[59] Many black families cautioned their sons returning from the war to be very prudent in direct confrontations with the old social system. Ministers, steeped in a fundamentalist philosophy, admonished their congregations to "wait on deliverance from the Lord," and to be patient in their suffering.[60] The same advice was being given by the leaders of the Elks and Masons to their members.[61]

The excessive caution characterized the mood among whites as well. Many of these white people in Tupelo were overwhelmed by the enormity and scope of the issues and participants. As early as 1948, when the Mississippi delegation bolted from the Democratic Presidential Convention, there was a sense that the drama of the changing racial patterns was to be played on a distant stage.[62] For all their personal interest in the events, the citizens of small communities like Tupelo felt that they were more a part of the audience than the main cast. The majority of whites in the town supported the practice of segregation, but the basic strategy was a wait-and-see policy. Consequently, the attempt to establish a local chapter of the Citizen's Council, a strongly pro-segregation organization, failed when only 60 people from the entire county appeared at the organizational meeting.[63]

Blacks, too, chose to continue a waiting game. Even efforts to bring a chapter of the NAACP to Tupelo were short-lived. The only major black organization formed in the decade was the Women's Service Organization, chartered in 1952.[64]

A pivotal event in the racial turmoil of the fifties occurred when a reactionary newspaper, founded by an established journalist, sprang up in opposition to the *Journal*. Aware that many subscribers and advertisers were dissatisfied with the *Journal's* moderate stand on racial matters, the fledgling *Lee County Tribune* offered a clear alternative. The *Tribune* exhorted the people of the area not to yield ground in matters of segregation. Moderation, it argued, was the vehicle that would lead to the destruction of the South.[65] Engaging in yellow journalism, the younger paper was able to exploit the emotional racial events as it played on the greatest fears of its readers. In typical fashion a major five-part series assailed the NAACP as a communist front organization.[66] In addressing itself to black grievances, the *Tribune* followed the well-established procedure of bathing the deep social wounds of blacks in benign bromides. In an earlier time, the strategy of the foundling newspaper might have been successful. Its formula was still standard in many prosperous newspapers across the state. The failure of the *Tribune* to undermine the support of the *Journal* reflects well on the support for the *Journal* and it also suggests the rejection by Lee countians of this confrontational style format of the *Tribune*.

The *Journal* had been the voice of racial moderation since George McLean assumed ownership in 1934. It had stood toe-to-toe against racists voices throughout the thirties and the forties. The following decade's editorials attacked the state legislature's attempts to subsidize the Citizen's Councils and other segregationist groups. Moreover, the newspaper withheld its support from candidates who ran on a platform that included racists planks. At every turn, Tupelo's citizens were counseled to exercise discreet judgment in their response to the racial issues of the day. Following the Supreme Court's landmark decision in *Brown v. Board of Education, Topeka, Kansas*, the *Journal* warned its readers, "Whatever solution we try, the important thing for us in the South to realize is that the politicians who lack qualities of natural leadership are almost certain to develop the South's new problem into a highly emotional issue in an effort to win office for themselves."[67] Later, when the state legislature discussed the possibility of abolishing public education, the *Journal* used a front-page editorial to oppose the plan.[68]

Aside from its more traditional influence as the area's largest newspaper, the community-sponsored projects of the *Journal* made it the hub of the communications network on a personal level as well as the more impersonal paper at the doorsteps. The newspaper was the primary sponsor of the Rural Community Development Council and, as such, George McLean was known personally in every rural community in the county. He spoke regularly to the groups and was the acknowledged leader in the agricultural programs that had brought Lee County national awards. The *Journal* had been a friend to the rural areas. It had featured the activities of even the smallest rural neighborhoods in its pages. The newspaper had served to link town and country. In this capacity, the racially moderate newspaper had been drawn very close to the longtime nemesis of blacks, the small white yeoman.

It was well known throughout the black community that George McLean had always supported the cause of the black man. Moreover, he was accessible to black leaders who wished to voice their grievances.[69] The black RCDC units provided McLean an entree into the rural black neighborhoods. Through his personal friendship with black leaders, McLean's influence stretched deep into the black community. Among his closest friends and aides had been Alice Little. A Cornell graduate and the daughter of one of Tupelo's best known black ministers, Ms. Little was the black home demonstration agent in Lee County for over 25 years. Upon her retirement from this position, she became directly involved with *Journal*-sponsored experimental programs in community development.[70]

One of the major conduits between the black and white communities was the friendship between George McLean and Amos Reece.[71] The acknowledged son of a prominent white man, Reece was reared in a white household before his movement to the black community as an adult. He was a large, imposing figure of a man whose presence radiated confidence and dignity. Well read, articulate, and unflinching in the face of intimidation, he was one of the most unique men ever seen in Tupelo. He was a familiar sight in the white community as well as the black. Moreover, it was well understood that he had access to many of the power figures in Tupelo. From the period of the thirties through the sixties, whenever an intermediary was needed it was Amos Reece to whom most blacks, individually and collectively, would turn.[72]

He understood that realistically he could only be the voice of local blacks articulating their grievances in higher places. He knew also that his only weapon was friendly persuasion and the interest of whites in maintaining stable, if not improved, race relations. Reece acknowledged that he could not remedy the injustices but he could attack their visible excesses.

Convinced that the informal channels of communication between the two races were not sufficient, Reece persistently urged blacks to register and vote.[73] Reece's efforts to register black voters at the end of World War II were without success. Some positive gains were made in the fifties but nothing of a major scope. Upon passage of the Voting Rights Act of 1965, Reece again took the lead in stimulating blacks to exercise their privilege to register. After a prominent white citizen provided the Elks Club with $500 to be used in the expense of transporting blacks to the courthouse to register, the redoubtable Reece claimed most of the money as he rushed almost 1,000 applicants to the circuit clerk's office.[74]

Registering more than 1,000 voters in a short span was a major step toward social justice, but it would take many future decades to convert this political clout into economic and social gains. Despite the fact that many blacks in the rural sections of Lee County had made important strides through RCDCs, those inside the city limits were still behind whites economically.

The traditional economic avenues most accessible to blacks have been in providing services within black neighborhoods that were not offered by white businesses. Black businesses that catered exclusively to white trade, such as barber shops, had disappeared during the reactionary years at the turn of the century.[75] There remained black-owned barber shops as well as beauty shops but they served black clientele only. The most significant legitimate black business in town, however, had been the funeral home.

For many years Tupelo had the only black-owned funeral home in northeast Mississippi. In 1916, J. W. Porter, an insurance salesman originally from Arkansas, bought the existing funeral parlor.[76] The assiduous Porter soon turned the business into one of the largest and most successful black-owned enterprises in the state. Combining his knowledge of insurance with his new enterprise, Porter worked with a black Methodist minister, Ben Rousser, to organize the Colored Benevolent Society whose stated purpose was to care for the poor and bury the black dead.[77] In time, more than 100 chapters, or camps as they were called, were organized throughout the northern section of the state.[78]

The camps held regular meetings and claimed a greater membership than any other single organization in the black communities of the area. This provided the politically moderate Porter with direct ties into every black neighborhood in the area. He was known by a majority of blacks in the town and the county. Porter was also the state treasurer for the Masonic Grand Lodge, adding to his prestige in Tupelo and giving greater range to his personal influence.[79] He and Amos Reece were cited as the two most outstanding black leaders in Tupelo during the post-World War II era.[80]

Porter's significance went far beyond his extensive ties within the black community. As one of the city's most successful businessmen, some whites regarded him as proof that the social system was not inordinately harsh and rewards would be forthcoming to those who were "willing to work."[81] His success prompted both pride and jealousy within the black community. In its entire history his achievements in business were without rival, but there were many blacks who resented his dominance in business, the Elks, the Masons, and the church.

Porter was indeed the exception. Entering the decade of the sixties, the income of blacks was only about half of that of whites.[82] But the 1960s signaled a transition. At this time, many of the members of the Community Development Foundation were segregationists. But they understood that racial harmony was necessary for continued economic and industrial development. One leading businessman, who requested anonymity, stated the case for many of his colleagues. "I grew up in Mississippi and accepted its values and principles of race relations. I thought the [racial] changes of the fifties and sixties would be detrimental to both races, but we had all seen what had happened in Little Rock and we knew that we couldn't afford that kind of disaster in our own town."

The traumatic events with the desegregation efforts at the University of Mississippi in nearby Oxford confirmed the need to change and to do so without accompanying violence. Thus, conservative businessmen in Tupelo and throughout the state urged that laws be obeyed and the transition be made peaceably. Biracial committees headed by George McLean and Amos Reece worked continuously to maintain channels of communication.

By the mid-sixties, the transition was under way. Black leaders responded to the change. The Elks Club assumed the responsibility of getting blacks registered to vote. Following this, it set itself up as a training center to educate the neophyte voters. As many as 500 people crowded their way into a single meeting to receive instructions in the basic procedure of the use of voting machines. Local candidates were invited to express their views before the organization and its guests.[83]

For years, many of the leading figures in the black community had been dues-paying members of the NAACP. Now, spurred by the swiftly changing events and the unchallenged activities of the Elks, a local chapter was founded in 1965. Much to the surprise of many of its members, the new group came into existence without any challenge from whites.[84]

In a bold move, the town's Park and Recreation Commission, chaired by white businessman Robert Leake, declared that all park and recreational facilities would no longer be segregated. The commission went further and declared that the city would not participate in state competition that was segregated.

Conscious of its role as a leader in the rapidly changing events, Tupelo's school officials acted to complete the desegregation efforts in hopes of being the first school in the state to sign the 1965 antidiscrimination agreement. Much to the chagrin of some local leaders, Greenville had signed the agreement the day before but Tupelo schools were desegregated in the fall of 1965 without incident.[85]

New economic opportunities were opened to blacks in the summer of 1965. Black women were employed in the factories on a mass basis for the first time. Segregation signs disappeared from the drinking fountains and restrooms. More importantly, the higher-paying jobs were now available to blacks. More than 80 percent of the blacks interviewed by the author cited the improved economic opportunities in the mid-sixties as the most important change in the black experience in Tupelo.[86]

One leading processing plant that had not hired any black workers since 1941 began to rehire blacks in late 1965. By 1970, the majority of the workers in the plant were black; many of them were women.[87] Not only did this mean that better-paying jobs were available, but more importantly it broke a 90-year caste system that had earlier employed black women only in domestic jobs. As late as 1960, three-fourths of the employed black women worked in private households or service jobs involving domestic skills.[88] A decade later, the number of black women working at these jobs was reduced by 40 percent.[89] The existence of alternative jobs also had the effect of raising the wages of those women who remained in domestic service.[90]

Unemployment among black males in 1970 was down to 1 percent.[91] The caste system had also been broken for black men during the mid-sixties. No longer were the men dependent primarily on unskilled day labor jobs. By 1970, 27 percent of the workers employed in Tupelo factories were black, even though blacks constituted only 21 percent of the county's population.[92] By contrast, blacks, both male and female, were still grossly underrepresented in white-collar occupations.[93]

Improvement in black housing paralleled the expanding job opportunities. Much of the federal monies that contributed so significantly to breaking the patterns of discrimination were used to develop a subsidized housing project.[94] "Shakerag," the town's largest black neighborhood and major slum area, was cleared to make room for a shopping mall. One-fourth of the town's black population was relocated to the north of a large existing black neighborhood.[95]

The demise of "Shakerag" and the construction of the new housing project had the immediate effect of dividing the black community into new and old sections, though it had no effect on the density of population. The black neighborhoods remained by far the most densely populated areas of town. Some of the black churches were relocated when the old section was destroyed and took on the appearance of recently acquired affluence in their new environs. Much of the original section looked old and overcrowded with the same narrow roads that were inadequate even at the turn of the century. There was, however, a new and important trend in the old sections. A number of small clusters of middle-class housing dotted the neighborhoods offering an incongruous contrast to the lines of small often unpainted houses that had characterized this section for almost three-quarters of a century.

Signs of change appeared like crocuses in spring, foretelling the broader changes to come. However, some of those shifts brought unanticipated problems. Because the leadership patterns were built around individuals rather than institutions there was no assurance of any continuity in leadership. J. W. Porter's death in 1967 and the failing health of Amos Reece caused a vacuum in leadership.

An intense struggle ensued as rivals bitterly sought positions of prominence within the black community. Robert Jamison, a native of Tupelo whose winning football teams had lifted him and his school to state prominence became the first black to seek a place on the town's Board of Aldermen. The attacks on his position by other blacks became so severe that Jamison was forced to withdraw from the race.[96] Concurrently, jealousy and infighting forced the recently established chapter of the NAACP to dissolve before 1970. Hard feelings developed between blacks contending for power and the Community Development Foundation over the latter's influence in the appointment of their rivals to positions of leadership. There were deliberate attempts of noncooperation in hopes that this would drive the appointees from office.[97] After the election of 1968, the Masons and Elks found their attendance dropping sharply as compared with that of the fifties.[98] The author's survey of leadership perception revealed clearly that there were no acknowledged leaders within black neighborhoods by the late sixties.

Efforts to organize were often unsuccessful. Several attempts to bring together a Street Improvements Committee in the late sixties all died at birth. No lasting political organization was assembled. Jealousy and infighting among blacks frightened away many good candidates.

There was also the fact that life within the city limits had lost some of its earlier advantages. Some of the blacks who had been born in the rural areas began to move back in the late sixties. Still others in the outlying regions who might have been drawn to Tupelo in an earlier time remained in the surrounding hamlets and commuted daily to work in the factories. Within Tupelo only small plots of land were available and suitable for black middle-class homes. The best land could be found only outside the city limits. By the late sixties, the majority of the more affluent black homes in Lee County were to be found outside Tupelo.

These rural hamlets, often built around existing churches, and the RCDC units seemed to have possessed greater unity than was found in town.[99] The NAACP chapter was reorganized outside Tupelo.[100] This rural-urban rivalry was one more schism among the area's black population.

The period 1965 to 1970, which began with grandiose hopes and expectations became in fact a transitional period. By the end of the period, the mood was complex but generally hopeful. The full employment, increased wages, and the demise of some of the old segregation patterns made it a time of guarded optimism. The inadequate housing, the more subtle forms of discrimination, and blacks' inability to organize, produced an antithetical frustration. There was, however, a newfound pride and a sense that history was working in favor of the black man for the first time in his experience.

Some of the hopes were fulfilled in the mid-1970s when blacks were finally able to unite politically and elect Boyce Grayson as the first African-American to the city's Board of Aldermen.[101] Each gain, even the smaller ones, tended to raise the level of expectation. Tupelo's buoyant optimism and "can-do" attitude had spread to the whole community.

Throughout the 1970s, blacks openly voiced their expectation that because Tupelo was different, all its citizens should seek and expect a higher quality of life. Black leaders freely confided that the caution of the 1960s was over and these leaders had become activists.[102]

Periodically, one of the first targets was the issue of police harassment and discrimination. Blacks had complained among themselves about police treatment for decades. As in many towns, blacks were convinced that some policemen had sought their position and had been hired to "keep blacks in line." Heretofore, blacks had never been able to organize in such a way as to present a united front against police harassment.

This prolonged inability to organize was caused in part by the lack of free time by black leaders. Organization requires a freedom from the long hours of most laborers. A few black ministers had enjoyed a flexible work schedule. Moreover, they had access to the church network, but they had never built an effective local protest organization. There were too few black professionals to provide a critical mass. Only A. M. Strange had been able to use his professional position to establish a meaningful coalition.

By the 1970s there was a new institution on the scene, the Rural Legal Services. In north Mississippi these were staffed by black attorneys, paralegals, and administrators. They were educated, organized, relatively insulated from the pressure of white conservatives, and eager to champion social change. They got that chance in the late 1970s in Tupelo.

The specific events began on March 18, 1976, when Eugene Pasto, a black prisoner in the local jail claimed to have been beaten by two white policemen, Dale Cruber and Roy Sandifer. One of the Rural Legal Service attorneys, Kenneth Mayfield, came to Pasto's defense. Mayfield represented him in a civil suit against Cruber and Sandifer. The plaintiff's position was upheld by Judge Orma R. Smith. Cruber and Sandifer were ordered to pay $2,500 in damages.[103]

The decision lit a fuse in the black community. Within two weeks of the court's decision, a group of angry black citizens met with city aldermen to insist on the permanent dismissal of the two detectives accused of the brutality.[104] With the exception of black Alderman Boyce Grayson, the Board of Aldermen did not fully appreciate the longstanding frustration of these protesters. The city fathers attempted to placate the group initially by reducing the rank of the detectives and creating a biracial committee to prevent future incidents. After this policy was dismissed, the Board of Aldermen offered an equally unacceptable proposal to transfer the offending officers to the fire department. Both proposals further fueled the anger and added insult to the legitimate efforts through established procedures.[105]

The day after the initial rebuff, Alfred "Skip" Robinson, a director of the Rural Legal Services and an executive with the United League of North Mississippi, from nearby Holly Springs, came forward to speak for the black community. Robinson called for a united march on downtown Tupelo in protest of the city's failure to remove the police officers. On March 11, 1978, the initial march was held. Even the most moderate black leaders joined the more than 400 protesting marchers.

Robinson, sensing the depth of the frustration and the breadth of the support, sought to increase the pressure by calling for a second march and boycott of all white-owned businesses in the town. Robinson had correctly judged the mood in the black community. More than 750 responded by joining in the second march. As in almost all community conflict, the issues were quickly enlarged. When addressing the marchers, Robinson added a second grievance to police brutality. He demanded that the downtown merchants increase the number of black employees to total 30 percent of the work force.[106]

The demands caught much of the white leadership off guard. Felix Black, the president of the Uptown Association, Jack Reed, George McLean, and other business leaders had been working behind the scenes from the outset urging the city officials to remove the police officers. This offstage maneuvering had become a test of power and some of the local officials vowed to resist the intrusions from public citizen McLean.[107]

Adding to the complications, Alfred Robinson himself had become a central issue. His demands for 30 percent employment of blacks in local shops were viewed by white leaders as unrealistic and calculated to heighten tensions. The black population constituted only 21 percent of the county's total population. Moreover, a recent survey by the state's Research and Development Center had shown that blacks constituted 31 percent of the county's factory workers and the black median income in Lee County ranked it in the top 5 percent of the black income in the state. Even with the most enthusiastic compliance to the demand, there were not enough black workers to fill the positions. Employed blacks could not afford to leave their existing industrial jobs to work in downtown shops.[108]

Tensions mounted. The white leadership could not achieve consensus to respond to the demands.[109] Additionally, Robinson refused to meet with the bira- cial committee. Consequently, this committee was unable to act. Meanwhile, membership in the county's United League was reported to have increased from 100 to more than 1,200, in only 2 months.[110] More fuel was added when the Ku Klux Klan's Imperial Wizard, Bill Wilkinson, arrived in town to organize any would-be supporters and to hold a public cross burning.[111] The town had become a tinderbox of emotions.

The Community Development Foundation sought to defuse the situation. At its annual meeting, the executive committee presented a formal position that was read to the gathering of more than 1,000 persons.

"The presence of the Ku Klux Klan is distressing and frightening. The Klan represents the worst possible form of racism and hatred. Its presence here is intol- erable and must be discouraged and condemned by Tupelo citizens concerned with the well-being and best interests of all our people — black or white. The Community Development Foundation stands in absolute, unalterable opposition to the Ku Klux Klan and its presence in Tupelo." The statement went on to "con- demn any inflammatory remark by black leaders from outside the city" (Meaning Skip Robinson). All persons supporting this statement were invited to stand. Without exception over 1,000 members pushed back their chairs and rose to express their endorsement of that position.[112]

Boyce Grayson, the city's only black alderman, was devoting himself tirelessly as the liaison between the city and the United League. Unfortunately, the city gov- ernment sometimes failed to provide him the empowerment he needed to be fully effective. Despite this, he was able to reduce some tension when he persuaded Robinson not to interrupt the annual Gum Tree Festival, the city's biggest single community celebration.[113]

Lewis Myers, the United League's attorney, and a staff member of the Rural Legal Service, helped to reduce some of the tension by meeting with the biracial committee. Subsequently, he attempted to enhance the credibility of the commit- tee by praising its efforts.[114]

But like a raging forest fire, every time the flames were controlled in one area, they resurfaced in another. Mayor Clyde Whitaker weakened the effort of the biracial committee by criticizing its work and composition. He argued that the committee did not represent the position of the common laborer.[115]

Alfred Robinson became even less flexible. He also stirred deep fears when his hard-line tactics were reprinted in the *Memphis Commercial Appeal*. Robinson told his audience, "Let me tell you, black folks, there's nothing wrong with a good dictatorship." He warned the audience not to talk to anyone on the other side, including members of the Justice Department. All questions and statements were to be addressed by Robinson personally.[116]

Robinson increased anxiety when he presented the city with a list of demands:
1. Removal of [officers] Cruber and Sandifer.
2. Adoption of an affirmative action plan by which up to 35 percent of the city's employees would be black.
3. A black would serve as a liaison between whites and blacks.
4. Set aside 20 percent of all federally funded grants for black contractors.
5. All Tupelo contractors were to file a report listing the number of black employees.
6. There would be a new youth center for blacks.
7. Establish a liaison committee to work with the United League's representatives and attorneys.[117]

Robinson punctuated his list of demands for still another march. This was the opportunity that the Klan had been waiting for. Bill Wilkinson, the Klan's Imperial Wizard, called for a national Klan rally in Tupelo on June 10, 1978 to coincide with the planned march.[118]

The city of Tupelo sought relief from the pressure by calling for a cooling-off period that would prevent both public demonstrations. Their efforts were soon challenged in court. The judge prefaced his opinion by commending Tupelo's outstanding record in the field of civil rights, but concluded by stating that the city could not prohibit the demonstrations.[119]

The stage was now set. Neither side showed signs of blinking and impotent Tupelo was bracing itself as the battleground. After more than two months of the sustained boycott and repeated marches and counterdemonstrations, nerves were raw. As the confrontation neared, a Klan spokesman predicted bloodshed.[120]

When June 10 arrived, the *Journal* urged everyone to stay home.[121] The *Journal's* fellow media certainly did not heed the advice. Representatives from ABC television, *Time* magazine, *The New York Times*, the *Chicago Tribune*, the *Washington Post, Rolling Stone,* as well as local reporters from the *Memphis Commercial Appeal* and the *Jackson Clarion Ledger* were on hand to document the events.[122]

The United League had scheduled its march for 1:00 p.m. to culminate at the courthouse. The Klan set a march time for 2:00 p.m. for the same destination. The Klan had sent the added threat that it would not share the courthouse lawn with any other group.[123]

The National Guard had been alerted to stand by. Sixty-five riot-clad policemen lined the march route armed with rifles and shotguns. Thirty-five state highway patrolmen were prepared just off Main Street in the Old Fairgrounds. The emergency room at the North Mississippi Medical Center was on full alert.[124]

At 9:00 a.m., 35 robed Klansmen began to distribute literature throughout downtown.[125] The confrontation seemed certain.

Six hundred marchers had come together at the Springhill Missionary Baptist Church in the predominantly black community. Then, in a surprise move, they began their march a half hour early at 12:30 p.m. instead of the announced 1:00 p.m. The marchers were preceded by a pickup truck with its rifles clearly displayed in the gun rack behind the passenger and the driver.[126]

The showdown was averted. The Klan, too, altered its march time and delayed their departure until 2:30 p.m. A disappointed Bill Wilkinson spoke to a group of only 150 to 200 supporters, a majority of whom were nonlocals. The small band of Klan supporters was surrounded by an equal number of black onlookers observing from across the street. Wilkinson acknowledged that, "We have been counting on this being the kicking off for the civil rights movement for the white people of the United States."[127]

The only physical confrontation occurred when a white lay minister was arrested for taunting the Klansmen when he shouted, "How dare you call yourselves Christians! You symbolize hatred."[128] After a scuffle ensued, a *Memphis Commercial Appeal* reporter, Joseph Shapiro, was also arrested but without specific charges. In time, both men had their cases dismissed in court.[129]

The boycott continued to drag on, though there were serious attempts to bring it to a conclusion. Jim High, grandson of bank president Jim High, acted boldly as the president of the Community Development Foundation when he called on the city to fulfill its public obligations by employing more blacks. High went on to say, "Some people simply have not received their fair share of this county's progress and simply do not believe that progress exists."[130] His efforts were applauded by Felix Black, the president of the Uptown Association, and Jack Reed, the city's most prominent merchant.[131]

Perhaps the most important work was performed by Kenneth Mayfield, the attorney who had represented Eugene Pasto at the beginning of the saga. Mayfield headed an Affirmative Action Committee. In that capacity, he drafted a 75-page plan to assure progress in minority employment with the city. In the end, the Board of Aldermen accepted the entire plan.[132] After more than eight months of confrontation the crisis began to subside.

While the affirmative action plan was accepted, its implementation required frequent prodding by the black community. Over the next four years, Kenneth Mayfield, Augustus Ashby, and Charles Penson continued to monitor the plan on behalf of the black community.[133]

Alfred "Skip" Robinson drifted from the area and converted to the Muslim faith. In time, he became a Muslim minister. He died in an automobile accident in 1986 under the name of Abdul Aziz Muhammed.[134]

Almost any discussion in the black community concerning recent history will cause Robinson's name to resurface, but it is A. M. Strange who remains a folk hero. During the 1980s, the black community sought to keep his memory alive by successfully collecting money for the maintenance of the A. M. Strange Library.[135]

In 1982, Mayfield attempted to build on the unity that had emerged in the black community during the boycott. He helped mobilize a coalition of the local chapter of the NAACP, the Henry Hampton Elks Lodge, The National Council of Negro Women, the United League of Mississippi, and the Tupelo Civic Improvement Club.[136] In time, the coalition grew apart and the effectiveness of the coalition diminished.

Other efforts to organize later in the decade were no more successful. As late as 1993, black churches remained the most influential organizations in the black community. Their role in providing political unity remains especially critical.

The major economic gains of the decade of the eighties were made without the assistance of communitywide organization. Black entrepreneurs during the decade followed the traditional path of serving business niches in ethnically oriented markets. In specific, the greatest wealth was earned in the manufacture and sale of hair products aimed at a national market of African-American women. Others focused on housing construction primarily for local blacks. Another entrepreneur is marketing rental-purchase appliances and furniture to a primarily ethnic population in north Mississippi. Kenneth Mayfield, the attorney/entrepreneur is now pushing beyond these markets by entering the manufacture of furniture, cracking a segment of the economy previously held by white businessmen.[137]

The distribution of wealth among African-Americans followed the national trend of the 1980s. There is obvious wealth at the top, the existence of which is documented by the 1990 census. The newer wealth already equals and exceeds that of J. W. Porter. Census data collected during 1990 also revealed that the single most affluent neighborhood in Tupelo, as measured by median family income, is a cluster of eight black homes.[138]

Despite these gains at the higher echelons, blacks as a whole remain the poorest segment of the Tupelo/Lee County population. They are especially the most likely to be among the very poorest. Moreover, economic growth among the average black family did not keep pace with the average white family during the eighties.[139]

This curtailment of economic growth at the middle level has caused concern among both black and white leaders. The *Daily Journal*, led by publisher Billy Crews worked during the 1993 campaign to encourage additional black representation on the city's Board of Aldermen. Discontent among the black constituency translated into the election of Steve Mayhorn who defeated the veteran, Boyce Grayson, for a seat on the Board of Aldermen. The transition seems to reflect that the black population is moving into a stage of development beyond the process of mere representation, to a level of equal voice within the city's policy-making board.

Despite sluggishness in some of the economic sectors, there were several notable social and economic changes during the 1980s. Two of the city's banks added African-American loan officers. Only the Jackson-owned bank had not followed that lead. Black leaders agree that the presence of black loan officers is an important signal to the black community. It indicates a sensitivity on the part of the banks that helps open the avenues of commerce between the banks and the black community.[140]

African-Americans are much more prominent on the city's payroll. By 1993, 24 percent of the city's full-time employees and 26 percent of the part-time workers were minorities. Within those numbers, blacks constitute 21 percent of the police and fire departments. They accounted for only 14 percent of the police and firemen in 1978 when the boycott marches began. In addition, the city's position of director of personnel has been an African-American since 1980.[141]

While blacks have been active in the membership of the Community Development Foundation since its inception, especially through participation in the Rural Community Development Councils, there is a feeling among some black leaders that CDF is neither sufficiently regional nor aggressive enough in assisting black business interests. Consequently, during the summer of 1993 more than 100 black business people from throughout north Mississippi came together for a dinner meeting to determine the interest in developing a regional economic development program, designed primarily for black businesses.[142] The groundwork for this fledgling attempt represents a generational transition in black economic development.

CHAPTER 9

How They Do It in Tupelo/Lee County: An Overview of the Tupelo Plan

A visitor to Tupelo in the 1990s, who saw only the surface features, might not be impressed. Looking only at the business districts there is little that is attractive. Many of the commercial strips are cluttered and aesthetically objectionable. Even neighboring towns are not quite sure why Tupelo's economy outstrips their own. They see the economic achievements, but are unable to view the community development from which the growth springs. Yet it is the underlying community development process that gives the town its economic advantages.

The community development process begins with leadership. Lee County's leaders are bright and energetic, as one would expect. They are also characterized by the same bottom-line pragmatism that is common in other towns. They judge the town by sound practical standards. By the most empirical measures (the workability and achievements of the community), they are not only comfortable but are enthusiastic with this community-based approach to economic and cultural development.

Some of these clear-eyed pragmatic leaders represent examples of transformational leaders as described by James McGregor Burns. Transforming leaders understand the wants and needs of the constituents and seek to meet those needs by involving the constituents in the solutions. In the process of so doing, followers are often converted to leaders themselves.[1]

While only a minority of Lee County's total leadership could be properly classified as transformational leaders, that group has been the most influential. George McLean stands as the prototype of such leadership. He drew on the most powerful of the cultural values of social justice and the role of the servant-leader. In the process, his goal was to help transform the existing culture to an environment in which community problems were recognized and addressed. This would be a culture in which community development flourished. The organizations he helped to create provided both the opportunity and vehicle by which other transformational leaders could function.

The Tupelo Plan that evolved from those principles of leadership begins with the development of people. This development took place on the two ends of the power spectrum. It provided grassroot-rural people with basic social tools and organization to address their own local issues. The success of this effort was instrumental in persuading existing leaders that economic prosperity would most likely come by enlarging the economic pie. Consequently, a leadership concerned with community development emerged. They promoted a cooperative spirit in which the whole community prospered.

The most basic principle in the Tupelo Plan is that local people must address local problems. The role of leaders, therefore, is to help people to help themselves, not tell them what to do, but to assist constituents in reaching the goals that are important to the constituents themselves.

This requires a mechanism or organization that can help facilitate consensus about a common direction for the community. This mechanism can also serve as the engine that drives the community development process. Lee County's driving organizations, because they have been experimental in nature, have evolved over an extended period of time. This has enhanced their effectiveness and ensured their flexibility to adjust to external social change.

At the heart of Lee County's organization are the coordinating associations that operate on four levels. The Community Development Foundation is the central point in the organization structure. The Community Development Foundation is concerned with every phase of the community from recreation to water supply to industrial development. It is a prototype of a generalist organization that seeks to improve the quality of life in all dimensions. To assist in that total community development, CDF works at the grassroots level with the Rural Community Development Councils which, while no longer as powerful as in its earlier stages, help to coordinate total community development in rural or unincorporated villages. Coordination at the level of incorporated communities is done through the Lee County Council of Governments (COG). At a regional level coordination is achieved through the Big Ten, composed of Lee County and the surrounding nine counties.

While these organizations vary in the degree of involvement and, therefore, the degree of effectiveness, they are each broad coordinating associations. These associations, especially the Community Development Foundation, explains in a large measure why Tupelo has so many generalist-leaders and generalist-constituents. The large number of generalist-leaders accounts for much of the town's distinctiveness and contributes to its community development success.

There is a reciprocal relationship between CDF and the generalist-leader. CDF, which was created by and for generalist-type leaders, actually produces still more generalist-type leaders because of the way it functions. By concerning itself with all phases of community life, CDF encourages and promotes generalist-leaders. These generalist-leaders, in turn, are the key to the community development process.

The Community Development Foundation pulls together key people from all phases of life, i.e., bankers, the superintendent of schools, the hospital director, retailers, factory managers, attorneys, journalists, physicians, etc. But in this setting they work in the role of community leaders, not corporate leaders. Bankers, for example, all agree that at the meetings they must not focus on their own bank's interests, but rather work for the best interests of the community. Once they leave this setting, they may and do compete aggressively with fellow banks for business. Based on hundreds of observations, these local cultural folkways are only rarely broken and when they are, unless the damage is repaired, the offender will lose his/her position of leadership within the community.[2] Only by acting in the best interest of the community can an individual retain trust and thereby retain a position of leadership. Trust holds this system together.

The newspaper, the *Northeast Mississippi Daily Journal*, is critical in this process. It is a vigilant watchdog that insists that the trust of the community not be abused or violated. But its role is even more central than that. Its primary focus is on the region and its development. Almost daily it keeps community development issues before the public. It is unrelenting in keeping problems and opportunities on the front page and throughout the newspaper.

The newspaper leads not only by words but by example. It invests more funds in community development than any other Tupelo business. Since all of the profits of the *Journal* return directly to the community through the community foundation CREATE, it may contribute more financial resources to its community and region than any other newspaper in the nation.

Its omnipresent concern for social justice is a signature characteristic of the newspaper. The newspaper was one of the first businesses in town to employ African-Americans in administrative positions. As both a promoter of social justice and community development, the *Journal* has sought to assure a broad spectrum of voices in the coordinating associations.

In order for these coordinating associations to work for all the community, they must have spokespersons from the basic segments of the whole community. When this occurs, CDF, the most prominent coordinating association does, in fact, represent the broad community. When it does not, CDF is seen by community members as being out of touch and its effectiveness is therefore reduced, as in the case of the boycotts and marches in the late 1970s. CDF, while the single most powerful organization, must continually remain sensitive to the whole community, or risk losing effectiveness.

These coordinating associations, especially those operating within Lee County — CDF, RCDC, and COG — have produced an ethic referred to in the area as "The Tupelo Spirit." The term itself is in constant use. The author has sometimes encountered its usage as often as 20 to 30 times in a single day of research. For purposes of this research, the term community spirit is being adopted to replace the more narrow term "Tupelo Spirit."

The characteristics of this community spirit began with the recognition by key leaders that community development is also good business. Leaders have become convinced through experience that community development enhances the probability of success for themselves and their business.

While many individuals may be drawn to the community development process by personal expectations, a majority of the leaders subsequently retain their involvement because of a greater satisfaction of being a part of a very successful program. It is a means of achieving personal satisfaction while providing a sense of accomplishment that is recognized on a state and regional basis. Many of these people may not achieve state and regional recognition within their own profession, but their community efforts are rewarded by state, regional, and even national awards. It is very common for community leaders to discuss the privilege of being a part of the success of a place like Tupelo.

This community spirit is characterized by high expectations. It begins with a sense of pride about past accomplishments and goes beyond that. There is a mood of expectation. William Beasley captured the essence of the mood a generation ago when he said, "Tupelo is the kind of place where when you wake up you expect something good to happen."[3] Even outsiders who have observed Tupelo's progress agree. The most common observation is that Tupelo does not just dream big dreams, they do the work necessary to achieve them.[4]

There is a cooperativeness found among the 1,200-member CDF and the community as a whole. Even individuals who do not like one another personally cooperate on community matters. Key leaders agree that the community leadership will not tolerate placing personal quarrels above community interest.

Lee County's leaders have worked effectively as team members for over a half-century. Many of the top leaders understand and practice teamwork and team building both in the workplace and the community arena. At least one leader has become so proficient that his efforts are of a path-breaking nature and he has begun to introduce his ideas into the school system through formal training.

Community involvement is expected of all persons in higher positions. Most of the newcomers to the community in prominent positions remark that it is almost impossible to be accepted socially unless you become active in the community development process. Although some approached this involvement reluctantly and skeptically, a majority noted that they, too, now consider their involvement as an opportunity and privilege.

It is not simply at the most prominent social levels that one finds extensive participation. One finds a large number of constituent involvement in the community development process. As Harold Kaufman noted 25 years ago, this broad-based involvement is the backbone of the community development process.[5] The high levels of voter turnout and the recent 96 percent vote to support the taxes for a new water system, and the 88 percent vote for the $17 million school bond issue are two of the most recent examples of this community spirit.

This community spirit is further characterized by the public/private cooperation that has been central to the community development process for almost 50 years. Former mayor James Ballard symbolized this cooperation during his 20 years as mayor, from 1952 to 1972. He was constantly in touch with all segments of the population, listening, adapting, and sometimes persuading. While CDF focused on economic development efforts, Ballard worked diligently to build a sound infrastructure that served the town and its economic growth.[6]

From the other perspective, the private sector has been willing to invest in public agencies. The $1.5 million investment in the Reading Aide program by George and Anna Keirsey McLean is reputed to be the largest contribution by an individual to an elementary school in the nation.[7] The city's Association for Excellence in Education has continued in that vein with its ten-year history of contributing to the school system.

The cooperation between Lee County's Board of Supervisors and the Community Development Association represents both public/private cooperation that has endured for almost 50 years. It also illustrates the cooperation between county and town. The industries that are scattered throughout the county demonstrate the gains to both county and town as a result of that cooperation.

As has been highlighted in this book, even the widespread cooperation has not prevented schisms or community conflict. Although the community development process has not eradicated these schisms, the community leadership recognizes the reality of conflict and attempts to address conflicts in an early stage. Conflict resolution is as much an ongoing process as is the effort at economic development.

The term "ongoing" characterizes almost every facet of the community development process. One of the most dominant characteristics is the constancy of the community development effort. There are, of course, high points of achievement when the work culminates in a milestone gain, but the process does not let up. Community development is done every day. Achievements raise the expectations and often reinvigorate the participants to aim still higher.

Community development energies are kept focused by omnipresent community assessments. The community or some component thereof is continually assessing its position and monitoring changes in the broader social and economic structure. Part of CDF's routine is to conduct a major community assessment at least every ten years, after which a strategic plan is developed by the Board of the CDF. Within the framework of this plan, the board identifies at least five or six major annual projects. The coming year's projects are announced at the Annual Banquet at which time the progress on the previous projects is also reported. In this way, the community development process stays focused. While the goals may not vary during a decade, the process is highly flexible, and different means remain an open possibility.

To assist in these assessments, the community engages some of the nation's top community and economic development practitioners and theorists. Their analyses and resulting plans follow in the initial tradition established by the Doane Agricultural Report almost a half-century ago. One of the current projects is to develop an areawide (at least ten counties) program for advanced vocational training. The community is also addressing its appearance during the 1990s. Concurrent with this, there are three other major assessments presently being undertaken. CREATE is sponsoring an assessment in the multicounty area surrounding Lee County. The Downtown Association is in the midst of a study and plan for a traditional downtown. The Tupelo school system is working with Philip Schlecty, author of the respected book, *Schools for the Twenty-First Century.* In this project, Tupelo's schools are one of five demonstration centers that are attempting to restructure the public schools.

In all of these and other visionary or planning projects, the community development process is information driven. The community assessments provide cornerstone data. In addition, the community seeks high-quality technical assistance. Community leaders are constantly looking to other communities and regions to borrow ideas. While Tupelo entertains many visitors seeking to learn from Tupelo's experience, Tupelo leaders are often on the road looking for new and innovative ideas.

In order to achieve those goals, the coordinating associations, especially CDF, work through a variety of service agencies. Since the most fundamental goal is to help people to help themselves, education and the educational system is a cardinal component of the community development process. As noted earlier, Lee County has developed an extensive educational system that includes day care, literacy programs, strong elementary and secondary school systems, vocational programs, branches of a community college, and a state university. Within this wide educational spectrum, the county seeks to meet the educational and training needs of all its people. In addition to formal educational systems, CDF sponsors other educational opportunities such as the economic symposium that is designed to enhance the skills of management.

Lee County's coordinating associations, CDF in particular, has long understood the need to create additional service associations that would complement the work of CDF. Many of the first agricultural associations, such as the dairying, poultry, and the short-lived marketing associations have served their role and are no longer central. However, other service associations meeting different needs are continually being established, some of which have been noted earlier.

Among the service agencies is the antipoverty agency, LIFT, Inc. The community also sponsored the Tennessee Valley Regional Housing Authority, and the more recent Northeast Mississippi Regional Water Supply District. It has promoted and supported the North Mississippi Industrial Development Association. CDF and the *Journal* helped give life to the educational facilities such as the Tupelo branches of Itawamba Community College and the University of Mississippi. The wide variety of art-supporting associations grew out of this same community development mode, although they were not conceived by CDF.

To pay for these and other service agencies, the community has relied initially on its own resources. As noted earlier, George McLean was sufficiently inventive to establish CREATE for the express purpose of building a reservoir that could capture local funds and utilize them for community development. However, the community has also sought to reach local goals by working in conjunction with regional development programs such as the Tennessee Valley Authority and the Appalachian Regional Commission.

Because the community has a history of upholding its side of the partnership by providing local funds, doing its homework and achieving the results promised, the community is better able to attract outside funds. Former U.S. Senator John Stennis confided, "When you got a request from a Tupelo leader, you knew they had done all their homework and that the community, not some self-serving individual, would be the beneficiary. So we always did everything we could to help them help themselves."[8] Moreover, most funding agencies knew that much of the money spent in these community development projects would eventually pay dividends in the form of job creation.

It is not by accident, but design, that Lee County's community development is focused on the creation of jobs. Here, too, the community leaders have done their research. Consequently, the county's economic development program parallels the pattern of other successful communities. Such patterns have been identified by other researchers in economic development, including Glenn Pulver. It is his work that provides the framework used in this section.

The five basic components of the economic development are: attract new basic employers; improve the efficiency of existing firms; encourage new business formation; improve the ability to capture income; and increase the aid from broader governments.[9]

To attract new employers, the community still uses some of the old approaches, sometimes described as "smokestack chasing," but this is only one part of the industrial recruitment plan. This older format includes seeking branch factories as existing industries. Like all communities that engage in attracting these factories, Lee County has built industrial parks as part of the enticement. As industries' needs change, so do the community's parks. Thus, there are existing parks to meet a spectrum of needs. There are those that are basic and look like other well-attended industrial parks. There is another park adjacent to the airport, which specializes in meeting the need of smaller employment centers. There are parks that are heavily wooded in rolling terrain and are much more aesthetically appealing. There are still other parks under construction that will meet the industrial needs in the twenty-first century. CDF always has plans in the drawing stage or under construction for future occupancy.

The county's economic development programs go far beyond traditional efforts of luring industries. CDF has been successful in attracting administrative units of corporations as the town moves in these new directions. The educational and cultural amenities, including good health care, are becoming even greater assets in attracting such employers.

CDF took the lead in attracting developers for the regional mall, which serves both as a large employer and a means of capturing much of the salaried income produced by industry and other sources.

Since most of the new jobs are created by existing firms, CDF spends the greatest portion of its time and energy serving existing business. One of CDF's professional staff works exclusively to meet the needs of existing industries.

In addition to this linkage, CDF and the community have a myriad of networks between themselves and the extant industries. Through CDF, community leaders serve as facilitators between industry and education. By means of these networks, the community helps to provide technical education for labor, managerial training, and technology transfer opportunities. The programs provide the flexibility of offering courses for academic credit, or shorter and more specific classes. Since the educational programs extend from high school vocational offerings to community college and university classes, almost all needs can be met locally. CDF's efforts to upgrade labor skills are a direct response to the request of existing industry.

CDF also serves as a facilitator by sponsoring monthly breakfast meetings at which all plant managers meet to discuss relevant issues and needs. This provides CDF a vehicle by which to recognize and to respond quickly to any current or future requirements. It is also a means of monitoring and improving employer/employee relations.

In its broadest role, CDF attempts to create an environment that maximizes production and profit. Thus, it may assist businesses in hurdling bureaucratic roadblocks or working to reduce transportation costs or even the removal of waste. It may serve as a mediator to prohibit the stealing of skilled laborers from fellow local industries. Such an industrial folkway is enforced primarily by assuring a steady stream of skilled laborers for all industries through the technical education programs.

The community and CDF promote new business formations. Beginning in 1958, George McLean helped to provide inexpensive business start-up space by building and renting warehouse space. Even in the 1950s, these small businesses employed more than 400 people. They have subsequently grown to be companies that employ more than 1,000 workers.[10] For over a decade, CDF has sponsored Industry/Education Day that attempts to assist in creating a total environment which understands and promotes economic growth. One such project encourages entrepreneurial effort among students even before they graduate from high school.[11]

Beginning in 1986, CDF sponsored an Entrepreneur's Forum modeled after similar successful programs in the northeast. CDF hired Frank Hull, currently at Fordham University, to produce and operate the forums. The basic idea was to assist in getting new businesses established, to assist in capitalization, and marketing.

The creation of new jobs is of maximum benefit to a community only if it can find ways to capture or retain the income of the area. This is, of course, one of the primary economic motives for business people to promote job creation. As described in earlier sections of this book, Tupelo merchants have long found ways of capturing the income of the area. The good roads program of post-World War I was one of the means of attracting more dollars through both retail and wholesale trade.

Lee countians remain adept at reducing economic leakage from the area. The regional mall captures income from a multicounty area. The regional trade of the banks and the outreach of the North Mississippi Medical Center are integral components of retaining local assets while capturing additional funds from the region. Both the banking and medical industries represent the area's trend toward service jobs.

The redevelopment and restructuring of the downtown represents an adjustment to current and future roles for the old commercial district. New housing is projected on the site of the old fairgrounds on the edge of the commercial zone. A newly constructed 8,000-seat coliseum will become an anchor for the redesigned function of the downtown.

East of the coliseum is the birthplace of Elvis Presley, which currently stands as the town's largest tourist attraction. To the northwest of town, the Natchez Trace Parkway Center is a tourist magnet as the town seeks to increase its share of tourist trade.

In addition to efforts at capturing individual income, the community is making progress toward capturing corporate income by having local businesses purchasing from one another. The most vital component is in the furniture industry where Lee County is both supplier and producer of furniture and furniture components. In addition, the large Wal-Mart and Sam's are major buyers of locally produced goods.

The final area of economic development is the attraction of financial aids from broader governments. Lee County has been especially adept at securing grants and other federal dollars for much of its infrastructure and many of its programs. Much of that success is due to the fact that Lee County has consistently been willing to generate local matching monies. Perhaps even more important, Lee County has a track record of being able to leverage outside funds to produce maximum results. As we've seen, Lee County fulfills its side of the contract. In so doing, it is the immediate winner in deriving the benefits of projects and infrastructure. It is the long-range benefactor because it enhances the probability of receiving future funds.

George McLean had always envisioned his part of the plan as regional in nature. From the beginning, the scope was designed to be inclusive. By the 1990s, that regionalism was becoming even more evident. Both the highway program and the water supply district are possible only through regional cooperation. A massive regional landfill program is on the verge of reality.

In the midst of this, the future role for Lee County is to be a regional hub. The Tupelo Plan was always designed as a regional plan and should serve the county and region well, if they hold to the principles described in this chapter.

Future challenges and problems will be a test of the foundation of this generation and whether subsequent generations can build on that groundwork. The goal of the Tupelo Plan has always been to create a community development environment that maximizes human energy. The nature of the specific problem it addresses is irrelevant. If the community development process is viable it should assist in addressing almost any problem.

George McLean's vision was never intended for this region only. His concern and reason for developing the model was to help people reach their full potential, wherever they might be. The key to success in the next century, McLean predicted, is to treat every person as a resource and to develop that resource to the maximum.[12] He also knew from experience that one must begin that effort in a specific locale. As he said, "We will start and demonstrate what can be done, and if it's good, maybe someone will copy it."[13]

APPENDIX

Key Leaders

Early Founders: Tupelo Before 1870

Baldwyn, M. F. D., early railroad builder, key figure in the creation of the Mobile and Ohio Railroad, which helped create all the towns in Lee County including Baldwyn, named in his honor.

Bell, John, son of an early Presbyterian missionary, land speculator, town builder, and partner of Robert Gordon.

Bolton, Richard, surveyor, land speculator, town builder, often worked with Gordon and Bell. Grandfather of Richard "Dick" Bolton, a prominent Tupelo attorney in the twentieth century.

Gordon, Robert, Scottish-born early land speculator, town builder, and one of the area's largest landowners. Began one of the first towns in northeast Mississippi and named it in honor of his hometown, Aberdeen, Scotland.

Harris, William, land speculator, town builder, created Harrisburg. Later with George Thomason and Christopher Orr, helped create the plat for Tupelo.

Orr, Christopher, land speculator, town builder, created the town of Palmetto and named same in honor of his native South Carolina. Partner with William Harris and George Thomason in creating Tupelo.

Thomason, George, land speculator, town builder. Along with Christopher Orr and William Harris, platted Tupelo.

Town Builders: Development of Tupelo and Lee County, 1870-1920

Allen, John Mills, perhaps the most visible and best known of nineteenth-century leaders in Lee County, nicknamed "Private" John Allen; served as congressional representative for the First Congressional District, leading businessman, a nationalist who helped the state of Mississippi and the South rejoin the nation after the Civil War. He always signed hotel registrations as John M. Allen, Tupelo, USA. Well known for his humor in Congress, some say one of the wittiest men ever to serve in Congress. Bitter opponent of Ku Klux Klan; subject of Claude Gentry's biography, *Private John Allen.*

Anderson, William Dozier, Tupelo mayor 1898-1906, later state senator, and ultimately a state supreme court justice. During his term as mayor, much of the electrical and water infrastructure of Tupelo was put in place.

Bonner, Dr. T. T., Tupelo physician, business leader at the turn of the century, and a member of the Board of Councilmen.

Clark, Berryman Turner (B.T.), leading businessman and brother of John Clark.

Clark, John, Tupelo and Lee County's most prominent businessman in the nineteenth century, served as a member of the Board of Councilmen, 1898-1906. The founder of the Lee County Bank, which evolved into the Bank of Tupelo and currently The Bank of Mississippi, one of the state's largest banks.

Clayton, Washington Lafayette (W. L.), businessman, landowner, chronicler of early Tupelo and Lee County.

Goodlett, Frank, business partner with Memory Leake in construction and lumber business; built many of the houses and businesses in Tupelo; used his construction interests to become leader in the "good roads" program.

Herndon, George, an original owner/publisher of *Tupelo Journal.*

Hood, C. B., business partner of John Clark.

Kincannon, Frank, owner, editor, publisher of the *Tupelo Journal,* provided a strong voice for the "good roads" program.

Kincannon, James, owner, publisher, editor of the *Tupelo Journal* at the turn of the century, helped to provide leadership during a progressive period of development.

Leake, Memory, business partner with Frank Goodlett in the construction and lumber industry; built many of the houses and businesses in Tupelo.

Long, Charles P., Tupelo attorney, businessman, one of the business leaders at the turn of the century who helped establish a small industrial base in Tupelo.

Medford, Harvey Clay, Tupelo's first mayor, educator, writer, and businessman.

Miller, John, owner, publisher, editor of *Tupelo Journal* in the 1880s and 1890s, a shameless booster of Tupelo. Lost favor with farmers during the Populist era and left town, under considerable pressure.

Robins, D. W. (Will), one of Lee County's largest landowners, one of the founders of the bank which became The Peoples Bank, nephew and business partner of John M. Allen, member of the Board of Councilmen, one of Tupelo's most influential mayors, key figure in the development of "good roads."

Rogers, J. J., Tupelo businessman, banker, wholesale grocer. Helped establish the wholesale business that sprang up after the construction of "good roads."

Troy, Corneilus (Neil), business partner of John Clark, member of the Board of Councilmen, 1898-1906.

Agrarian Revolt: 1870s-1900

Ballard, Joseph, co-owner with James Gillespie of the *Tupelo Ledger,* a farmer-oriented newspaper and rival of the *Tupelo Journal* during the Populist revolt.

Burkitt, Frank, major Populist leader in the 1880s-1890s. Active in the Grange and Farmers' Alliance, editor of the *Okolona Chickasaw Messenger,* an important voice for the farmer's movement in the late nineteenth century.

Freeman, R. D., one of the leaders of the farmers' movement in Lee County in the 1880s and 1890s; brother of Thomas Freeman.

Freeman, Thomas, one of the leaders of the farmers' movement in Lee County in the 1880s and 1890s; brother of R. D. Freeman.

Gillespie, James, co-owner with Joseph Ballard of the *Tupelo Ledger,* a farmer-oriented newspaper and rival of the *Tupelo Journal* during the Populist revolt.

Hansell, John, Lee County leader in the Greenback Party, later active in the farmer's revolt near the end of the nineteenth century.

Agricultural Development and Diversification: 1920s-1950

Bolton, Richard (Dick), grandson of Richard Bolton, leading attorney and business leader; respected for his sound judgment and community involvement.

Carr, Gale, dairyman, developer of the Tupelo Area Artificial Insemination Association, later developer of Carr Acres, south of Tupelo.

High, James (Jim), president of The Peoples Bank, perhaps the most active and visible business leader in Lee County from the end of World War I to the Great Depression; father of the first agricultural diversification program at the end of World War I; cited by the *Memphis Commercial Appeal* as the most visible and effective leader in northeast Mississippi.

Little, Alice, daughter of a prominent African-American leader. In her position as home demonstration leader, she was one of the most influential women leaders in this century.

McLean, George, owner/publisher of the *Tupelo Journal,* which name evolved into the *Northeast Mississippi Daily Journal,* moved to Tupelo in June 1934, became active in every facet of community and economic development for the next half-century, father of the "Tupelo Model" and Community Development Foundation; in 1971 established CREATE, the community foundation for northeast Mississippi.

Nanney, Phil, president of the Bank of Tupelo; mayor of Tupelo; key business leader in the infancy of the Tupelo Model.

Porter, J. W., key business leader, he was one of the first African-American economic leaders in Tupelo. He helped to establish many African-American organizations.

Rankin, John, native of Tupelo, United States congressman, active proponent of T.V.A., very influential in making Tupelo the "First T.V.A. City."

Reece, Amos, community leader; key member of the biracial organizations.

Reed, Robert W. (Bob), one of Tupelo's leading merchants for the first half of the twentieth century; respected for his sound business judgment and civic activity; there were perhaps no progressive activities in the first half of the century in which he did not participate.

Reed, Rex, brother of Bob Reed, major industrialist and owner of Lee County's largest farm in the first half of the twentieth century.

Rutherford, Harry, editor of the *Tupelo/Northeast Mississippi Daily Journal* from the late 1930s until his death in the late 1970s. A trusted colleague of George

McLean, he was active in almost all phases of community life; took particular interest in the promotion and development of "affordable housing."

Strange, A. M., educator; trained a generation of talented African-American leaders; one of the most revered leaders in the community's history.

Whitesides, Josh, bank president, key leader in the early development of the "Tupelo Model."

Industrial Development: 1950s-1990s

Ballard, James, mayor of Tupelo from 1950s-1970s; was a public leader in the public-private partnership that became a cornerstone in the Tupelo Model.

Clark, Grace, still another example of the youngest generation of leaders, serves on almost all key committees in Tupelo; one of the founders of the Gardner-Simmons Program for Women, which offers assistance to victims of abuse.

Crews, William Lowrey (Billy), publisher of the *Northeast Mississippi Daily Journal,* is one of the bright young leaders who are the latest generation of leaders; helped implement the Reading Aide program as a young employee of the *Daily Journal;* groomed to succeed George McLean; coordinated the creation of the Neighborhood Development Corporation, an effort to regenerate housing in an old racially mixed neighborhood.

Grayson, Boyce, first African-American to serve on the Board of Aldermen, former president of NAACP.

Holliman, Wilbert G. (Mickey), along with partner, A. E. (Bo) Bland, left Morris Futorian's furniture industry to become one of the first local businessmen to establish a furniture industry in 1970. This company, Action Industries, joined with Lane Furniture and is one of the nation's largest furniture manufacturers. Mickey Holliman now serves as its president.

Leake, Robert, descendant of Memory Leake; active civic leader. As chairman of the recreation committee, he was key to the desegregation efforts in the 1960s.

Martin, Harry, president and director of the Community Development Foundation from the mid-1950s to present time, 1999; widely regarded as one of the nation's foremost industrial developers; key participant in all industrial development for the past half-century.

Mayfield, Kenneth, attorney, successful businessman, early civil rights leader.

Mayhorn, Steve, son of Ulyssus Mayhorn, member of the Board of Aldermen; executive director, Habitat for Humanity for northeast Mississippi.

Mayhorn, Ulyssus, merchant; well-respected leader, especially in the African-American community.

McCullough, Jr., Glenn, current mayor, previous director of Mississippi's Appalachian Regional Commission. Like his friend, Billy Crews, he, too, represents the most recent generation of leadership.

McLean, George, coordinated the creation of the Neighborhood Development Corporation, an effort to regenerate housing in an old racially mixed neighborhood. (See Agricultural Development.)

McLean, Anna Keirsey, wife of George McLean, who succeeded her husband on his death. As the leader of the *Journal,* her ten-year tenure represented more than a transition. The newspaper prospered more than at any point in its almost 130-year history.

Morse, True D., former president of Doane Agricultural Services of St. Louis, MO. Consultant who helped shape the Tupelo Model, later undersecretary of Agriculture.

Otis, Larry, first president of the Tupelo branch of Itawamba Community College; helped organize the Neighborhood Development Corporation.

Patterson, Aubrey, president of The Bank of Mississippi; civic leader; former president of the Community Development Foundation.

Penson, Charles, another of the new breed of civic leaders; president of the Black Business Association of Mississippi; human resource director at the *Northeast Mississippi Daily Journal.*

Prince, Julian, superintendent of Tupelo schools; helped lay the foundation for public support for strong schools.

Reed, Jack, son of Bob Reed; leading merchant, industrialist, one of the most active and respected civic leaders in the history of the community; central to almost every community project in the last half-century; probably the most widely recognized and respected leader at the current time.

Savery, James M. (Ikey), owner of local insurance company; for many years was chairman of the industrial development committee of the Community Development Foundation.

Smith, John, president of The Peoples Bank with its rich history of community development; just completed his term as president of the Community Development Foundation.

Whitehead, J. C., former president of Bank of Tupelo; active in almost every facet of community life from the 1950s to present.

Whitfield, Lewis, bank president of Deposit Guaranty; leader in state economic matters. In the tradition of a long line of bank president-civic leaders, he established the Association for Excellence in Education, which the Ford Foundation and Harvard's Kennedy School of Government cited as one of the ten best examples of private-public partnerships in the nation.

ENDNOTES

Chapter 1 — An Introduction to Tupelo, Mississippi, and the Community Development Process

1. The Community Development Foundation was selected by the Industrial Development Research Council as one of the nation's top ten economic development agencies. *Northeast Mississippi Daily Journal,* April 10, 1987.

2. Community Development Foundation, "1992 Business and Economic Facts," Tupelo, MS, 1992, pp. 9 and 13.

3. Tupelo Public School records.

4. National Civic League, "Applications, Rules, and Instructions," Denver, CO, 1992, p.1. The awards are given to communities that are examples of "collaborative, grassroot efforts to improve the quality of life."

5. J. Mac Holladay, *Economic and Community Development: A Southern Exposure,* An Occasional Paper of the Kettering Foundation, Dayton, OH, 1992.

6. Community Development Foundation, "Part of CDF's Success Story," Tupelo, MS, Community Development Foundation, 1992, p. 5.

7. Department of Agriculture, *Yearbook, 1901.* Washington: Government Printing Office, 1902, p. 93.

8. Holladay, 1992, p. 7.

9. The phrase "town and country" was used throughout the South in the 1800s. It marked the distinction between town and rural areas.

10. Ron Shafer and Gene F. Summers, "Community Economic Development," in James A. Christenson and Jerry W. Robinson, Jr., eds., *Community Development in Perspective.* Ames, IA: Iowa State University, 1989, pp. 173-174.

11. The phrase was coined by Harry A. Martin, the president of the Community Development Foundation and is also the title of a paper deliv-

ered by Mr. Martin at the University of Illinois, 1992. A copy of the paper is in the possession of the author.

12.   Leonard S. Cottrell, Jr., "The Competent Community," in Roland L. Warren, ed., *New Perspectives on the American Community: A Book of Readings,* 3d ed., Chicago: Rand McNally, 1977, p. 548.

13.   Ronald L. Warren, and Larry Lyon "Basic Approaches to the Community," in Roland L. Warren and Larry Lyon, eds., *New Perspectives on the American Community: A Book of Readings,* 5th ed., Chicago: Dorsey Press, 1988, p. 6.

14.   One of the best discussions of the interactional approach is, Harold F. Kaufman, "Toward an Interactional Conception of Community," *Social Forces,* 1959, 38(1), 8-17. See also Kenneth P. Wilkinson, *The Community in Rural America.* Westport, CT, 1991, pp. 13-40.

15.   Page Smith, *As A City Upon a Hill: The Town in American History.* New York: Alfred A. Knopf, 1966.

16.   One of the most important discussions of the importance of boundaries in community life is Gerald D. Suttles, *The Social Construction of Communities.* Chicago: University of Chicago Press, 1972, pp. 233-234.

17.   Charles J. Galpin, *Rural Life.* New York: The Century Company, 1918, p. 87.

18.   During the time periods covered in this history, people of African descent bore several different names. Because the term, "African-American" was not in popular use until the late twentieth century, the author has chosen, in most instances, to use the word "black" when referring to African-Americans.

19.   Ronald L. Warren, *The Community in America,* 3d. ed. Chicago: Rand McNally, 1978, pp. 52-95.

20.   James A. Christenson, Kim Fendley and Jerry W. Robinson, Jr., "Community Development," in James A. Christenson and Jerry W. Robinson, Jr., eds., *Community Development in Perspective.* Ames, IA: Iowa State University, 1989, p.14.

21.   Ibid., "Themes of Community Development," pp. 32-38.

22.   Lorraine E. Garkovich, "Local Organizations and Leadership in

Community Development," in Christenson and Robinson, 1989, pp. 203-206.

23.   Harold F. Kaufman, "Coordinating Associations in Community Development." Lecture given at the University of Mississippi, October 1972.

24.   Max DePree, *Leadership Is an Art.* New York: Dell Publishing Co., 1990.

25.   Southern Growth Policies Board, *Halfway Home and A Long Way to Go.*

26.   M. J. Esman and N. T. Uphoff, *Local Organizations: Intermediaries in Rural Development.* Ithaca, NY: Cornell University Press, 1984.

27.   A. E. Luloff, "Community and Social Change," in A. E. Luloff and Louis E. Swanson, eds., *American Rural Communities.* Boulder, CO: Westview Press, 1990, p. 227.

28.   Kaufman, 1959.

29.   Vaughn L. Grisham, Jr., Tupelo, Mississippi, "From Settlement to Industrial Community, 1860-1970." Unpublished doctoral dissertation. University of North Carolina, 1975, pp. 82-85; 98-105; 108-111; 152-173.

30.   Ibid. 1975, pp. 184-196.

31.   *The Wall Street Journal,* December 18, 1923.

32.   George McLean was named *Progressive Farmer's* Man of the Year, 1948.

33.   Harold F. Kaufman and Louis H. Bluhm, *Leadership Structures in Three Small City-Centered Communities,* Technical Bulletin #78. Mississippi Agriculture and Forestry Experiment Station. Mississippi State University, 1976.

Chapter 2 — Town Building

1.   John Hebron Moore, *Agriculture in Antebellum Mississippi.* New York: Bookman Associates, 1958, p. 9.

2.   Sam Bass Warner, *The Private City: Philadelphia in Three Periods of Its Growth.* Philadelphia: University of Pennsylvania Press, 1968, pp. 3-4.

3. Henry S. Halbert, "The Story of Dancing Rabbit Creek," *Mississippi Historical Society Publications*, VI (1902). pp. 373-377; and Lucie H. Craig, "The Removal of the Chickasaw Indians," (unpublished master's thesis, The University of Mississippi, 1939), p. 97.

4. Mary Elizabeth Young, *Redskins, Ruffleshirts and Rednecks: Indian Allotments in Alabama and Mississippi.* Norman: University of Oklahoma Press, 1961, p. 115.

5. John Edmond Gonzales, "Flush Times, Depression, War, and Compromise," pp. 284-309, in Richard Aubrey McLemore, ed. *A History of Mississippi Vol. I.* Hattiesburg: University and College Press of Mississippi, 1973, p. 284.

6. Joseph Glover Baldwin *The Flush Times of Alabama and Mississippi: A Series of Sketches,* 2d ed., New York: D. Appleton and Company 1853, pp. 82-83.

7. Ibid., p. 238.

8. Reuben Davis, *Recollections of Mississippi and Mississippians.* Hattiesburg: University and College Press of Mississippi, 1972, pp. 103, 111.

9. Paul Wallace Gates, "The Role of the Land Speculator in Western History," *Pennsylvania Magazine of History and Biography,* LXVI (July 1942) p. 315.

10. Interview and materials supplied by Richard Bolton, the grandson of the original Richard Bolton. Interview September 3, 1971 in Tupelo, MS. Also Young, *Redskins,* pp. 116-117; and *Mississippi Laws,* special session, 1837, pp. 205- 213; and materials in the Evans Memorial Library, Aberdeen, MS.

11. E. T. Winston, *Story of Pontotoc.* Pontotoc, MS: Pontotoc Print, 1931, pp. 109-110; and Young, *Redskins,* p. 118.

12. James Wesley Silver, "Land Speculation Profits in the Chickasaw Cession," *Journal of Southern History,* X (February 1944), p. 86.

13. Harold D. Woodman, *King Cotton and His Retainers, Financing and Marketing the Cotton Crop of the South, 1800-1925.* Lexington: The University of Kentucky Press, 1968, viii.

14. Hubert H. McAlexander, "Flush Times in Holly Springs," *Journal of Mississippi History, 48,* (February 1986), pp.1-13.

15. Davis, *Recollections,* p. 9.

16. McAlexander, "Flush Times in Holly Springs," p. 2.

17. Young, *Redskins,* p. 145.

18. *Laws of Mississippi, 1836,* pp. 301-307; *1837,* pp. 205-213, 305-309; *1838,* pp. 154-157, 236-243, 287-290, 398-404.

19. *Itawamba County Deedbook, II,* 53; *III,* 488 and Roger Mabry, "History of Palmetto Community," (unpublished paper in the Lee County Library, Tupelo, MS, p. 1.

20. Avery O. Craven, *Soil Exhaustion as a Factor in the Agricultural History of Virginia and Maryland, 1806-1860.* Urbana: University of Illinois Press, 1926, pp. 19-21.

21. Hernando, *Phenix,* March 19, 1842.

22. McAlexander, "Flush Times in Holly Springs," p. 3.

23. Young, *Redskins,* p.145.

24. *Laws of Mississippi, 1824-1838,* pp. 215-233, 651-659, 700-741, 888; *1841,* pp. 219-233.

25. Lewis Cecil Gray, *History of Agriculture in the Southern United States to 1860.* 2 volumes, New York: Peter Smith, 1941, II, pp. 900 and 1027.

26   United States Census, Seventh Census, 1850, Compendium, p. 261.

27. Seventh Census, 1850, pp. 260-261 and Eighth Census, 1860, pp. 270-271.

28. Hernando, *Phenix,* November 19, 1842.

29. Davis, *Recollections,* p. 105.

30. James H. Stone, "The Economic Development of Holly Springs During the 1840s" *Journal of Mississippi History, 32,* January 1970, p. 347.

31. *Laws of Mississippi, 1840,* p. 2, 22-25.

32. Winston, *Pontotoc,* p. 135.

33. Clare Leslie Marquette, "The Life and Letters of a Pontotoc Pioneer, Charles Hathaway Larrabee," *Journal of Mississippi,* 20, (April 1958) pp. 77-98; and William B. Hesseltine, "The Mississippi Career of Lyman C. Draper," *Journal of Mississippi History, 15,* (July 1953), pp. 165-180.

34. J. A. Orr, "A Trip from Houston to Jackson, Mississippi in 1845," *Mississippi Historical Society Publications, 9,* 1906, pp. 174-175.

35. Seventh Census, 1850, p. 448.

36. James A. Ward, "A New Look at Antebellum Southern Railroad Development," *Journal of Southern History, 39* (August 1973), pp. 409-420.

37. James Hutton Lemley, *The Gulf Mobile and Ohio, A Railroad That Had to Expand or Expire.* Homewood, IL: Irwin, 1953, pp. 308-309; and Lewis Troost, "Mobile and Ohio Railroad," *DeBow's Review, III* (April 1847) p. 328.

38. Ibid.

39. *Laws of Mississippi, 1842,* pp. 269-270.

40. *Laws of Mississippi, 1848,* pp. 83-95.

41. *Laws of Mississippi, 1850,* pp. 189-190.

42. *United States Statutes at Large, 1851, IX,* pp. 466-467.

43. Young, pp. 145-148.

44. Dawson A. Phelps, "Travel on the Natchez Trace: A Study of Its Economic Impacts," *Journal of Mississippi History, XV* (July 1953) pp. 155-164.

45. *Laws of Mississippi, 1840,* pp. 70-71.

46. Ephrain Noble Lowe, *Economic Geography of Mississippi,* Oxford: The University of Mississippi, 1928, p. 50.

47. Franklin L. Riley, "Extinct Towns and Villages of Mississippi," *Mississippi Historical Society Publications, V* (1902), pp. 351-352.

48. "Mobile and Ohio Railroad," *DeBow's Review, XIII* (July 1852) pp. 87-88.

49. *Itawamba County Deedbook, XVI,* p. 231.

50. Ibid., p. 232.

51. *Itawamba County Platbook, I,* p. 79.

52. *Itawamba County Deedbook, XVI,* p. 347.

53. *Itawamba County Platbook, I,* p. 79.

54. *Itawamba County Deedbook, XVI,* pp. 453-454.

55. Ibid., pp. 487-489.

56. Riley, "Extent Towns," p. 352.

57. John Hill Aughey, *Tupelo.* Lincoln, NE: State Journal Company Printers, 1888, p. 1.

58. Stephen Dill Lee, "The Battle of Tupelo or Harrisburg, July 14, 1864," *Mississippi Historical Society Publications, VI* (1902), pp. 38-52.

59. W. L. Clayton, "Pen Pictures," *Tupelo Journal,* August 17, 1906.

60. Lemley, *Gulf Mobile and Ohio,* p. 311.

61. *Laws of Mississippi, 1866-1868,* p. 26.

62. Ibid., pp. 29-35.

63. Daniel Joseph Boorstin, *The Americans: The National Experience,* New York: Random House, 1965, pp. 164-168.

64. Ibid., p. 164.

65. *Laws of Mississippi, 1866-1868,* pp. 33-34.

66. *North Mississippian,* April 26, 1867.

67. *Tupelo Journal,* February 15, 1873.

68. *Tupelo Journal,* February 22, 1873.

69. George Herndon, "Early Tupelo," *Tupelo Journal,* November 3, 1918.

70. Mrs. S. J. High, "History of Tupelo and Lee County," (unpublished paper in the Lee County Library, Tupelo, MS) p. 7.

71. *Tupelo Journal,* August 31, 1906 and April 8, 1932.

72. Tupelo Board of Councilmen Book, I, p. 221.

73. *Tupelo Journal,* February 22, 1873.

74. Housing patterns were determined by U. S. Census data, Ninth, 1870, and Tenth, 1880, Census and a Sanborn Map.

75. Figures were compiled from raw data of the Ninth, 1870, and Tenth, 1880, Census.

76. Ninth Census, 1870, pp. 184-185; and Tenth Census 1880, p. 91, 231, 233.

77. *Tupelo Journal,* November 1, 1873; and June 23, 30, 1873.

78. *Tupelo Journal,* April 8, 1873.

79. *Tupelo Journal,* September 14, 1877.

80. Stephen Thernstrom, *Social Mobility in a Nineteenth Century City.* Cambridge: Harvard University Press, 1964, p. 85; Blake McKelvey, *Rochester, the flower city, 1855-1890.* Cambridge: Harvard University Press, 1949, p. 3; Peter Knight's, "Population Turnover, Persistence, and Residential Mobility in Boston, 1830-1860," in Stephen Thernstrom and Richard Sennett, eds., *Nineteenth Century Cities.* pp. 258-274; and Clyde Griffin, "Workers Divided: The Effect of Craft and Ethnic Differences in Poughkeepsie, New York, 1850-1880," in Stephen Thernstrom and Richard Sennett, eds., *Nineteenth Century Cities: Essays in New Urban History.* New Haven: Yale University Press, 1969, pp. 56-59.

81. Davis, *Recollections,* p. 19.

82. Claude Gentry, *Private John Allen, Gentleman-Statesman-Sage-Prophet.* Decatur, GA: Bowen Press, 1951.

83. *Tupelo Journal,* February 2, 1900 and April 8, 1932.

Chapter 3 — Expanding the Economic Base

1.   John P. Blair, *Urban and Regional Economics,* Homewood, IL: Irwin, 1991, p. 140.

2.   David R. Goldfield and Blaine A. Brownell, *Urban America: A History,* second edition, Boston: Houghton Mifflin Co., 1990, p. 179.

3.   Robert Wieke, *The Search for Order, 1877-1920.* New York: Hill and Wang, 1967. The emergence of the Urban network that served to unite the "island communities" is a major theme in the book.

4.   Gerald Mortimer Capers, Jr., *Biography of a River Town — Memphis: Its Heroic Age.* Chapel Hill: University of North Carolina Press, 1939, pp. 216-218.

5.   Blaine A. Brownell, "Urbanization in the South: A Unique Experience?" *Mississippi Quarterly XXVI* (Spring 1973), p. 112.

6.   Capers, *Memphis,* p. 218.

7.   Charles Nelson Glaab, *Kansas City and the Railroads: Community Policy in The South of a Regional Metropolis.* Madison: State Historical Society of Wisconsin, 1962, p. 187.

8.   *Laws of Mississippi, 1886,* Jackson: R. H. Henry State Printers, 1886, pp. 203-208.

9.   Rebecca W. Smith and Marion Mullins, eds., "The Diary of H. C. Medford, Confederate Soldier, 1864," *Southwestern Historical Quarterly, XXXIV* (October, 1930), p. 107.

10.   Reuben Davis, *Recollections of Mississippi and Mississippians* (Hattiesburg, MS, University and College Press of Mississippi, 1972) p. 179, W. L. Clayton, "Pen Pictures," Tupelo, Mississippi, August 6, 1906, and Claude Gentry, *Private John Allen, Gentleman-Statesman-Sage-Prophet,* Decatur, GA: Bowen Press, 1951, p. 159.

11.   John Miller's age is based on his reported age in The Tenth Census, MS, 1880.

12.   Thomas D. Clark, "The Country Newspaper: A Factor in Southern Opinion, 1865-1920," *Journal of Southern History, XIV* (February 1948), 3-

5; Robert R. Dykstra, *The Cattle Towns.* New York: Alfred A. Knopf, 1968, pp. 149-150. One of the best examples of the role of the newspaper editor to unite a movement for railroads is Robert T. Van Horn in Glaab, *Kansas City and the Railroads.*

13. *Tupelo Journal,* December 25, 1885 to October 29, 1886.

14. *Tupelo Journal,* November 27, 1885.

15. *Mississippi Laws, 1886,* pp. 207-208.

16. Author's interview with Kathleen Mitts, a local historian whose father was active in bringing the railroad to Tupelo; Tupelo, MS, June 3, 1970.

17. *Tupelo Journal,* February 19, 1886; and *Mississippi Laws, 1886,* pp. 207-208.

18. The *Tupelo Journal* had occasional references to Verona's efforts to secure the route for itself; see *Tupelo Journal,* August 7, 1885; September 11, 1885, October 16, 1885; January 8, 29, 1886; February 22, 1886.

19. Ibid., September 4, 11, 1885; October 9, 1885.

20. Ibid., September 26, 1885; December 11, 1885; January 15, 1886.

21. *Birmingham Age,* November 18, 1887.

22. Glaab, *Kansas City and the Railroads,* pp. 114-115.

23. *Tupelo Journal,* April 16, 1886.

24. Ibid., May 20, 1886.

25. Ibid., October 7, 1886.

26. Ibid., March 4, 25, 1887.

27. "A History of The Bank of Tupelo," *Tupelo Journal,* April 1, 1930.

28. *Tupelo Ledger,* September 18, 1890. The article provides a brief historical sketch of J. J. Rogers Company.

29. *Tupelo Journal,* March 18, 1887.

30. C. W. Troy, "History of Early Tupelo," *Tupelo Journal,* April 18, 1932.

31. High, "History of Tupelo and Lee County," [n.p.].

32. Tupelo Board of Councilmen, Minutes, February 18, 1890, p. 285; March 19, 1890, p. 287; Book "A" July 13, 1891, p. 12.

33. *Tupelo Journal,* December 2, 1887.

34. Ibid., March 16; April 13, 1888.

35. Ibid., March 23, 1888.

36. Ibid., March 16; April 13, 1888; July 11, 1889; May 1, 1890.

37. Ibid., September 18, 1890.

38. Ibid., October 2, 1890.

39. Ibid., March 25, 1892.

40. Mary E. Rodgers, "The City of Tupelo, Mississippi," (Tupelo: *Tupelo Journal,* 1907), [n.p.].

41. *Birmingham News,* November 18, 1887.

42. Rodgers, "The City of Tupelo," [n.p.].

43. *Tupelo Journal,* March 3, 15, 22, 29, 1890.

44. Ibid., April 25, 1889.

45. Tupelo Board of Councilmen, Minutes, October 12, 1889, p. 272.

46. United States, Bureau of The Census, Eleventh Census of The United States: 1890, Agriculture, Washington: Government Printing Office, 1892, p. 50.

47. Matthew Brown Hammond, *The Cotton Industry: An Essay in American Economic History,* New York: The Macmillan Company, 1897, Appendix; and Dunbar Rowland, *Mississippi: The Heart of the South,* 4 Volumes, Jackson: S. J. Clark, 1952, II, pp. 256-260.

48. Stephen E. Ambrose, "Cotton Prices and Costs: A Suggestion," *Georgia Historical Quarterly*, XLVIII (March 1964), pp. 78-80.

49. James Scaborough Ferguson, "Agrarianism in Mississippi, 1871-1900: A Study in Nonconformity," (Unpublished doctoral dissertation, The University of North Carolina, 1952), p. 5.

50. *Tupelo Journal*, January 31, 1887.

51. Lee County's 1880 population was counted at 20,410. A decade later it had declined to 20,040. Using a low estimate of a birthrate of 25 and a deathrate of 10, the county should have experienced a natural rate of increase in excess of 3,000. United States Bureau of The Census, Eleventh Census of The United States 1890, Population Part I. Washington: Government Printing Office, 1892, pp. 27, 241.

52. Tupelo Board of Councilmen, Minutes, December 2, 1889, p. 280; January 3, 1890, p. 284.

53. Ibid., December 2, 1889, p. 280; January 14, 1891, p. 304; Book "A," July 13, 1891, p. 12; January 12, 1892, p. 20.

54. Troy, "History of Early Tupelo," *Tupelo Journal*, April 18, 1932.

55. *Tupelo Journal*, December 5, 12, 19, 1892.

56. Ibid., January 20; February 3, 10, 17, and 24, 1893.

57. Ibid., March 3, 1893.

58. Ibid., February 3, 10, 17, 24, 1893.

59. For the use of this tactic in other small towns, see Lyle W. Dorsett, "Town Promotion," *New England Quarterly*, XL (June, 1967), pp. 275-277.

60. *Tupelo Journal*, March 17; October 6, 13, 1893; July 13, 1894.

61. United States Department of Agriculture, *Yearbook, 1911*, Washington: Government Printing Office, 1912, p. 500.

62. *Tupelo Journal*, October 20, 1899.

63. United States Bureau of The Census, Twelfth Census of The United States: 1900 Population, Part I, Washington: Government Printing Office, 1902,

pp. 232-233.

64. See for example, *Tupelo Journal*, February 16, 1894.

65. Stanley Elkins and Eric McKitrick, "A Meaning for Turner's Frontier," *Political Science Quarterly*, LXIX (September 1954), pp. 325-326.

66. *Tupelo Journal*, August 12, 19, 26, 1898.

67. For a description of the progressive sentiment in the state as a whole see Martha Bigelow, "Mississippi Progressivism," *Journal of Mississippi History*, XXIX (August 1967), pp. 202-209.

68. The quest for a structural reform rather than social reform was common to cities throughout the region. See David R. Goldfield, *Cotton Fields and Skyscrapers: Southern City and Region, 1607-1980*. Baton Rouge: Louisiana State University Press, 1982. p. 101. For a similar pattern throughout the nation, see Steven C. Swett, "The Test of a Reformer: A Study of Seth Low," *New York Historical Quarterly*, XLIV (January 1960) pp. 5-41; George Edwin Mowry, *The California Progressives*, Berkeley: The University of California Press, 1951, pp. 23-25; William D. Miller, *Mr. Crump of Memphis*, Baton Rouge: Louisiana State University Press, 1964; Constance McLaughlin Green, *Holyoke, MA: A Case History of the Industrial Revolution*, New Haven: Yale University Press, 1939, pp. 267-269.

69. *Tupelo Journal*, "The Industrial Review," Tupelo, 1902, [n.p.].

70. Van C. Kincannon, Jr. and W. H. Milam, *Tupelo: Premier City of North Mississippi*, Tupelo: Kincannon and Milam, 1921, p. 20.

71. Ibid.

72. Dunbar Rowland, *Mississippi: Heart of the South*, 4 Volumes, Jackson: S. J. Clark Publishing Company, 1925, III 637-638; and *Tupelo Journal*, January 7, 1952.

73. *Memphis Commercial Appeal*, January 15, 1899.

74. Clyde J. Faries, "Redneck Rhetoric and The Last of The Redeemers: The 1899 McLaurin-Allen Campaign," *Journal of Mississippi History*, XXXII (November 1971), 283-298.

75. The rivalry is manifested in the newspaper accounts from the period. See for example, *Tupelo Journal* March 2, 1900. The author was given addi-

tional insight into the rivalry in an interview with Sam H. Long, the son of Charles P. Long, an active participant in the events at the turn of the century. Interview March 3, 1973 in Tupelo, MS. Sam Long was both a political rival and subsequently an ally of Will Robins.

76. Tupelo Board of Councilmen, Minutes, Book "A," February 3, 1899, pp. 582-583.

77. *Tupelo Journal*, March 17, 1899.

78. Ibid., November 3, 1899.

79. Ibid., June 9, 16, 1899.

80. See for example, James C. Cobb, *The Selling of the South: The Southern Crusade for Industrial Development 1936-1990*, 2d ed., Urbana: University of Illinois Press, 1993 and Goldfield, *Cottonfields and Skyscrapers*, pp. 123-124.

81. *Tupelo Journal*, November 10, 1899.

82. Cobb, *The Selling of The South*, and Goldfield, *Cottonfields and Skyscrapers*.

83. A list of the men and the amount of their investment is given in the *Tupelo Journal*, November 10, 1899.

84. Papers of Charles Philip Long, one of the leaders of the industrial project, in the possession of his son, Sam H. Long of Tupelo, MS.

85. *Memphis Commercial Appeal*, "The Hub of the Universe," November 22, 1903. This article was a history of Tupelo's Industrial Development from 1899 to 1903.

86. *Tupelo Journal*, July 18, 1902.

87. *Memphis Commercial Appeal*, November 22, 1903.

88. Kincannon and Milam, "Tupelo," p. 2.

89. Rodgers, "The City of Tupelo, Mississippi," [n.p.].

90. *Memphis Commercial Appeal*, November 22, 1903.

91. Tupelo Board of Councilmen, Minutes, Book "B," June 12, 1902, p. 39.

92. *Tupelo Journal,* June 10, 1904.

93. Rodgers, "The City of Tupelo," [n.p.].

94. William Fowler Holmes, *The White Chief, James Kimble Vardaman,* Baton Rouge: Louisiana State University Press, 1970. p. 107.

95. Ibid., pp. 387-388.

96. Ethridge Cotton, Jr., "Major Changes in the Mississippi Labor Force, Their Causes and Effects," (unpublished doctoral dissertation, The University of Pittsburgh, 1962), p. 2.

97. John Knox Bettersworth, *Mississippi: A History,* Austin, TX: The Steak Company, 1959, p. 394.

98. Charles Philip Long Papers.

99. Gerald M. Capers, "The Rural Lag of Southern Cities," *Mississippi Quarterly, XXI* (Fall 1968), 255-256.

100. Tupelo Deedbooks. The list of the most active participants in the industrial development was determined by a simple count of the number of activities reported in the newspaper. This list corresponds roughly to that reported in the *Tupelo Journal,* November 10, 1899. The Index to the Deedbook was used to determine their land holdings and subsequently the Deedbooks themselves.

101. Rodgers, "The City of Tupelo, Mississippi," [n.p.].

102. William R. Thompson, *A Preface to Urban Economics.* Baltimore: The Johns Hopkins Press, 1965, pp. 18-21.

103. *Tupelo Journal,* June 10, 1904.

104. Ibid., May 26, 1905.

105. *Mississippi Laws, 1886,* pp. 320-325; *Amended Mississippi Laws, 1896,* p. 162; Lee County Supervisors Minutes, VI, pp. 37; 79-81; 110, 354. For the increased yields see United States Bureau of The Census, Thirteenth Census of the United States, Agriculture, 1910, Washington: Government Printing Office, 1912, p. 334.

106. Tupelo Board of Councilmen, Minutes, Book "A," October 2, 1900,

p. 240.

107. Ibid.

108. *Tupelo Journal*, October 19, 1900.

109. Ibid., October 16, 1947.

110. A year after his death, John Clark was remembered as the "leading spirit" in the town's growth.

111. Rowland, *Mississippi*, p. 637.

112. Thirteenth Census, 1910 Abstract With Supplement for Mississippi, p. 598.

Chapter 4 — The Agrarian Revolt: A Study in Community Conflict

1. Lewis A. Coser, *The Functions of Social Conflict*, Glencoe, IL: Free Press, 1971.

2. Matthew Brown Hammond, *The Cotton Industry: An Essay in Economic History*, New York: The Macmillan Company, 1897, appendix.

3. Comer Vann Woodward, *Origins of the New South*, 1877-1913, Baton Rouge: Louisiana State University Press, 1951, p. 264.

4. *Tupelo Journal*, April 17, 1931.

5. Jerry W. Robinson, Jr., "The Conflict Approach" in James A. Christensen and Jerry W. Robinson, Jr., eds., *Community Development in Perspective*, Ames, IA: Iowa State University Press, 1989, pp. 93-94.

6. Stanley B. Parsons, *The Populist Context: Rural Versus Urban Power on a Great Plains Frontier*. Westport, CT: Greenwood Press, 1973, pp. 37-41.

7. *Tupelo Journal*, February 10, 17, 24; March 3, 1873.

8. Ibid., June 8, 1875.

9. Ibid., April 11, 1879.

10. Ibid., May 17, 1880.

11. Ibid., February 24, 1882.

12. *Aberdeen Examiner*, May 17, 1883.

13. Robinson, "The Conflict Approach," p. 90.

14. Albert D. Kirwan, *Revolt of the Rednecks: Mississippi Politics, 1876-1925*, Gloucester, MA: Peter Smith, 1964, pp. 54-55.

15. *Tupelo Journal*, November 20, 1885.

16. Ibid., December 11, 1885.

17. Ibid., April 16, 1886.

18. Robinson, "The Conflict Approach," pp. 96-97.

19. James S. Coleman, "The Dynamics of Community Controversy" in Roland L. Warren and Larry Lyon, *New Perspectives on the American Community*, fifth edition, Chicago: Dorsey Press, 1988, pp. 334-336.

20. *Tupelo Journal*, July 20, 1888.

21. United States, Bureau of the Census, Tenth Census of the United States: 1880. Lee County Manuscript and *Tupelo Journal*, July 20, 1888.

22. *Tupelo Ledger*, July 17, 1890.

23. William David McCain, "The Populist Party in Mississippi" (unpublished master's thesis, The University of Mississippi, 1931), p. 10.

24. *Tupelo Ledger*, May 1, 1888.

25. *Tupelo Journal*, April 27, 1888.

26. Ibid., January 7, 14, 1880.

27. *Aberdeen Examiner*, July 24, 1891.

28. Theodore R. Mitchell, *Political Education in the Southern Farmers' Alliance, 1887-1900*, Madison: University of Wisconsin Press, 1987, pp. 4-5.

29. *Tupelo Ledger*, July 18, 1889.

30. Ibid., November 7, 21, 1889.

31. Ibid., January 16, 1890.

32. Coleman, "The Dynamics of Community Controversy," p. 339.

33. *Tupelo Journal,* February 29, 1890.

34. *Tupelo Journal,* quoting the *Okolona Chickasaw Messenger,* March 17, 1890.

35. Roland L. Warren, *The Community in America,* 3d ed., Chicago: Rand McNally, 1978, pp. 287-294.

36. United States Bureau of Census, Eleventh Census of the United States: 1890. Population. Washington: Government Printing Office, 1891, I. p. 208.

37. See especially, *Tupelo Journal,* October 11, 25; November 15; December 13, 1889.

38. Thomas D. Clark, "The Furnishing and Supply System in Southern Agriculture since 1865," *Journal of Southern History, XII* (February 1946), p. 34.

39. Intercounty family ties were determined by weekly reports printed in the *Tupelo Journal* from rural communities throughout Lee County.

40. *Tupelo Ledger,* July 25, August 1, 1889; *Tupelo Journal,* January 9, 16, 25, 1890.

41. Woodward, *Origins of the New South,* p. 169.

42. This observation is supported by weekly reports from the rural hamlets printed in the *Tupelo Journal.* See for example *Tupelo Journal,* March 14, 12; April 4, 11, 18; May 2, 9, 1890.

43. Ibid., February 21, 1896. This pattern held true for much of the South. See Eleventh Census, Statistics of Churches. Washington: Government Printing Office, 1893, p. 69.

44. *Tupelo Ledger,* May 11, and May 18, 1888.

45. Ibid., May 25, 1888.

46. *Tupelo Journal,* June 15, 1888.

47. Ibid., June 22, 1888.

48. Claude Gentry, *Private John Allen, Gentlemen-Statesman-Sage-Prophet.* Decatur, GA: Bowen Press, 1951, p. 159.

49. David G. Sansing, *Mississippi: Its People and Culture.* Minneapolis: T. S. Denison and Company, 1981, p. 252.

50. Kirwan, *Revolt of the Rednecks,* p. 61.

51. *Tupelo Journal,* April 18, 25, 1890.

52. Ibid., May 2, 1890.

53. Ibid., July 19, 1890.

54. Ibid., April 4, 11, 18; May 2, 9, 1890.

55. Ibid., June 6, 1890.

56. Mitchell, *Political Education in the Southern Farmers' Alliance,* p. 76.

57. Ibid., p. 77.

58. Writers Project Administration, "Lee County: Races and Nationalities," typewritten copy in the Lee County Library in Tupelo, MS, 1937, X, p. 59.

59. *Tupelo Journal,* June 27, 1890.

60. Ibid., July 11, 1891.

61. Robinson, "The Conflict Approach," p. 97.

62. For a discussion of avoidance as a defense mechanism in coping with political cross-pressures, see Paul F. Lazarsfeld, Bernard Berelson, and Hazon Gaudet, *The People's Choice.* New York: Columbia University Press, 1948, Chapter 10.

63. *Tupelo Journal,* August 1, 1890.

64. Mitchell, *Political Education in the Southern Farmers' Alliance,* p. 161.

65. Ibid., and Theodore Saloutos, *Farmer Movements in the South, 1865-1933.* Lincoln: University of Nebraska Press, 1964, p. 120.

66. Kirwan, *Revolt of the Rednecks,* p. 86.

67. Saloutos, *Farmer Movements in the South,* p. 119.

68. *Tupelo Ledger,* February 12, 1891.

69. Ibid.

70. Ibid., February 26, 1891.

71. Coleman, "The Dynamics of Community Controversy," pp. 334-335.

72. *Tupelo Journal,* March 5, 1891, March 13, 1891.

73. Kirwan, *The Revolt of the Rednecks,* p. 86.

74. *Tupelo Ledger,* April 9, 1891.

75. *Tupelo Journal,* April 10, 1891.

76. Tupelo Board of Councilmen, Minutes, Book "A," (May 14, 1891), p. 4.

77. *Tupelo Journal,* May 15, 1891.

78. *Tupelo Ledger,* May 21, 1891.

79. Ibid., April 20, 30, 1891.

80. Ibid., May 7, 1891.

81. *Tupelo Journal,* July 24, 1891.

82. *Aberdeen Examiner,* July 24, 21, 1891.

83. *Tupelo Ledger,* July 30, 1891, quoting *The Jackson Clarion Ledger, Greenville Democrat, Oxford Globe,* and *Corinth Democrat,* [n.d. for the quoted newspapers].

84. *Tupelo Ledger,* July 23, 1891.

85. Coleman, "The Dynamics of Community Controversy," p. 338.

86. Ibid., July 30, 1891 and August 6, 1891; and *Tupelo Journal,* July 31 and August 7, 1891.

87. *Tupelo Journal,* August 28, 1891.

88. *Tupelo Journal,* November 6, 1891.

89. Ibid., August 7, 21; September 18, 1891; and *Tupelo Ledger,* August 13, 20, 1891.

90. *Tupelo Journal,* October 2, 1891.

91. Ibid., November 6, 1891.

92. Ibid., April 1, 1892.

93. Ibid., July 9, 1892.

94. *Tupelo Ledger,* August 12, 1892.

95. Ibid., September 15, 1892.

96. *Tupelo Ledger,* September 22, 1892; *Tupelo Journal,* September 30 and October 7, 14, 1892.

97. *Tupelo Journal,* September 16, 1892.

98. *Tupelo Ledger,* September 15, 1892.

99. Ibid., September 20, and October 6, 1892.

100. *Tupelo Ledger,* September 9, 1892.

101. *Tupelo Journal,* October 14, 1892.

102. Ibid., October 28, 1892.

103. Ibid., October 29, 1892 and November 4, 1892.

104. Ibid., November 11, 1892.

105. Ibid., November 11, 1892.

106. Ibid., November 8, 1895.

107. Ibid., November 16, 1896.

108. Ibid., February 21, 1896.

109. Ibid., July 2, 1897.

110. Tupelo Board of Councilmen, Minutes, February 3, 1890, p. 234 and W.P.A. Files, Race and Nationalities, V. 10, p. 4.

111. *Tupelo Journal,* August 7, 1883.

112. Sansing, *Mississippi,* p. 252.

113. *Tupelo Ledger,* July 23 and 30, 1891; *Tupelo Journal,* October 28, and November 4, 1892.

114. Tupelo Board of Councilmen, Minutes, Book "A," October 2, 1894, pp. 130-131.

115. *Tupelo Journal,* April 10, 1896.

116. Ibid., April 1, 8, 14, 1898.

117. Tupelo Board of Councilmen Minutes Book "A," April 5, and May 3, 1898, pp. 177-179.

118. Horizontal ties held the races together as equals as opposed to vertical ties that link superordinates to subordinates.

Chapter 5 — The Development of Good Roads: Tying the Community Together

1. Thomas D. Clark, "Changes in Transportation," in Richard Aubrey McLemore, ed., *A History of Mississippi,* two volumes, Hattiesburg: University and College Press of Mississippi, 1973, II, 278.

2. The description of the wagon yard is drawn from Charles Philip Long, "A History of Tupelo," unpublished paper in the Lee County Library, Tupelo, MS, pp. 4-6.

3. Author's interview with Richard Bolton in Tupelo, MS, June 3,1972, and *Tupelo Journal,* January 9, 1909.

4. For a comparable pattern see Bessie Louise Pierce, *A History of Chicago,* three volumes, New York: Alfred A. Knopf, 1937, I, 52-53.

5. John P. Blair, *Urban and Regional Economics,* Homewood, IL: Irwin, 1991, p. 87.

6. Amos Henry Hawley, *Human Ecology: A Theory of Community Structure.* New York: The Ronald Press, 1950, p. 405.

7. For a discussion of the development of mass transportation and its expression of the "walking City" to the modern metropolis surrounded by its satellite suburbs, see Sam Bass Warner, Jr., *Streetcar Suburbs: The Progress of Growth in Boston,* Cambridge: Harvard University Press, 1962.

8. For examples of lengthy editorials on the need for good roads in Lee County, see *Tupelo Journal,* January 30,1885; May 28, 1886: December 4, 1891; May 26, 1893; February 22, 1895; July 29, 1898; February 6, 20, 1903.

9. Department of Agriculture, *Yearbook, 1901,* Washington: Government Printing Office, 1902, p. 414.

10. Ibid.

11. Logan Waller Page, "Objective-Lesson roads," Department of Agriculture, *Yearbook, 1906.* Washington: Government Printing Office, 1907, pp. 137-150.

12. Ibid., p. 145.

13. Logan Waller Page, "Necessity for Road Improvement in the South," *South Atlantic Quarterly,* IX (April, 1910), 155-160.

14. Joseph Hyde Pratt, "Good Roads Movement in the South," *Annals of the American Academy of Political and Social Sciences, XXXV* (January 1910), 109.

15. Clark, "Changes in Transportation," p. 277.

16. George H. Ethridge, *Mississippi Constitutions,* Jackson: Turner Printing House, 1928, pp. 310-314.

17. Ibid.

18. Cecil Kenneth Brown, *The State Highway System of North Carolina, Its Evolution and Present Status,* Chapel Hill: University of North Carolina Press, 1931, p. 9.

19. Dunbar Rowland, *Mississippi: The Heart of the South.* 4 volumes, Jackson: S. J. Clark Publishing Company, 1925, II, 295. (Hereinafter cited as Rowland, *Mississippi.*)

20. Supervisors, Minutes, VIII, May 9, 1907, pp. 248-251; August 3, 1907, pp. 471-472.

21. Mississippi State Highway Department, *Pictorial Review: A Supplemental Report for the Mississippi State Highway Department,* Jackson: Hederman Bros. Press, 1940, p. 21.

22. Ethridge, *Mississippi Constitutions,* p. 310.

23. Rowland, *Mississippi, II,* 295.

24. *Tupelo Journal-Review,* September 11, 1925.

25. *Tupelo Journal,* September 29, 1905.

26. Among the civic developments were a new city hall, a Y.M.C.A. building, and a town beautification program. Between 1909 and 1911 the activities of the city government were greatly enlarged. The mayor's annual salary was increased from $500 to $900 and he was expected to work at the job on a regular basis. See Tupelo Board of Aldermen, Minutes II, December 8, 1910, 260; and *Tupelo Journal,* September 10, 17, 24, 1909.

27. *Tupelo Journal,* January 2, 1909.

28. Tupelo Board of Aldermen, Minutes II, June 7, 1909, pp. 103-109.

29. Ibid., September 13, 1909, p. 146.

30. *Tupelo Journal,* October 1, 1909.

31. United States Bureau of Census, Thirteenth Census: 1900, Abstracts With Supplement for Mississippi, Washington: Government Printing Office, 1912, p. 616.

32. *Tupelo Journal,* March 13, 1908.

33. Brown, *The State Highway System of North Carolina,* p. 53. Brown lamented that "after twenty years 'Good Roads' enthusiasts had still not gained farmer support for the movement."

34. *Mississippi Senate Journal,* 1910, pp. 7-8.

35. Ibid., p. 88.

36. Ibid., p. 501.

37. Lee County Board of Supervisors, Minutes, X, March 10, 1910, pp. 14-16.

38. Lee County Board of Supervisors, Minutes, X, May 6, 1910, p. 69.

39. Ibid., July 5, 1910, pp. 123-127.

40. *Tupelo Journal,* May 5, 1910.

41. Tupelo Board of Aldermen, Minutes, II, May 7, 1912, pp. 444-445.

42. *Tupelo Journal,* February 2, 1912.

43. Ibid., May 3, 1912.

44. Tupelo Board of Aldermen, Minutes, III, September 7, 1915, pp. 266-268.

45. *Tupelo Journal,* March 1, 1912. Many southern railroads were acting in concert with the Department of Agriculture in sponsoring these trains.

46. Ibid., May 24, 1912.

47. Mississippi Planning Committee, *Today and Tomorrow,* Jackson: Hederman Bros., 1949, p.16.

48. For descriptions of the visiting tours of the road system see *Tupelo Journal,* August 26, 1912, September 12, October 24, 1913 and passim.

49. For Frank Goodlett's role in the road program see *Tupelo Journal,* July 21, 1914.

50. Ibid., May 8, 15, 22, 29; June 5, 12, 19, 26; July 3, 10, 1914.

51. Ibid., June 19, 1914.

52. Ibid., July 10, 1914.

53. Mississippi State Highway Department, *Pictorial Review*, p. 33.

54. David R. Goldfield, *Cotton Fields and Skyscrapers: Southern City and Region, 1608-1980*, Baton Rouge: 1982, p. 101.

55. Mississippi State Highway Department, *Pictorial Review*, p. 33.

56. Jane Jacobs, *The Death and Life of Great American Cities*, New York: Random House, 1961, p. 29.

57. Prior to the paved streets the town seemed to take little pride in its appearance; now there was reason to be proud. John Allen lamented to the Civic Improvement League in 1909 that he had tried unsuccessfully at earlier periods to beautify the town or to get others interested in such a project. See *Tupelo Journal*, September 10, 1909.

58. The expression "city beautiful" seemed to come into popular usage shortly after the completion of the streets and was later frequently used to contrast the wreckage of the 1936 tornado with what had existed earlier. For a cursory but useful discussion of the city beautiful movement in the nation see Lewis Mumford, *Sticks and Stones: A Study of American Architecture and Civilization*, New York: Dover Press, 1955, pp. 127-131.

59. *Memphis Commercial Appeal*, March 27, 1920.

60. *Tupelo Journal*, January 5, 1912.

61. Ibid., November 5, 1915 and October 20, 1916.

62. Ibid., January 5, 1912 and January 2, 1914.

63. Ibid., January 23, 30, 1914.

64. Ibid., July 3, 1914.

65. Ibid., May 27, 1923.

66. Ibid., May 27, 1923.

67. Ibid., September 12, 1921.

68. Ibid., June 24, 1923.

69. Tupelo Chamber of Commerce, "Industrial Survey of Tupelo, Mississippi," *Tupelo Journal,* June 1, 1938, p. 13.

70. Kathleen Mitts, "Where Hominy and Grits Met," *See Tupelo,* March-April, 1967, p. 9.

71. R. Richard Wohl and A. Theodore Brown, "The Usable Past: A Study of Historical Past," *Huntington Library Quarterly, XXXIII* (May 1960), pp. 237-259.

72. Author's interview with George A. McLean, June 4, 1973.

73. Lecture given by George A. McLean, September 19, 1970, at the University of Mississippi.

74. *Tupelo Journal,* July 10, 1972.

75. Kingsley Davis, "The Origin and Growth of Urbanization in the World," *American Journal of Sociology, LX,* (March 1955), pp. 429-437.

76. Hawley, *Human Ecology,* pp. 409-417; Nicholas J. Demerath and Harlan W. Gilmore, "The Ecology of Southern Cities," in Rupert B. Vance and Nicholas J. Demerath, editors, *The Urban South,* Chapel Hill: University of North Carolina Press, 1954, pp. 145-146.

77. Roderick Duncan McKenzie, "Spatial Distance and Community Organization," *Social Forces, V* (June 1927), p. 625.

Chapter 6 — Community Development and the Agricultural Transition

1. United States Bureau of the Census, Thirteenth Census, 1910, Agriculture. Washington: Government Printing Office, 1913, VI, p. 868.

2. James Henry Street, *The New Revolution in the Cotton Economy: Mechanization and Its Consequences,* Chapel Hill: University of North Carolina Press, 1957, pp. 36-37.

3. James H. Shideler, *Farm Crisis, 1919-1923,* Berkeley: University of California Press, 1957, p. 5.

4. Rupert Bayless Vance, *Human Factors in Cotton Culture: A Study in the*

Social Geography of the American South, Chapel Hill: University of North Carolina Press, 1929, p. 11; and D. A. McCandliss, *Base Book of Mississippi Agriculture,* Jackson: Department of Agriculture, 1955, pp. 121-122. (Hereinafter cited as *Base Book.*)

5. Gilbert Fite, "Voluntary Attempts to Reduce Cotton Acreage in the South, 1914-1933," *Journal of Southern History, XIV,* November 1948, p. 482.

6. Edwin Griswold Nourse, *American Agriculture and the European Market,* New York: McGraw-Hill, 1924, pp. 283-286.

7. United States Department of Agriculture, *Yearbook, 1915.* Washington: Government Printing Office, 1916, p. 18.

8. *Tupelo Journal,* September 25, 1914.

9. The "Buy-a-Bale" movement swept the entire South. See David L. Cohn, *The Life and Times of King Cotton,* New York: Oxford University Press, 1956, pp. 233-234; and James L. McCorkle, "The Louisiana 'Buy-a-Bale' Cotton Movement, 1914," *Louisiana History, XIV* (Spring 1974), pp. 133-152.

10. *Tupelo Journal,* September 11, 25; October 2, 9, and 16, 1914.

11. Fite, "Voluntary Attempts to Reduce Cotton Acreage in the South," p. 483.

12. Hearings before the House Committee on Agriculture Regarding the Boll Weevil, p. 29, cited in Vance, *Human Factors in Cotton Culture,* p. 92.

13. "The Cotton Situation," *Agriculture Yearbook, 1921,* p. 35.

14. *Base Book,* p. 121.

15. Floyd Hunter, "Community Organization: Lever for Institutional Change?" in Rupert R. Vance and Nicholas J. Demerath, eds., *The Urban South,* Chapel Hill: University of North Carolina Press, 1954, p. 252.

16. An earlier editor offered the warning, "Hard times have befallen those farmers who have not seen the errors of their ways and cling to their king cotton! cotton! cotton!" *Tupelo Journal,* January 24, 1874.

17. Author's interview with Richard Bolton in Tupelo, Mississippi, November 12, 1972.

18. Kenneth P. Wilkinson, *The Community in Rural America,* Westport, CT: Greenwood Press, 1991, p. 92.

19. *Pontotoc Chickasaw Union,* February 15, 1838.

20. Charles Patrick Joseph Mooney, *The Mid-South and Its Builders,* Memphis: Thomas W. Briggs Company, 1920.

21. David G. Sansing, "Peoples Bank and Trust Co.: In Partnership with the Community," Fulton: *Itawamba County Times,* 1989, p. 29.

22. The Peoples Bank and Trust statement in the *Tupelo Journal,* January 7 and October 6, 1916.

23. Harold Severson, "Land of Milk and Money," *Southern Farmer,* January, 1949, [n.p.].

24. Author's interview with one of Tupelo's premier storytellers, Samuel H. Long, in Tupelo, MS, March 9, 1973.

25. Bradford Knapp, "Diversified Agriculture and the Relation of the Banker to the Farmer," United States Department of Agriculture, Office of the Secretary, Circular No. 50 (Washington 1915).

26. Ibid., pp. 1-2.

27. Ibid., pp. 3-12.

28. Willie D. Halsell, "L. Q. C. Lamar's Taylor Farm: An Experiment in Diversified Farming," *Journal of Mississippi History, V* (October 1943), pp. 185-196.

29. Ibid., p. 188.

30. *Tupelo Journal,* February 1885.

31. Jack Gunning, "Tupelo, Mississippi: Dairy Farming Proves Tops in Cotton Community," *The Kraftsman,* May-June, 1947, p. 4.

32. *Tupelo Journal,* June 2 and June 30, 1916.

33. Ibid., July 14, 1916.

34. *Tupelo Weekly News,* "Dairying and Progress Edition," March 1929.

35. *Tupelo Journal,* November 12, 1918.

36. United States Bureau of The Census, Thirteenth Census: 1910. Agriculture. Washington: Government Printing Office, 1912, pp. 868 and 884; United States Bureau of The Census, Fourteenth Census, 1920. Agriculture, 1922, VI, Washington: Government Printing Office, part 2, pp. 534 and 542.

37. *The Wall Street Journal,* December 18, 1923.

38. Sansing, *The Peoples Bank,* p. 32.

39. *Tupelo Weekly News,* "Dairying and Progress Edition," March 1929.

40. Hodding Carter, "Tupelo, Mississippi," *The Saturday Evening Post,* CCXXI-II (February 17, 1951), p. 78. High apparently got this first slogan from railroad-sponsored diversification trains in the Midwest called "The Cow-Sow-and-Hen Trains." Mildred Thorne, "Suggested Research on Railroad Aid to the Farmer, with Particular Reference to Iowa and Kansas," *Agricultural History, XXI* (October 1957), pp. 50-66.

41. *Tupelo Journal,* December 19, 1949.

42. Ibid., January 20, March 17, and June 16, 1922.

43. For one of the best of the special issues see the *Tupelo Journal-Review,* February 23, 1926.

44. For an excellent account of Mooney's efforts in behalf of diversification see James Wesley Silver, "C. P. J. Mooney of the *Memphis Commercial Appeal,* Crusader for Diversification," *Agricultural History, XVII* (April 1943), pp. 81-89.

45. The *Memphis Commercial Appeal* column was headed "Farmers Attention!" and offered reminders of the selling price of various crops or provided other pieces of practical advice. See Thomas Harrison Baker III, "The Memphis Commercial Appeal" (unpublished doctoral dissertation, The University of Texas, 1965), pp. 271-273. Sam Durham, the local dairy specialist, wrote the variously titled columns for the *Tupelo Journal.*

46. *Tupelo Journal,* November 12, 1918.

47. Ibid., June 22, August 24, 1928.

48. Ibid., January 29, 1926.

49. Tupelo Board of Aldermen, Minutes, V (August 6, 1929), pp. 389-390.

50. *Tupelo Journal,* May 1, 1927, November 15, and December 3, 1929.

51. Ibid., January 26, 1927.

52. *Tupelo Weekly News,* "Dairying and Progress Edition," March 1929.

53. *Tupelo Journal,* January 16, 1927.

54. Ibid., February 9, 1927.

55. Ibid., March 6, 1927.

56. Ibid., March 16, 19, and April 24, 1927.

57. Ibid., May 15, 1927.

58. Mooney, *The Mid-South and Its Builders,* p. 139.

59. Dunbar Rowland, *Mississippi: The Heart of the South,* 4 volumes, Jackson, MS: S. J. Clark Publishing Company, 1925, III, pp. 20-23.

60. Sansing, *The Peoples Bank,* p. 32.

61. Ibid., p. 46.

62. Ibid., pp. 50-51.

63. Tupelo Board of Aldermen, Minutes, V (October 27, 1933), pp. 622-623. The terms of the contract are cited in ibid., November 13, 1933, pp. 626-635.

64. Richardson Wood, "The Community Goes into Business," *Harvard Business Review, XXVI* (January 1948), pp. 149-150.

65. *Tupelo Daily News,* November 18, 19, 1934; *Memphis Commercial Appeal,* November 19, 1934.

66. All discussions of George McLean and his work were drawn from numerous personal conversations with George McLean and from hours of video-

and audiotaped interviews conducted by the author.

67. Based on the author's conversations and experiences with Harry Rutherford and Bill Stroud.

68. Harold Severson, "How a Cotton-sick Area Got Well," *Banking, XLI* (July 1948), p. 52.

69. The small Lee County farms prohibited the early development of beef cattle on a large scale. See Carter, "Tupelo, Mississippi," p. 78.

70. Wilson Whitman, "Three Southern Towns, Tupelo: Feudalism and the T.V.A.," *Nation, CXLVIII* (December 31, 1938), p. 12.

71. Author's interview with Gale Carr in Verona, MS, June 7, 1972.

72. *Tupelo Journal,* April 6, 1936.

73. Ibid., April 3, 1936.

74. Ibid., April 10, 1936.

75. The master plan was originally proposed two months before the tornado. *Tupelo Journal,* February 5, 1936; and author's interview with George McLean in Tupelo, MS, August 7, 1973.

76. *Tupelo Journal,* June 3, 1936.

77. Ibid.

78. Ibid., March 13, 1941, and author's interview with George McLean in Tupelo, MS, August 7, 1973.

79. *Tupelo Journal,* February 12, 24; June 17, 1943.

80. Ibid., February 24, 1943.

81. Ibid., April 8, 1937. A more complete discussion of the textile mill strike is given in Chapter 7.

82. Jack Gunning, "Tupelo, Mississippi: Dairy Farming Proves Tops in Cotton Community," *The Kraftsman, Producer's Edition,* May-June 1947, p. 5.

83. Author's interview with Gale Carr in Verona, MS, June 5, 1973.

84. Ibid.

85. Gunning, "Tupelo, Mississippi," p. 5.

86. Ibid.

87. *Tupelo Journal,* July 30, 1941.

88. Ibid., February 12, 1942.

89. Gunning, "Tupelo, Mississippi," p. 6; and author's interview with Gale Carr in Verona, MS, June 5, 1973.

90. *Tupelo Journal,* March 31, 1951.

91. Ibid., May 24, 1941.

92. George McLean, "It Can Be Done!" A keynote speech to the Agricultural Committee of the Chamber of Commerce of the United States of America, at St. Louis, MO, October 9, 1969.

93. George McLean, *Rural Community Development,* an eight-page leaflet, no date, but written in 1946.

94. Ibid.

95. Ibid.

96. Ibid.

97. Ibid.

98. George McLean, "Private Initiative at Work." Speech to the North Carolina Bankers Association. [n.d.].

99. Ibid.

100. "Community Development Foundation: 40 Years of Job Growth and Economic Development," Tupelo: *Northeast Mississippi Daily Journal,* 1986, pp. 4-5.

101. *Tupelo Journal,* January 10, 1948.

102. Ibid., December 3, 1949.

103. Paul Chapman, *Progressive Farmer,* March 1948, pp. 48-50.

104. The number of foreign nations represented among the tours of the area is drawn from accounts in the local newspaper.

105. *Tupelo Journal,* June 28, 1967.

106. Author's separate interviews with Gale Carr, former Lee County dairy specialist, in Verona, MS, June 7, 1972; and Harry Martin, former assistant county agent for Lee County, in Tupelo, MS, July 9, 1973.

107. Figures drawn from the files of the county agent for Lee County, Tupelo, Mississippi.

108. Author's separate interviews with Gale Carr, in Verona, MS, June 7, 1972; Harry Martin, in Tupelo, MS, July 9, 1973; and Charlie Metts, former small dairyman, in Etta, MS, June 14, 1971. For a detailed analysis of the impact of technological changes in agriculture see Wayne D. Rasmussen, "Impact of Technological Change on American Agriculture, 1862-1962," *Journal of Economic History, XXII* (December 1962), pp. 585-591.

109. John A. Hamilton and Kay King, "Mississippi's Changing Economy," Jackson: Mississippi Research and Development Center, 1969, p. 11.

110. United States Bureau of the Census, Eighteenth Census of the United States: 1960. Population, Part 26, Mississippi. Washington: Government Printing Office, 1962, pp. 11-14.

111. Ibid., p. 12.

112. United States Bureau of the Census, Nineteenth Census of the United States: 1970. Population, Part 26, Mississippi. Washington: Government Printing Office, 1962, p. 16.

113. McLean, "Private Initiative at Work."

114. "Community Development Foundation: 40 Years of Job Growth and Economic Development," Tupelo: *Northeast Mississippi Daily Journal,* 1988, p. 6.

115. United States Bureau of the Census, "Selected Labor Force and Community, 1990, Table 2."

116. *Community Development Foundation Bulletin,* October/November 1986.

Chapter 7 — The Industrial Transition

1. A good study of this time period as the turning point in southern industrialization is James C. Cobb, *The Selling of the South: The Southern Crusade for Industrial Development, 1936-1990,* 2d ed., Urbana: University of Illinois Press, 1993.

2. National Emergency Council, *Report on Economic Conditions of the South,* Washington: Government Printing Office, 1938, p. 1.

3. Ibid., p. 8.

4. *Industrial Status of Mississippi,* prepared and printed by the Mississippi State Planning Commission, Jackson, MS, 1935, pp. 21-24.

5. Charles Philip Long, "A Short Description of the Tornado of April 5th, 1936," unpublished paper in the Lee County Library, Tupelo, MS, pp. 11,14.

6. Cobb, *Selling of the South,* pp. 8-12.

7. George Brown Tindall, *The Emergence of the New South, 1913-1945,* Baton Rouge: Louisiana State University Press, 1967, pp. 459-463.

8. William R. Schriver, "The Industrialization of the Southeast since 1950: Some Causes of Manufacturing Relocation, with Speculation about Its Effects," *American Journal of Economics and Sociology, XXX* (January 1971), pp. 67-68.

9. Charles Tilly, "Do Communities Act?" *Sociological Inquiry, XLIII* (Winter, 1973), p. 207; Roland L. Warren and Herbert H. Hyman, "Purposive Community Change in Consensus and Dissensus Situations," in Terry N. Clark, ed., *Community Structure and Decision-Making: Comparative Analyses,* San Francisco: Chandler Publishing Company, 1966, pp. 407-424; Michael Aiken and Robert Alford, "Community Structure and Innovation: The Case of Urban Renewal," in John Walton and Donald E. Carns, eds., *Cities in Change: Studies on the Urban Condition,* Boston: Allyn

and Bacon, 1973, pp. 369-388.

10. Donald Crumpton Mosley, "The Labor Union Movement," in Richard Aubrey McLemore. ed., *A History of Mississippi,* two volumes, Hattiesburg: The University and College Press of Mississippi, 1973, II, pp. 258-259.

11. *Tupelo Journal,* March 15, April 1, 1937; and Irving Bernstein, *The Lean Years: A History of the American Worker, 1920-1933,* Boston: Houghton Mifflin Company, 1960, pp. 1-43.

12. *Tupelo Journal,* February 23, 24, March 10, 12, 15, 16, 18, 30, 31, 1937.

13. Ibid., March 16, 18, 1937.

14. Ibid., April 8, 9, 10, 1937.

15. Ibid., April 10, 11, 1937.

16. Author's interview with Sam H. Long, the commander of the National Guard unit which staged the artillery drill in Tupelo, MS, March 3, 1973.

17. *Tupelo Journal,* April 14, 1937.

18. Ibid., April 23, 1937.

19. Wilson Whitman, "Three Southern Towns, I, Tupelo: Feudalism and the T.V.A.," *Nation, CXLVIII,* December 31, 1938, p. 13.

20. Author's interview with James M. Savery, Sr., in Tupelo, MS, March 18, 1973.

21. Whitman, "Tupelo," p. 14.

22. See for example, Arthur J. Vidich and Joseph Bensman, *Small Town in Mass Society: Class, Power, and Religion in a Rural Community,* revised edition, Princeton, NJ: Princeton University Press, 1968, pp. 132-136. The Minutes of the Tupelo Board of Aldermen are devoid of any reference to the strike at the Tupelo Cotton Mill.

23. Tupelo, Mississippi, Board of Aldermen, Minutes, III, October 26 and November 3, 1937, pp. 340-341, pp. 349-351.

24. Whitman, "Tupelo," p. 14.

25.   *Tupelo Journal,* February 9, 1938.

26.   Ibid., December 16, 1938, and January 7, 1938; author's interview with James M. Savery, Sr. in Tupelo, MS, March 8, 1973.

27.   Wyatt Winton Belcher contrasts the activities of St. Louis leaders who relied on the town's natural advantages with the aggressive style of Chicago's businessmen. *The Economic Rivalry between St. Louis and Chicago, 1850-1880,* New York: Columbia University Press, 1947.

28.   Author's interview with George McLean in Tupelo, MS, August 7, 1973; also Jack Edward Prince, "History and Development of the Mississippi Balance Agriculture with Industry Program,1936-1958," unpublished doctoral dissertation, The Ohio State University, 1961, p. 1,333.

29.   *Tupelo Journal,* May 28, 1941.

30.   The South as a whole made economic gains through military camps. See Tindall, *The Emergence of the New South,* pp. 695-700. The failures of Mississippi are noted in the Agricultural and Industrial Board, First Biennial Report, July 1, 1944 to June 30, 1946 (Jackson, Mississippi, July 1946), p. 7.

31.   James S. Coleman, *Community Conflict,* New York: The Free Press, 1958, p. 4.

32.   Author's interview with Gale Carr, former head of Lee County's dairy program, in Verona, MS, June 5, 1973.

33.   "Business Activity in Mississippi by Districts," *Mississippi Business Review, III-VIII,* January 1942-June 1947.

34.   George McLean, "Private Initiative At Work," A speech delivered to the North Carolina Bankers. (Location not given). 1967.

35.   George McLean, "It Can Be Done!" A Speech delivered to Agriculture Committee Chamber of Commerce of the United States of America at St. Louis, MO, October 9, 1969.

36.   U. S. Census. 1930, 1940, 1950.

37.   A. E. Luloff "Small Town Demographics" in A. E. Luloff and Louis E.

Swanson, ed., *American Rural Communities,* Boulder: Westview Press, 1990, p. 14.

38. Interview with Harry Clark, the first director of the North Mississippi Industrial Development Association and later director of the Texas Department of Economic Development, August 1992.

39. George McLean, "Your Responsibility for the Development of Your Community," *Delta Kappa,* The University of Mississippi, May 15, 1947.

40. Ibid.

41. Ibid.

42. McLean, "Private Initiative At Work." This story appears in all of McLean's major speeches outside of Mississippi between 1947 and 1969.

43. George McLean, "Community Development in Mississippi." A speech given at the University of Mississippi, February 1982.

44. McLean frequently used this as a closing statement in his speeches between 1969 and 1981.

45. Interview with M. M. Winkler in Tupelo, MS, September 19, 1975.

46. A copy of the *Doane Agricultural Report* is located in the offices of the Community Development Foundation.

47. Background data on the Community Development Foundation is located in the Community Development Foundation Resource Library.

48. Chamber of Commerce Industrial Survey of Tupelo, Mississippi, 1938, p. 14.

49. *Tupelo Journal,* February 28, 1946.

50. Tupelo Board of Aldermen, Minutes, VII, March 15, 1946, p. 295.

51. Community Development Foundation Files.

52. This is an often-cited quotation — See, for example, Community Development Foundation, "A Part of CDF's Success Story," Tupelo, MS. 1992, p. 1.

53. *Tupelo Journal,* February 8, 1951.

54. Harry A. Martin, "Economic Advancement Through Community Unity," Speech to the 21st Century Council of Lawrence County, TN, October 21, 1987, p. 3.

55. Ibid.

56. North Mississippi Industrial Development Association, "A Progress Report on North Mississippi," West Point, MS, 1953.

57. Tupelo, Board of Aldermen, Minutes, June 30, 1956, 75 and *Tupelo Journal,* July 16, 1955.

58. United States Bureau of the Census, Sixteenth Census of The United States, 1950 Characteristics of the Population, II Part 24 Mississippi. Washington: Government Printing Office, 1952, 84; United States Bureau of the Census, Seventeenth Census of The United States, 1960, Characteristics of the Population, I Part 26, Mississippi, Washington: Government Printing Office, 1963, p. 154 and Community Development Foundation, Economic Facts on Lee and Adjoining Counties. Tupelo: Community Development Foundation, April 1972, p. 7.

59. Roger W. Schmenner, *Making Business Location Decisions,* Englewood Cliffs, NJ: Prentiss-Hall, 1982, p. 124 and 154.

60. George McLean, "How Can We Plan and Carry Out Economic Development in a Rural Area?" Speech given by George McLean, neither the place nor the date is given, p. 7.

61. Louis M. O'Quinn, "Tupelo and Why," *Mississippi Business Review, XXXV* (March 1964), p. 10.

62. Author's interview with Dr. W. O. Benjamin, President of Itawamba Community College, Tupelo, MS, April 4, 1990.

63. Community and Economic Progress in the Tupelo Area, Leaflet, CDF, October 1991.

64. Author's interview with William Young, former Director of LIFT, Inc., October 3, 1988.

65. Author's interview with Mr. J. C. Whitehead, former president and CEO of the Bank of Mississippi, July 7, 1991.

66. Author's interview with Mr. Jack Reed, president of Reed, Inc., July 21, 1991.

67. Based on author's observations over a 21-year period. For a similar observation, see Harold F. Kaufman, *Team Leadership: A Key to Development; Another Chapter in The Tupelo Story*, Mississippi State, MS: Mississippi State University, 1970, p. 9.

68. Based on more than 500 interviews in Tupelo.

69. Author's interview with Mr. Amos Reece, October 7, 1971, in Tupelo, MS.

70. Kaufman, *Team Leadership*, p. 7.

71. *Tupelo Journal*, November 2, 11, 1965; January 22, 1965.

72. Ibid.

73. Community Development Foundation Files.

74. Community Development Files and files of North Mississippi Industrial Development Association.

75. Data drawn from United States Census.

76. "A Part of CDF's Success Story," p. 2.

77. The author participated in some of these meetings.

78. Council of Governments, "Three Year Overall Program Design, Fiscal Years, 1979-1982," April 1979.

79. *Northeast Mississippi Daily Journal*, June 25, 1971.

80. Harry Martin, "The Growth of The Furniture Industry in Mississippi," Presentation to Mississippi Manufacturers Association, October 9, 1986.

81. Author's interviews with furniture entrepreneurs from around the ten-county area.

82. Ibid.

83. Harry Martin, "Economic Development: Fundamentals in Building More

Momentum," Speech delivered in Selma — Dallas County, AL, November 20, 1987.

84. Interview with Tracey Lord, former plant manager, Tecumseh, August 2, 1992.

85. Ibid.

86. David L. Birch, *Job Creation in America: How Our Smallest Companies Put the Most People to Work,* New York: The Free Press, 1987, p. 136.

87. *Tupelo Area Daily Journal,* May 26, 1971.

88. *Northeast Mississippi Daily Journal,* December 26, 1971. (A brief description of the origin of CREATE.)

89. Community Development Foundation, Bulletin, June 24, 1985. (Contains a brief history of the origin of the Tupelo branch of The University of Mississippi.)

90. *Northeast Mississippi Daily Journal,* April 30, 1976.

91. Author's interview with Governor William L. Winter, March 1, 1982 in Jackson, MS.

92. *Northeast Mississippi Daily Journal,* February 25, 1976.

93. Community Development Foundation, Year in Review, 1988-89.

94. Community Development Foundation Files, See for example, Industry-Education Day, January 27, 1988.

95. Community Development Foundation Files and author's interview with Ms. Betty Scott, a coordinator for the National Model for Career Technical Education, July 12, 1991; author's interview with Mr. Jimmy Young, Director of the Lee County Vocational Education Program, July 18, 1991; and videotape developed by CDF.

96. CDF Files. The author has toured the PALS Lab.

97. CDF Files.

98. Author's interviews with Lewis Whitfield on numerous occasions.

99. Author's interview with Mike Walters, superintendent of Tupelo Public Schools, June 3, 1992.

100. Ibid.

101. Author's interview with Claude Hartley, chairman of the school board of Tupelo, MS, concerning the effort to pass the school bond issue October 5, 1990.

102. National Civic League, *All-America City Award Yearbook, 1989,* pp. 18-19.

103. Diane Gore Pittman, "Tupelo at The Crossroads," unpublished manuscript in the possession of the author.

104. Jackson, Mississippi, *Clarion Ledger.*

105. *Northeast Mississippi Daily Journal,* April 10, 1987.

106. One of the best descriptions is in *Shadows in the Sunbelt,* MDC, (formerly Manpower Development Corporation): Chapel Hill, NC, p. 19.

107. Raw data drawn from the end of the year reports of Mississippi Employment Security Commission.

108. Author's interview with five plant managers who requested that they remain anonymous.

109. Almost all annual publications carry the logo "The Tupelo Area's Global Connection."

110. Data drawn from the Mississippi Employment Security Commission end of the year reports and CDF Files.

111. *Northeast Mississippi Daily Journal,* July 6, 1993.

112. Community Development Foundation, "1993 Business and Economic Facts," Tupelo, Community Development Foundation, 1993, p. 27.

113. Ibid., p. 26.

114. CDF Files.

115. Audit Bureau of Circulation. The figures were obtained from the *Northeast*

Mississippi Daily Journal.

116. *Northeast Mississippi Daily Journal,* July 6, 1993.

117. Ibid.

118. Author's interviews with chairpersons of Tupelo Symphony, Theater and Art Program.

119. CDF "A Part of CDF's Success Story," p. 18.

120. Max DePree, *Leadership Is an Art,* New York: Dell Publishing Co., 1989, p. 12.

121. Harold F. Kaufman and Louis H. Bluhm, "Leadership Structure in Three Small City-Centered Communities," Technical Bulletin #78 Mississippi Agricultural and Forestry Experiment Station, Mississippi State University, 1976.

122. Glenn D. Israel and Lionel J. Beauliew "Community Leadership" in A. E. Luloff and Louis E. Swanson, eds. *American Rural Communities,* Boulder: Westview Press, 1990, pp. 188-190.

123. Pittman, "Tupelo at the Crossroads."

Chapter 8 — The Last to Organize:
The Black Experience in Tupelo/Lee County

1. United States, Bureau of the Census, Ninth Census of the United States: 1870, Washington: Government Printing Office, 1872.

2. Ninth Census, p. 418.

3. Ninth Census, MS.

4. Ibid., and "History of the Spring Hill District Association," Program of the Seventy-Fifth Anniversary of the Spring Hill District Association, 1946, pp. 9-10. Copy in the possession of the Reverend Ethel Page, minister of the Spring Hill Baptist Church of Tupelo, MS.

5. Washington Lafayette Clayton, "Pen Pictures of Olden Times," *Tupelo Journal,* November 3, 1906.

6. Wharton, *The Negro in Mississippi,* p. 96.

7. Carl Schurz, *Speeches, Correspondence and Political Papers,* edited by Frederic Bancroft (New York: G. P. Putnam's Sons, 1913), p. 307.

8. The survey relied on the original manuscripts of the census of 1870 and 1880. The focus was on households rather than heads of households. In this way, any children who might have been listed in the 1870 census and whose names appear on the 1880 list would be considered as persistence for the original household. As indicated in Chapter 2, there are no death certificates for this period, hence the number of persons who disappeared from the survey had to be estimated based on the existing death rate.

9. Records of deaths within the state were not kept until 1912.

10. William Tudor, "Post Civil War Migration of Former Slaves" (unpublished paper prepared at Vanderbilt University, 1966).

11. A summary of the mobility rates for all four communities is provided in Stephan Thernstrom's *The Other Bostonians: Poverty and Progress in the American Metropolis, 1880-1970,* Cambridge: Harvard University Press, 1973, Table 9.2, p. 226.

12. Ibid., Table 9.1, p. 222.

13. *Tupelo Journal,* March 9, 1883.

14. Ibid., May 11, 1882.

15. Ibid., August 7, 1883.

16. Ibid., October 19, 1883.

17. Ibid.

18. Photographs of railroad construction during this period depict almost total Negro laborers.

19. Tupelo Board of Councilmen, Minutes, February 3, 1890, p. 284.

20. *Tupelo Ledger,* October 17, 1889.

21. For an example of the verbal assault by politicians in Tupelo see William David McCain, "The Populist Party in Mississippi" (unpublished master's

thesis, the University of Mississippi, 1931), p. 19.

22.   See, for example, *Tupelo Ledger,* July 23 and 30, 1891 and *Tupelo Journal,* October 28 and November 4, 1892.

23.   Tupelo Board of Councilmen, Minutes, Book "A," October 2, 1894, pp. 130-131.

24.   *Tupelo Journal,* November 14, 1894.

25.   William A. Mabry, "Disfranchisement of the Negro in Mississippi," *Journal of Southern History, IV* (August 1938), pp. 318-333.

26.   Vladimer Orlando Key, Jr., *Southern Politics in State and Nation,* New York: Alfred A. Knopf, 1949, p. 7.

27.   Harold Underwood Faulkner, *The Quest for Social Justice,* 1898-1914, New York: The Macmillan Company, 1931, p. 10.

28.   Emmet J. Scott, *Negro Migration during the War,* New York: Oxford University Press, 1920, p. 52.

29.   St. Clair Drake and Horace R. Cayton, Black Metropolis, New York: Harcourt, Brace and Co., 1945, p. 58.

30.   Major emphasis on the role of the Chicago Defender is found in "The Migration of 1916-1918," in Richard E. Sherman, ed., *The Negro and the City,* Englewood Cliffs, NJ: Prentice-Hall, 1970, pp. 6-9.

31.   Carter G. Woodson, *A Century of Negro Migration,* Washington, D.C.: The Association for the Study of Negro Life and History, 1918, pp. 168-170.

32.   *Tupelo Journal,* August 16, 1918.

33.   Scott, *Negro Migration during the War,* pp. 163-164, and Homer C. Hawkins, "Trends in Black Migration from 1863 to 1960," *Phylon, XXXV* (June 1973), pp. 144-145.

34.   Fred McGehee Wrigton, "Negro Migration and Incomes in Mississippi," unpublished Ph.D. dissertation, Mississippi State University, 1972, p. 17.

35.   United States, Bureau of the Census, Fourteenth Census of the United States: 1920, Population, III, Washington: Government Printing Office, 1922, p. 537.

36. Everett S. Lee, "A Theory of Migration," *Demography, III,* 1 (1966), p. 54.

37. August Meier, *Negro Thought in America, 1880-1915: Racial Ideologies in the Age of Booker T. Washington,* Ann Arbor: University of Michigan Press, 1963, p. 146.

38. *Tupelo Journal,* October 18, 1918.

39. Tupelo Board of Aldermen, Minutes, III (October 11, 1918), p. 609. The lengthy ordinance is discussed on pages 606-610.

40. Ibid., p. 610.

41. Fourteenth Census, III, p. 542. There were 1,719 blacks over 10 years of age; 502 were illiterate.

42. Works Project Administration, "Schools of Today," Lee County, 20 volumes. Compiled and written by the staff of the Works Project Administration. (Typewritten copy in the Lee County Library, 1937), XIX, p. 6.

43. Documentation is available in the annual inventory of school-age children in the Minutes of the Board of Aldermen.

44. Author's interview with Ms. Hattie Debro, a former student and teaching colleague of A. M. Strange, in Tupelo, MS, October 7, 1974.

45. W.P.A., "Schools of Today," p. 51.

46. *Tupelo Journal,* January 29, 1924.

47. Author's interview with Ms. Hattie Debro in Tupelo, MS, October 7, 1974.

48. Author's interview with Halbert Smith, a friend and former student of A. M. Strange, in Tupelo, MS, October 9, 1974.

49. *Tupelo Journal,* November 6, 1928.

50. Ibid., October 31, 1928.

51. Author's interview with Ms. Fred Louis Kirksey, one of Tupelo's leading businesswomen and civic leader, in Tupelo, MS, September 18, 1974.

52. This point was emphasized in the author's interviews with Ms. Fred Louis

Kirksey, Ms. Hattie Debro, and Mr. Halbert Smith in Tupelo, Mississippi, September 18, October 7, October 9, 1974, respectively.

53. *Tupelo Journal,* February 21, 1930.

54. Twenty-six of the 29 persons over 60 years of age who were interviewed by the author cited A. M. Strange as one of the three most outstanding black leaders within the span of their memory.

55. Author's interviews with Ms. Hattie Debro, Ms. Alice Little, Ms. Fred Louis Kirksey, and Mr. Halbert Smith in Tupelo, MS, September 18, October 7, and October 9, 1974, respectively.

56. Author's interview with Ms. Fred Louis Kirksey in Tupelo, MS, September 18, 1974.

57. Author's interview with A. L. Radcliff, who replaced A. M. Strange as the principal of the school, in Tupelo, MS, on September 19, 1974.

58. The role of the Elks Club is discussed at a later point in this chapter.

59. Author's interview and discussion with more than 25 persons at the Henry Hampton Elks Lodge in Tupelo, MS, on January 5, 1975.

60. Author's interviews with the Reverends James Wilson, Ethel Page, and E. C. Cayson in Tupelo, MS, on October 4, 1974; December 19, 1974; and January 3, 1975, respectively. Reverends Wilson and Page were ministers at the end of World War II. Reverend Cayson's father was a minister of a local church at the time.

61. Author's interviews with leaders of the Masons and Elks clubs in Tupelo, MS, on December 12, 1974, and January 4, 1975.

62. For an insider's view of these events, see J. Oliver Emmerich, *Two Faces of Janus: The Saga of Deep South Change,* Jackson, MS: University and College Press of Mississippi, 1973, pp. 88-103.

63. *Tupelo Journal,* October 20, 1955.

64. Ibid., April 4, 1952.

65. This view is expressed in the majority of the editorials dealing with race relations in the *Lee County Tribune.* See for example, March 15, 29, and April 19, 1956.

66. Ibid., January 5, 12, 19, 26 and February 2, 1956.

67. *Tupelo Journal,* May 18, 1954.

68. Ibid., December 1954.

69. Thirty-two persons of a selected sample of 42 blacks who had lived in Tupelo for at least 20 years expressed to the author the belief that race relations were less tense and more open in Tupelo than in other communities with which they were familiar. Of those persons, 27 (88 percent) cited George McLean as the key figure in promoting moderate race relations.

70. Author's interview with Ms. Alice Little in Tupelo, MS, on October 19, 1974.

71. Much of the discussion of the role of Amos Reece in Tupelo is based on the author's three-year acquaintance with Amos Reece.

72. Based on author's interviews with 42 long-term residents of Tupelo.

73. Author's interview with Halbert Smith in Tupelo, MS, on October 9, 1974.

74. Author's interview with Augustus Ashby, president of the Henry Hampton Lodge of the Elk's Club, in Tupelo, MS, on November 3, 1974.

75. The last such barbershop closed in 1902. *Tupelo Journal,* January 4, 1902.

76. Author's interview with Ms. Valerie Grayson, daughter of J. W. Porter and current owner of the Porter Funeral Home, in Tupelo, MS, on September 19, 1974.

77. Author's interview with the Reverend James Wilson in Tupelo, MS, on October 19, 1974.

78. Author's interview with Ms. Valerie Grayson in Tupelo, MS, on September 19, 1974.

79. *Tupelo Journal,* March 26, 1951.

80. Based on a random sample within Tupelo and among members of the Rural Community Development Councils in the surrounding rural areas. Both J. W. Porter and Amos Reece were named by more than 80 percent of those persons who had lived in Tupelo for at least 20 years. No other person was named by more than 50 percent of the respondents.

81. This view was expressed by a majority of whites who commented on the success of J. W. Porter to the author.

82. Claudette E. Bennett, *The Black Population in the United States: March 1991*, Washington: U.S. Department of Commerce, Bureau of the Census, 1992, p. 13.

83. Author's interview with Augustus Ashby in Tupelo, MS, on November 12, 1974.

84. Author's interview with Robert Jamison, former president of the Tupelo Chapter of the NAACP, in Tupelo, MS, on January 9, 1975.

85. *Tupelo Area Daily Journal,* August 18, 1965.

86. Ninety-seven persons (83 percent) of the 117 persons interviewed cited improved job opportunities as the most important event with which they were familiar in Tupelo.

87. Author's interview with ten black women who worked at the processing plant. Records of the race of plant workers were not made available to the author.

88. United States, Bureau of the Census, Eighteenth Census of the United States: 1960, Mississippi, Part 26, Washington: Government Printing Office, 1962, p. 160.

89. There were 601 Negro women working at jobs using domestic skills in 1960 and 367 similarly employed in 1970. See United States, Bureau of the Census, Eighteenth Census of the United States: 1960, Mississippi, Part 26, p. 160; and idem, Nineteenth Census of the United States: 1970, Mississippi, Part 26, Washington: Government Printing Office, 1972, p. 251.

90. There were no records relating to the salaries of domestic workers in Tupelo. Sixteen women who had been maids or cooks in 1960 were interviewed by the author. None of these women were paid more than $40 a week and most earned between $15 and $25 per week. Only four of those remained in domestic service by 1970 and all received more than $50 per week. There was no attempt by the author to do a systematic sample among domestic workers.

91. There were only eight unemployed male Negroes according to the 1970 census. United States, Bureau of the Census, Nineteenth Census, p. 249.

92. Statistics drawn from the records of the Community Development Foundation.

93. Nineteenth Census, p. 251.

94. Tupelo Board of Aldermen, Minutes, XI (November 29, 1962), p. 37.

95. *Tupelo Area Daily Journal,* January 31, 1968.

96. Author's interview with Robert Jamison in Tupelo, MS, on January 9, 1975.

97. Based on the author's interviews conducted within the black neighborhoods.

98. Author's interviews with leaders of the Masons and Elks Clubs in Tupelo, Mississippi, on December 12, 1974 and January 4, 1975, respectively.

99. Based on the author's interviews and impressions in six rural Negro communities.

100. Author's interview with Thomas Morris, current president of the Lee County Chapter of the NAACP, in Nettleton, MS, on December 14, 1974.

101. Author's interview with Boyce Grayson, July 18, 1992.

102. Author's interview with more than 100 black citizens during the decade of the 1970s.

103. A brief summary of the events is provided in the *Northeast Mississippi Daily Journal,* February 18, 1978.

104. *Northeast Mississippi Daily Journal,* February 13, and February 22, 1978.

105. *Memphis Commercial Appeal,* March 11, 12, 18, 1978.

106. Ibid., March 19, 1978.

107. Author's interview with George McLean, March 20, 1978.

108. *Northeast Mississippi Daily Journal,* April 26, 1978.

109. Author's interview with downtown merchants and other civic leaders, March 21, 1978.

110. *Memphis Commercial Appeal,* March 24, 1978.

111. Ibid., April 8, 1978.

112. *Northeast Mississippi Daily Journal,* May 9, 1978 and CDF Files.

113. *Memphis Commercial Appeal,* May 13, 1978.

114. Ibid., May 12, 1978.

115. Ibid., May 18, 1978.

116. Ibid., May 13, 1978.

117. *Northeast Mississippi Daily Journal,* May 19, 1978.

118. Ibid., May 22, 1978.

119. *Jackson Clarion Ledger,* May 20, 1978.

120. *Memphis Commercial Appeal,* June 7, 1978.

121. *Northeast Mississippi Daily Journal,* June 10-11, 1978.

122. Ibid., June 12, 1978.

123. *Memphis Commercial Appeal,* June 10, 1978.

124. *Northeast Mississippi Daily Journal,* June 12, 1978.

125. Ibid.

126. *Memphis Commercial Appeal,* June 11, 1978.

127. Ibid.

128. *Northeast Mississippi Daily Journal,* June 12, 1978.

129. Ibid., and August 23, 1978.

130. *Northeast Mississippi Daily Journal,* September 21, 1978.

131. Ibid.

132. *Memphis Commercial Appeal,* November 18, 1978.

133. See *Northeast Mississippi Daily Journal,* March 4, 1979; April 5-6, 1980; April 8, 1980; December 16, 1981; January 30-31, 1982.

134. Ibid., December 19, 1986.

135. Ibid., September 26, 1983.

136. *Memphis Commercial Appeal,* March 31, 1982.

137. Author's interviews with black businessmen in 1991, 1992, and 1993.

138. Census data was provided by the Center for Population Studies at the University of Mississippi.

139. Ibid.

140. Data supplied by the Tupelo Director of Personnel.

141. Ibid.

142. Author's interview with Charles Pearson, July 26, 1993.

Chapter 9 — How They Do It in Tupelo/Lee County: An Overview of the Tupelo Plan

1. James McGregor Burns, *Leadership,* New York: Harper and Row, 1978.

2. All bank presidents over the past 25 years described this cultural expectation of placing community interest first. The author has both observed and been told of the expectations and sanctions involved in working on behalf of the community.

3. Author's interview with William Beasley, October 17, 1978.

4. The author interviewed 34 key leaders from northeast Mississippi during the summer of 1992. Almost all used similar language in describing Lee County's achievements.

5. Harold F. Kaufman, *Team Leadership: A Key to Development, Another*

Chapter in the Tupelo Story, Mississippi State, MS. Mississippi State University, Applied Series, 1, March 1970, pp. 3-5.

6. Based on the author's study of the Minutes of the Board of Aldermen and many interviews. Especially insightful were the interviews with the former city attorney Frank Riley.

7. Diane Gove Pittman, "Tupelo at the Crossroads." Unpublished Paper in the possession of the author.

8. Author's interview with Senator John C. Stennis in DeKalb, MS, August 12, 1987.

9. George C. Pulver, "A Theoretical Framework for the Analysis of Community Economic Development Policy Options," in *Nonmetropolitan Industrial Growth and Community Change,* Gene F. Summers and A. E. Selvik, eds. Lexington; MA: Lexington Books, 1979.

10. George McLean, "It Can Be Done!" Speech to the Agricultural Committee of the U.S. Chamber of Commerce, St. Louis, MO, October 9, 1969.

11. The program was described at the annual Industry/Education Day January 27, 1988, Material is part of CDF Files.

12. *Northeast Mississippi Daily Journal,* May 8, 1970.

13. George McLean, filmed interview, March 1, 1972.

INDEX

Cottrell, Leonard, 5
Counties: Big Ten, 159; consortium of, 87; establishment of, 21-22; new, 30; seats of, 30-31
Cox, Jimmy, 106
Craven, Avery, 24
CREATE. *See* Christian, Research, Education, Action, Technical Enterprise (CREATE)
Crews, William Lowrey (Billy), 137-138, 156, 172
Crime: early, 31-32; organized, 115
Cronin, Tom, 13
Cruber, Dale, 152, 154
Crump, Edward Hull, 85
Cultural activities, 3, 136
Cunningham, R. C., 61

D

Dabbs, L. H., 61
Daily Journal. See Journal
Dairy industry, 75, 83, 100, 101, 108; artificial insemination and, 88-89, 102; promotion of, 80-81, 82, 83, 87
Davis, Reuben, 26, 34
Daybrite factory, 112-113
Day care center, 117
Democratic Party: African-Americans and, 140; agrarianism and, 54, 56, 57-63
Department stores, 74
Desegregation, 146, 148-149
DeSoto County, 21, 22
Diversification: agricultural, 12, 79-89, 101, 108-109; industrial, 111, 117, 129, 130; leaders of, 79-83
Doane Agricultural Service, 89, 90, 92, 112; report by, 112, 162
Dougherty, M. C., 95
Douglas, Stephen, 27-28, 35
Downtown Association, 163
Drainage program, 49, 71
Draper, Lyman, 26
Durham, Sam, 82, 83

E

Economic development, 3, 14-19; African-Americans and, 156-157; boundaries and, 7-8, 14-15; community development and, 5, 123, 162, 164; history of, 11-15; principles of, 110-112, 164. *See also* Industrialization

Tupelo Journal. See Journal

Tupelo Model, 3, 89, 91-92, 93, 94, 99-100

Tupelo Plan, 99-100, 103, 110, 158-167; elements of, 160-167; leaders and, 158-159, 160-161; organizations and, 158-160; regionalism and, 166-167

"Tupelo Spirit," 6, 117, 160-161

T.V.A. *See* Tennessee Valley Authority (T.V.A.)

U

Union County, 116

United League of North Mississippi, 152, 153, 154

Unity, 61-62

Universities, 123-124; early, 24-25

University of Mississippi, 123-124, 163; desegregation of, 149

Uptown Association, 152, 155

U.S. News & World Report, 3

V

Van Buren, Martin, 25

Vardaman, James K., 48

Vegetables, 108-109

Verona, 31, 34, 39, 40, 117, 119

Vocational training, 117, 122, 123, 125, 162, 165

Volunteerism, 93-94, 117-118

Voting Rights Act, 147

W

Wagon yards, 32, 68-69

Wall Street Journal, The, 2, 12, 81

Wal-Mart, 166

Warner, Sam Bass, 20

Warren, Roland, 8

Water supply, 11, 12, 46, 136

Watson, Tom, 58

Weaver, James, 62, 63

Whitaker, Clyde, 114, 154

White, Cecil, 114

White, Hugh, 105, 107

White supremacy, 58, 59-60, 61, 62

Whitehead, J. C., 117, 137, 174

Whitesides, Emmett, 72

Whitesides, Josh, 112, 172

Whitfield, Lewis, 125, 137, 174